The Soul of Justice

The Soul of Justice

Social Bonds and Racial Hubris

Cynthia Willett

Cornell University Press

Ithaca and London

First published 2001 by Cornell University Press
First printing, Cornell Paperbacks, 2001
Printed in the United States of America

Library of Congress Cataloging-in-Publication Data

Willett, Cynthia, b. 1956
    The soul of justice : social bonds and racial hubris / Cynthia Willett.
        p.   cm.
    Includes bibliographical references and index.
    ISBN 0-8014-3891-8 (cloth : alk. paper) — ISBN 0-8014-8715-3 (pbk. :
alk. paper)
        1. Social justice. 2. Liberalism. 3. Individualism. 4. African Americans
    Race identity. 5. African Americans—Social conditions. I. Title.
    HM671 .W54 2001
    303.3'72—dc21   2001001716

Cornell University Press strives to use environmentally responsible suppliers
and materials to the fullest extent possible in the publishing of its books. Such
materials include vegetable-based, low-VOC inks and acid-free papers that
are recycled, totally chlorine-free, or partly composed of nonwood fibers.
Books that bear the logo of the FSC (Forest Stewardship Council) use paper
taken from forests that have been inspected and certified as meeting the highest standards for environmental and social responsibility. For further information, visit our website at www.cornellpress.cornell.edu.

Cloth printing   10 9 8 7 6 5 4 3 2 1
Paperback printing   10 9 8 7 6 5 4 3 2 1

For my father and mother,
Joseph and Ellen Willett

Contents

Acknowledgments

Two little free spirits by the names of Liza and Joe presided over the writing of this book. These little spirits have made me wonder what vision of justice lies beyond the narrow contours of our ordinary lives. My husband, Stefan, has shared with me the adventure of raising the children as well as many of the conversations that hold this book together.

The structure of the book took shape in an excellent workshop on gender as concept and method organized by Janet Sharistanian and Ann Schofield at the University of Kansas in the fall of 1995. Since those days at Kansas, I have benefited much from engaging conversations with Amy Coplan on the Greek concepts of eros and hubris, and on Toni Morrison's mesmerizing novels. Oleta Prinsloo's Ph.D. dissertation on the cultural fictions of slavery in a Missouri border community has been educating me about the moral ambivalence of whites. Dawn Jakubowski has developed in clear and powerful terms the impact of care ethics on liberalism in her dissertation on multiculturalism and social justice. And Namita Goswami's dissertation research on the black body never lets me forget the political force of racial fantasy.

Among my many outstanding colleagues at Emory, Pam Hall, David Carr, Thomas Flynn, Rudolf Makkreel, Mark Risjord, and Michael Sullivan have been especially generous with their advice during various stages of writing this book. A University Research Committee Grant at Emory in the fall of 1999 freed me from teaching so that I could complete a draft of the manuscript. Emory's Women's Studies Program sponsored my research assistants, Jennifer Shaw and Sara Puotinen, who tracked down missing sources. I am also grateful to Beth Butterfield for the index, as well as for her outstanding assistance with several of my classes, and to Eric Schramm for his expert job at copyediting the text.

Duane Davis, Linda Bell, Tim Craker, David Jones, Roy Martinez, Shawn Smith, Jim Winchester, and Jason Wirth have sustained me with the warmth of their friendship and philosophical community in Atlanta (Duane, you are an honorary member!). Many of my friends have helped me to better understand the ancient Greek culture, but I am especially grateful to Deborah Achtenberg, Mitch Miller, Thomas Tuozzo, Steven Strange, Cynthia Patterson, and Richard Patterson. Howard McGary, Patricia Huntington,

Martin Matustik, and my editor at Cornell University Press, Catherine Rice, have guided me in the process of revision with their own excellent insights into my project. Fused into the composition of the project is the spirit of my father's jazz music and my mother's political passion and local activism, and it is to my parents, Joseph and Ellen Willett, that I dedicate the book.

CYNTHIA WILLETT

Atlanta

The Soul of Justice

Prologue
Eros and Hubris
Social Justice in Old and New World Settings

Hubris is a form of slighting, since it consists in doing and saying things that cause shame to the victim ... simply for the pleasure involved.... The cause of the pleasure thus enjoyed by the insolent man is that he thinks himself greatly superior to others when ill-treating them.

Aristotle

It was only on the third day, when they could no longer bear the hunger and the insults, that they began to talk about giving in.

Chinua Achebe

To meditate on the fraudulent, self-destroying philosophy of that superiority ... was ... work.

Toni Morrison

Every individual possesses an inviolability that lies at the heart of justice. This sentiment has been central to prevailing theories of justice since the Enlightenment, and defended most strongly in liberalism. Liberal theorists challenge traditional beliefs in social hierarchies, arguing that no individual is meant to serve the needs of others. This strong commitment to the individual makes it difficult to understand the impressive contradictions of modern liberal states. Among these contradictions is at least one simple fact: High standards of living among the middle and upper classes require massive numbers of people to serve as poorly paid laborers, sentencing these workers and their families to lives of despair and degradation. Does the contradiction between the liberal principle of the individual and the reality of massive degradation reflect the inability to put our liberal ideas into practice? Or is there something amiss in the principle itself?

My hypothesis is that the problem, in part, resides in the principle itself. Formulations of liberalism vary, but as a whole these formulations converge toward a central moral claim regarding the individual. According to this claim, the individual is a rational decision maker who should value above all else his autonomy. In the political sphere, this core principle of autonomy translates into a liberal doctrine of human rights. The aim of these rights is to secure protective barriers against external forms of coercion for the sake of individual or group freedom. This liberal aim minimalizes a fact about the human situation that is becoming ever more significant in the era of globalization. This is the fact of interdependency. Major environmental decisions affect not only local populations, but also the role that our species plays in the larger ecosphere. Consumption or investment patterns of the middle classes can have a significant impact on the life-chances of countless others. At this time, but also for the foreseeable future, the freedom of the wealthy middle classes in Europe and America will depend upon the reality of disenfranchised workers inside and outside of our national borders.[1] Could it be that we modernists have misconceptualized the very notion of freedom? Could it be that we do not even know ourselves?

Social, environmental, and economic interdependency is hardly a recent development. It is a characteristic of our species. We are not solitary hunters. We are social creatures ever in search of psychic meaning and economic sustenance from others.[2] Liberal interpreters of moral rights have not come to terms with the fact of psychic and economic interdependency, and as a consequence have difficulty addressing persuasively a whole spectrum of injustices. These theorists have observed that unbounded claims to private wealth allow some individuals to acquire godlike powers over the lives of others, and they argue that such powers need to be curbed through redistributive economic policies. This liberal argument, however, is losing its persuasive power in Europe and America, where neoliberal policies since the Reagan era have weakened or dismantled the welfare state while

Special thanks to Amy Coplan, Mitch Miller, Steven Strange, Richard Patterson, Cynthia Patterson, and Thomas Tuozzo for helping me to understand the significance of hubris in ancient Greek culture, and for pointing me toward many of the crucial sources. Equally special thanks to Lina Buffington, Fereydoon Family, Thomas Flynn, Bill Lawson, David Reidy, Michael Sullivan, Shawn Smith, and Jim Winchester, as well as members of the Departments of Philosophy at the University of Central Arkansas, Emory University, and University of Georgia, for helping me to clarify my arguments.

[1] For a further discussion of the philosophical implications of this fact, see Enrique Dussel's *The Underside of Modernity*, trans. Eduardo Mendieta (Amherst, N.Y.: Humanity Books, 1998), esp. 5.

[2] Frans de Waal, *Good Natured: The Origins of Right and Wrong in Humans and Other Animals* (Cambridge: Harvard University Press, 1996), 167.

increasing the differences between the rich and the poor. At the same time, liberal free trade agreements empower corporations to amass degrees of wealth and power that threaten the sovereignty of entire nation states. To be sure, unbridled rights to free speech within liberal countries, and especially in the United States, protect critical discourse. These rights to speech, however, also protect forms of communication (at major cultural and economic sites of consumption, including network news programs and Hollywood cinema) that can insult and silence alternative voices. These simple facts suggest that Enlightenment liberalism needs substantial rethinking.

My central contention is that while liberal theory is absolutely right to raise the individual to the ultimate principle of justice, liberalism cannot resolve the contradictions of modern life because of the way in which it conceives of the individual. Based in the Enlightenment, liberalism interprets the person through an oppositional scale with autonomy at one end and dependence at the other. This scale is used to measure moral maturity, and to construct and justify legal rights. While contemporary liberal thinkers (including John Rawls and Jürgen Habermas) argue that individuals thrive only in a social context, these thinkers nonetheless envision the individual in traditional Enlightenment terms. The liberal doctrine of equality is based on the human capacity to exercise reason and make choices for one's own life. The moral psychology of liberalism overemphasizes the importance of reason in individual lives, while the valorization of the capacity to make choices undervalues what I will argue to be our more important need, the need to cultivate diverse relationships based on friendship, emotional intimacy, and economic cooperation in a thriving social milieu.

While Enlightenment liberalism aims to promote equality, liberalism in fact perpetuates massive social inequalities. These inequalities grow out of the fact that liberal theory categorizes individuals into those who are viewed as responsible for their own lives and those who are entangled in relationships of dependency. One consequence of this division is that those who perform carework, raising children or caring for elders, are evaluated as not contributing fully to the productivity of society. The liberal model of the self as the rational decision maker sets up carework as different in kind from work based on autonomy, and recognizes only the latter as value-creating labor worthy of decent pay. As I argue in Chapter 4, the failure to recognize the caregiver as a normative model of the individual conspires with the high rates of poverty for single mothers and their children, while rendering these families dependent upon the state. Liberal individualism makes it difficult to see any original sources of value outside of the rational capacity of the individual. This excessive valorization of reason excludes as original sources of value connections with our children and our elders as well as our immersion in nature, culture, and history.

Local citizenship for a democracy in an era of threatening globalization should not be grounded in rights to autonomy (including bare rights to privacy, property, or rational self-choice). Citizenship should be defined first of all in terms of the rights, responsibilities, and emotional capacities of the social person. This reformulation of a universal and egalitarian doctrine of individual rights shifts the center of identity away from monotonous discourses of ownership and merit toward the diverse discourses of the lover, the working family, and the cosmopolitan friend.

Major contemporary traditions of social and political theory have taken significant steps toward revaluing the social dimension of the individual. Anglo-American and Habermasian philosophers have tempered the excessive individualism and rationalism of Enlightenment liberalism by drawing upon what psychologist Carol Gilligan calls an ethics of care, and I examine these views in Part 1. In Part 2, I turn to post-Hegelian philosophers who unmask the postures of rationalism through the legacy of Freud. While these two major branches of normative philosophy do not agree on the basic facts of human psychology, they teach us about the limits of Enlightenment liberalism. Both traditions urge us to look deeper into the social drama of the modern subject than the liberal theorist usually does. Still, neither tradition challenges autonomy as the ultimate meaning of individuality. There is, however, another well-developed tradition of literature and thought on what it means to be a human being. In the African-American pragmatist tradition, the normative conception of the individual in need of legal protection is not based primarily on the rational capacity to make decisions for oneself, although this conception of the individual does not exclude this capacity. This alternative conception integrates the rational capacity into a whole person, who is first of all defined in terms of the social capacity to flourish with others in history, culture, and a work-based community.

It is difficult to grasp the everyday battles of racism without understanding the impact of social forces on personal identity and normative thinking. African-American thinkers do not focus their accounts of human relationships on what I would describe as quasi-biological needs for nurturing and trust. I believe that this minimalist view of sociality hinders Anglo-American efforts to reform Enlightenment liberalism (see Part 1). Nor do major African-American thinkers focus their accounts of individual identity on quasi-biological drives for erotic satisfaction as neo-Romantic, continental thinkers tend to do (Part 2). These thinkers focus directly and forcefully on the "social eros" of human relationships (Part 3). They tell of how racism can challenge the human spirit and distort the capacity to desire. They explore the social pathos experienced by the black in an anti-black world. And they trace this pathos to crimes of arrogance and power.

The social pathos of arrogance is not a category that can be articulated fully and persuasively within an Enlightenment model of liberal rights (see Chapter 7). Interestingly, this category of crime did play a significant role in older ideas of democracy. The working poor and subsistence farmers who were citizens of classical Athens understood the crime of arrogance as *"hubris,"* and they enjoyed various legal and moral codes against it.[3] An ancient view of democracy reemerges in the African-American context, but in a radically egalitarian guise. From within this context emerges a challenge to the basic paradigm of Enlightenment liberalism as well as its Hegelian, or Romantic and post-Romantic, offshoots. It is a mistake to conceptualize the bearer of rights in terms of the needs of the rational agent; the moral defense of individual rights should be anchored in the material needs and intellectual capacities of the social person.[4]

---

[3] My discussion of hubris grows out of Drucilla Cornell's argument for "degradation prohibition" in her inspiring book, *The Imaginary Domain* (New York: Routledge, 1995). Cornell draws the parameters for her discussion of degradation from Lacan. I discuss hubris through an alternative philosophical anthropology in order to emphasize diverse sources of human sociality. This anthropology shifts away from Enlightenment liberal issues of self-ownership (including Cornell's account of the rights to the imaginary domain) toward the social person's right to nonhubristic economic and philic relationships. I worry about Cornell's separation of economic and cultural issues from her defense of individual freedoms.

My project also aims to contribute to the work of Iris Young, and, in particular, to her fine analysis of five categories of oppression. See especially "Five Faces of Oppression" in her classic work on social justice, *Justice and the Politics of Difference* (Princeton: Princeton University Press, 1990), 39–65. As I understand these categories, hubris involves a synthesis of elements of two of them, cultural imperialism and violence. Drawing upon this synthesis, I would categorize rape as a crime of hubris, and not violence per se. In her analysis, Young demonstrates that oppression is not the result of individual decisions but of systemic constraints on social groups. She argues that an "individualist social ontology usually goes together with a normative conception of the self ... as autonomous, unified, free, and self-made" (45). She also argues that freedom needs to be redefined in terms of "exercising one's capacities and ... participating in determining one's action.... To these two general values correspond two social conditions that define injustice: oppression, the institutional constraint on self-development, and domination, the institutional constraint on self-determination" (37). I focus on the rights of the individual to participate in erotic and philic bonds rather than self-development or self-determination per se. Damage to these bonds involves elements of both oppression and domination.

[4] I will emphasize the emotional needs that are missing from the prevailing liberal valorization of rational decision making; however, the need to find a more powerful model of the individual requires understanding the way in which reason and emotions are integrated in the experience of the nonpathological person. My understanding of the relation between reason and emotion owes much to Amy Coplan's analysis of the "integration model" in her Ph.D. dissertation (in progress) at Emory University.

Since the Enlightenment, political philosophers have emphasized one of two extreme poles of human subjectivity. At one pole is the subject who defines himself through active self-agency or possessive self-ownership and claims as his prize the rights and privileges of autonomy. At the center of these concerns is the right to protect a private space from governmental interference and criminal violation. This pole is at the center of Enlightenment-based, Anglo-American, liberal theory. At the other pole is the subject who discovers who he is through the recognition bestowed upon him by other persons. This view is represented in Romantic, continental thought, and especially in the philosophical anthropology of Hegel. While the first model presents the modern individual as a private subject or rational agent whose decisions are immune from social force, the second model fuses the rational values and purposes of the individual with the community, nation-state, or other larger social or historical processes. Neither position fully lends itself to grasping how individuals discover who they are in relationships with others by negotiating a range of social forces.

The social forces that impinge upon the life of an individual are diverse and dissonant. The individual wades through these forces in every zone of modern life. Neither the intimate pleasures of private sexual fantasy nor the quiet reflections of the intellectual operate in a space devoid of the images, rhythms, and techno-curves of consumer culture or corporate-sponsored infotainment. As theorists, we cannot grasp the impact of diverse social forces without an eclectic weave of disciplines, methods, and traditions. The demand for such a synthesis is not new. It can be found in the philosophical tradition of critical theory.

First Wave Critical Theory and Freud's Theory of Sexual Drives

As a European movement, critical theory traces back to the Frankfurt School. The aim of first generation thinkers Adorno, Benjamin, Horkheimer, and Marcuse was to bring together psychoanalytic theories of alienation and unconscious desire with leftist critiques of capitalist exploitation. While these thinkers accepted the Enlightenment's valorization of autonomy, and never found an exit from the brutal contradictions of modern political systems, they nonetheless refused to relegate these contradictions to secondary concerns in the application of liberal theory. More recently, Jürgen Habermas has taken up the Frankfurt School's expansive interests in social critique while severely narrowing the scope of leftist moral and political philosophy. As a result of this narrowing of the critical project, the contradictions of the modern liberal state have fallen into the margins of normative theory. If we are to take seriously the failures of modernization, we will need to bring its contradictions to the center of justice theory, shift the paradigm for the individual, and redefine human rights in a larger narrative of social justice— or so I will argue. In many ways, this revision of the critical theory that we inherit from Habermas entails returning to the insights of the first generation.

The first wave critical theorists aimed to salvage the liberal ideals of the Enlightenment while accounting for anti-Semitism in the rapidly modernizing Germany of the 1920s and 1930s and the empty materialism of the middle classes in post–World War II America. It was not immediately clear how the ideal of rational autonomy could survive the nonrational forces that shape the political landscape of the well-developed countries and hollow out the meaning of our modern lives. The early Frankfurt theorists worked to correct the naive rationalism of the Enlightenment by appropriating elements of a philosophical anthropology from Hegelian and Marxian romanticism, but even more from the postromantic pessimism of Freud. From Freud they borrowed the idea that basic human drives are asocial and sexual, or even savagely destructive. While Freud's theory of the unconscious allowed critical theorists to explain aspects of the irrational in modern life, Freudian psychology also made it difficult to see how modernization could avoid substantial forms of social and psychological repression. For these theorists (with the strongest exception of Marcuse), there would be no clear way out of what contemporary writer Jamaica Kincaid describes as the loneliness and the emptiness that is "the European disease."[5] The question is whether classic psychoanalytic theory adequately articulates the deepest desires and sources of angst for the modern psyche. Enlightenment rationalism has vanquished from our consciousness the emotional life that earlier ages recognized as central. How do we understand what unacknowledged desires lie hidden in the modern heart? Perhaps, less by what he says than by what he does not say, Habermas gives us the first clue.

Second Wave Critical Theory and Habermas's Rationalism

Habermas narrows the scope of moral and political philosophy by restricting the normative task to setting up the correct procedures for debating the principles of justice. This procedure provides the terms for what he

---

[5] Jamaica Kincaid, *A Small Place* (New York: Penguin, 1988), 80.

calls communicative, or discourse, ethics. Habermas's claim is that if we were to set up a potentially worldwide debate in accordance with the rules that he lays out, the debate would yield universalizable moral principles. The concern I share with most of Habermas's critics is that the rules are not, and can never be, as value-free as Habermas would claim.

Behind Habermas's proposal for discourse ethics is an important insight into the value of democractic communication and oral culture for making basic moral decisions that affect us all. The first generation critical theorists did not have a strong interest in either democratic theory or oral culture. Less clear, however, is whether or not Habermas has determined the best avenues for public discourse and moral persuasion. He construes moral debate as a "contest" (or *agon*), and argues that only those individuals who possess the requisite moral intelligence merit inclusion in the debate. I will examine the normative standards presupposed by discourse ethics in Chapter 2. Even apart from his theory of moral intelligence, however, Habermas gives us hints as to which populations his standards would exclude.

In a contribution to the anthology *Multiculturalism*, edited by Amy Gutmann, Habermas states explicitly that fundamentalists are to be excluded from public debate. While it is not clear who Habermas has in mind, I would think the term might include members of the Nation of Islam, as well as other controversial religious groups. If I am right, then I wonder how many individuals would be effectively disenfranchised through a series of rules that, much like the use of literacy tests to prevent African Americans from voting until 1965, purport to have universal relevance but in fact do not. Habermas offers reasons for the exclusion of these types of people from our moral debates. He explains that fundamentalism "is based on ... interpretations of the world that claim exclusiveness for a privileged way of life," while Western secularism allows for civilized debate among those who disagree.[6]

Having sung the praises of the West, Habermas stumbles across what must be a troubling claim to a man of such tremendous powers of reflection. Agreement among the co-combatants on rules for a civilized debate cannot rest on neutral grounds. What counts as reasonable depends upon "loyalty to [a] common political culture." Habermas explains that this is because rules and principles require interpretation, and interpretation is rooted in "the perspective of the nation's historical experience." Underlying a people's sense of the reasonable is the libidinal affect of loyalty. But then one has to

---

[6] Jürgen Habermas, "Struggles for Recognition in the Democratic Constitutional State," in *Multiculturalism: Examining the Politics of Recognition*, ed. Amy Gutmann (Princeton, N.J.: Princeton University Press, 1994), 133; this edited collection is henceforth cited as *M*.

wonder if Habermas can safely distinguish between the loyalty that we attribute to civilized people like ourselves and the fundamentalism that we attribute to others.

It is important at this juncture to listen to those who speak from the other side of the cultural and religious divides of our time. Network news programs owned by American-based corporations (at this moment, Westinghouse, Disney, and General Electric) filter these voices through American interests, making it difficult to know if we have properly understood their point of view. In a recent *New York Times* essay, however, a journalist gives insight into anti-Western sentiments by pointing out a certain zeal lurking behind the discourse of the West: "We Americans are the apostles of the Fast World, the prophets of the free market and the high priests of high tech. We want 'enlargement' of both our values and our Pizza Huts. We want the world to follow our lead and become democratic and capitalistic, with a Web site in every pot, a Pepsi on every lip, [and] Microsoft Windows in every computer."[7] Is it clear who the "fundamentalists" are? I am not so sure. The journalist continues: "No wonder, therefore, that resentment of America is on the rise globally." Sometimes we tend to see exaggerated in the Other what we most deny in ourselves.

The journalist reports on a subtle change in the moral language of our critics in the Middle East. "In 1996 I visited Teheran.... A short time later, I noticed that Iran's mullahs had begun calling America something other than the 'Great Satan.' They had begun calling it 'the capital of global arrogance.'"

"The Iranian leadership had grasped the important distinction between 'global arrogance' and old-fashioned notions of imperialism, when one country physically occupies another," the journalist explains. "Global arrogance is when your culture and economic clout are so powerful and widely diffused that you don't need to occupy other people to influence their lives." The Other of the West has grasped a sophisticated moral distinction between new and old forms of power. The question is, have we?

But, you may be thinking, the Islamic fundamentalists in Iran have imprisoned Jews and liberal reformers for their activities against the state, and used state power to threaten liberal presses. While the United States does not imprison Jews or liberals, one out of three black men in their twenties is under criminal justice supervision (prison, parole, or probation) on any

---

[7] Thomas L. Friedman, "From Supercharged Financial Markets to Osama bin Laden, the Emerging Global Order Demands an Enforcer. That's America's New Burden," *New York Times Magazine*, March 28, 1999, 43.

given day.[8] How could it be that so many young black men bear the status of criminal in our liberal political system?

Liberal theory determines what kinds of assaults on individuals count as crimes, and which ones do not. We think, and in part rightly so, that physical acts of violence should count among the more serious crimes. We fear Islamic fundamentalists because they threaten violence in the name of unyielding principles. We refuse, however, to understand how economic and cultural forces of powerful nations can damage citizens of weaker nations by destroying their culture and livelihood, and by rendering their nations dependent upon foreign powers. The unrestrained power of reactionary Islamic regimes brings misery to the lives of many, but so too does the unrestrained economic and cultural power of the overdeveloped nations. When culture and economic relations accomplish oppression, there is no need to violate individual rights—or at least not as these rights are defined by liberal theory.

After World War II, the defeated German state was forced to acknowledge guilt for the Holocaust and to begin reparations. The United States, however, has not made substantial reparations for the bondage, genocide, or wrongful incarceration of people of color. Reparation policies, in contrast with liberal redistributive tax policies and the neoliberal preference for private charity, acknowledge debts owed by dominant groups to those who have been oppressed. The Islamic fundamentalists refuse to accept limits on the authority of their religion and their historical point of view. Do we Americans accept limits on the authority of our style of capitalism and our concept of rights? Without accepting such limits, are we not fundamentalists too?

Habermas not only finds demons who threaten our "common culture" from without, in the same essay but on a different front he censures internal critics of the West. He distinguishes between two types of internal critics, the "traditionalists" and the "deconstructionists." The "traditionalists" are described as calling "for a return to classical traditions of the West." The deconstructionist position is identified as having "'nothing more to say for the view that intellectual standards are masks for the will to political power than that it too reflects the will to power of deconstructionists.'"[9] "We can leave this debate aside," Habermas remarks, "since it contributes little to an analysis of struggles for recognition."[10] Careful reflection, less on the content than on the gesture of Habermas's remark, however, reveals a

---

[8] Council of State Government's Report, "Responding to Racial Disparities in Prison and Jail Populations," presented on June 12, 1998, in Hartford, Connecticut. http://www.csgeast.org/programs/criminal_justice/cj_racial.html.

[9] Habermas is citing Amy Gutmann in *M*, 120.

[10] Ibid.

certain moral blindness in what Habermas calls discourse ethics. For how could Habermas's dismissal of his major philosophical rivals not be seen as a gesture of power, in fact, as an insult against communities internal to European and Euro-American alliances? Could it be that discourse ethics too masks a certain will to power?

If communication is to be recognized as core to a global system of justice, it cannot proceed without registering the moral force of those who are its critics from inside and outside the West. The gesture of setting aside the debates of those who dissent is one of the unjust privileges of power. The discourse ethicist is not any more immune from this kind of gesture than the rest of us. What the discourse ethicist lacks are the tools to grasp how the dismissive gesture constitutes a central moral issue. Habermas separates moral philosophy from an analysis of the games of power and the desires that these games conceal, and this is, I think, a mistake. Nonviolent communication presupposes that the limits of power have already been well established. A theory of justice has to begin by articulating these limits.

Moral Rights and Tragic Hubris

Liberal theorists understand the necessary limits on power in terms of the modern notion of individual rights. The modern, liberal notion of right, however, does not capture everything that might be included within the concept of the limit. This failure stems from a blind spot in our liberal theories of justice and morality. This blind spot does not center on the substance but on the gestures (or, more generally speaking, as I will argue, the social forces) that lie behind our moral disagreements. What the deconstructionist unmasks as the will to power, and what at least one of the West's critics terms "arrogance," is not a category that appears in modern legal or moral theory. Interestingly, such a category does appear in the classical tradition.[11] In ancient Greek traditions of law and literature, crimes of arrogance constitute an actionable offense and a basis for understanding tragic violence. The Athenian *demos*, or working poor citizens of Athenian democracy, understood the offense as a serious crime of the elite against the masses, and they termed this crime *hubris*.[12]

---

[11] At this point, it is also important to remember that the ancient Greeks learned much from older cultures, including Persia and Egypt. Lucius Outlaw explains the racist implications of concealing the links between these cultures in his fascinating essay "The Future of 'Philosophy' in America," in *On Race and Philosophy* (New York: Routledge, 1996), 183–204.

[12] Josiah Ober, *Mass and Elite in Democratic Athens* (Princeton, N.J.: Princeton University Press, 1989), 208–212; henceforth cited as *DA*.

Modern liberal theories of justice have borrowed much from classical theories of democracy. Interestingly, however, these modern bourgeois theories have neglected entirely that category of crime that was of central importance for the working poor in ancient Athens. Political theorists have relegated the significance of hubris to literary scholarship, while literary theorists have neglected the political implications of what they view as a religious crime or moral vice. Hubris was understood by the Greeks as an assault against a multiple weave of social relationships. Modern scholars, often interpreting hubris as a character flaw, have not paid sufficient attention to the significance of these social relationships in Athenian democracy and literature.

The translators of a group of Euripides' plays explain that hubris does not refer exclusively "as is often supposed, to an arrogant attitude towards the gods, but to status violations against one's fellow mortals. These usually take the form of specific acts of verbal or physical abuse, including assault and rape. Thus Medea [in Euripides' play] uses 'hubris' to refer to Jason's mistreatment of her, and also for his insulting language."[13] Medea murders her own children not only out of insane rage, but also out of the desire to protect her children from the horror of humiliation. In the play she exclaims: "There's no way this can be—that I should leave my sons alive to suffer outrage [hubris] from my enemies. In any case, it's necessary that they die" (l. 1060). Some acts of hubris are comical and even salutary. Rebellious acts of hubris (e.g., the mocking laughter of the slave) serve as occasions for upsetting obscene imbalances of power. Other acts of hubris are cruel and lead to fates that are worse than death. Euripides' portrayal of outrage and madness can help us to grasp the unnamed excesses of power as well as the responses that these excesses provoke in modern social systems.

The crime of hubris plays a significant role in the literature and law of Athenian democracy. By legal and cultural means, the *demos* of the ancient city-state checked the outrages of the rich or powerful against the working

---

[13] Ruby Blondell, Mary-Kay Gamel, Nancy Sorkin Rabinowitz, and Bella Zweig, eds., *Women on the Edge: Four Plays by Euripides* (New York: Routledge, 1999), 19; henceforth cited as *WE*. Mitch Miller suggests that hubris might function simultaneously as an offense against the gods and as an abuse of power against those situated below one in the social hierarchy. For example, the suitors in the *Odyssey* violate the codes of proper deference to the host (in their consumption of the resources of the household against the will of Penelope) as well as to Zeus, god of strangers. The traditional reading of hubris as arrogance toward the gods may be based on an inattention to the gods' function as sanctioning restraint in relations with those who are (relatively) powerless. This inattention blinds us to the primarily social character of hubris. I thank Miller for these helpful comments, offered in e-mail correspondence May 28, 2000.

poor.[14] For the Greeks, crimes of hubris were acknowledged as a significant cause of internal unrest and revolution. Hubris against strangers was acknowledged as a cause of war (*H*, 2). Like the modern notion of right, classical codes against hubris establish limits on outrageous forms of power. Modern Enlightenment-based democracies appear to be blind to the social and economic forces of dangerous elites, and fail to theorize social and economic rights as basic to freedom. Unlike the bourgeois, liberal notion of right, the ancient codes recognize the social life of the individual as the soul of justice.

Popular Greek culture was a complex mix of democratic and aristocratic traditions. Ancient conceptions of manhood were tied to ideas about honor (*DA*, 10–12, 250). "The rhetoric of ideal 'masculine' conduct, even in democratic Athens, was derived to a significant degree from the norms of heroic behavior on the battlefield. The word *arete* ('excellence'), which came to mean any kind of goodness, has the same root as the word for a man (*aner*) and originally referred primarily to excellence in battle" (*WE*, 50). In sixth- through fourth-century Athens, those who could afford the risks to their status and property would strive for gains of honor through the contests reserved for the elite (*DA*, 112). These contests were staged as zero-sum games, one man's gain in status entailing another man's loss. Those men who were publicly dishonored were expected to express rage, and to seek retribution through acts of revenge.

The working poor citizens voted directly on political issues and had considerable power in ancient Athens. Still, Athenian democracy failed to develop an egalitarian ethic. The masses did not speak in the verbal contests at the Assembly. These contests (or *agons*) were reserved for those who were, in the requisite sense, "excellent." The masses did enjoy legal and social codes to protect them from the worst excesses of the elite. Citizens could seek retribution against the arrogance of the rich in the law courts. For the ninety or so percent of the Greek citizens who counted among the common laborers and subsistence farmers, charges of hubris functioned as a form of social control. As Josiah Ober explains, "The Athenian democratic constitution ensured that the legal and political advantages enjoyed by the wealthy few in oligarchic states were minimalized at Athens" (*DA*, 193). While the wealthy elite were viewed as a constant source of tension in the democracy, the ancient Greeks assumed that the working poor "due to their lack of means, are forced to act moderately (*sophronein*)" (*DA*, 212). Legal and social codes against

---

[14] N. R. E. Fisher, *Hubris: A Study in the Values of Honour and Shame in Ancient Greece* (Warminster, Eng.: Aris and Phillips, 1992), 1; henceforth cited as *H*. Thanks much to Amy Coplan for pointing me toward this valuable source.

hubris aimed to assure that the rich did not make wealth or power more important than the demands for mutual aid within kinship and between social groups (*DA*, 211–213). While it is not clear how effective these codes were in practice, working-class codes against hubris do offer a tool of democracy that is missing in modern bourgeois theory.

Codes against hubris are absent in liberal democracies today despite the persistence of major social inequities. Perhaps the closest legal equivalent that we have to the classical concept of hubris is the hate crime.[15] However, recent efforts to introduce legislation against hate crimes have not always succeeded. As in the case of affirmative action, Enlightenment-oriented theorists have difficulty mounting persuasive arguments for the liberal social policies they espouse. Opponents of hate-crime legislation argue that the emotion of hate is not adequate to distinguish one type of crime over another, and that all types of crime are hate crimes. These claims miss the point that hate crimes (motivated by racial, ethnic, or other rivalries) do not target the individual but the social status of the target's perceived group-affiliation. This type of crime does not only damage the individual but also reinforces large-scale social inequalities. Opponents of the legislation claim that "hate is only foiled when the hated are immune to the bigot's power, not when the haters are punished. A hater cannot psychologically wound if a victim cannot be psychologically wounded. And that immunity to hurt can never be given; it can only be achieved."[16] I do not know to what degree individuals can inoculate themselves from humiliation without suffering from pathological symptoms of denial. The denial of pain often only deepens it. This narrow focus on psychological responses, however, obscures ways in which some social groups can control powerful institutions or economic and cultural policies in ways that severely damage other social groups. If modeled on ancient laws against hubris, hate crime legislation would offer a means to establish limits on the powers of dominant social groups. Why has this classical tool of a working-class democracy not survived into modern times?

Even contemporary scholars who discuss the role of hubris in drama undervalue its significance, and focus instead on the body and its appetites. For example, after the Euripides scholars elaborate upon the role of hubris in plays like *Medea*, they locate the major themes of Greek drama elsewhere: "Comedy makes crude jokes about food, drink, and sex, while tragedy exposes deep anxieties surrounding these same features of

---

[15] One might also consider the race-based hubris involved in flying the confederate flag.

[16] These arguments against hate-crime legislation are developed by Andrew Sullivan in "The Fight Against Hate: Why We Can't—and Shouldn't—Win It," *New York Times Magazine*, September 26, 1999, 50.

mortality" (*WE*, 46). Aristotle has made quite clear that the focus of drama is not on mastering our desires but, more centrally, on our "friendly relationships."[17] He proceeds, however, to exclude the politics of hubris from his study of tragic drama. Elaborating on classical scholarship, I will argue that classical tragedy served as a means for the masses to communicate to the elite a fundamental principle of social justice. According to these Greeks, when we mess with our relationships, we mess with ourselves. This is a moral message that we have trouble understanding today.

Foucault, perhaps better than any other recent European scholar, draws our attention to the ways in which external sources of power (and especially modern institutional norms) can invade the mind of the individual and constitute who we are. In *The Use of Pleasure*, he indicates his concern for the freedom of our erotic life by suggestively juxtaposing the Greek "arts of existence" with the "system of interdictions" that characterize an authoritarian, Christian morality.[18] Foucault describes the Greek arts of existence as styles of moderation in food, diet, and, to a lesser extent, sex, while interpreting the virtue of moderation strictly in terms of its difference from excess (*UP*, 45). Foucault invites the reader to ponder the emancipatory potential in these ancient "practices of the self" over more authoritarian Christian models of the self. His portrayal of antiquity, however, underestimates the central role of friendship and social intimacy in the erotic life of the Greek citizen. By focusing on the "quantitative" difference between moderation and excess, and not on the social crime of hubris, Foucault forecloses from contemporary social theory the codes and prohibitions used by the masses in order to limit the power of the elites.[19]

---

[17] Aristotle, *Poetics*, trans. Richard Janko (Indianapolis: Hackett, 1987), 53b20. A recent book promises to discuss these relationships in full; see Elizabeth S. Belfiore, *Murder Among Friends: Violation of Philia in Greek Tragedy* (New York: Oxford University Press, 2000).

[18] Michel Foucault, *The Use of Pleasure: Vol. II* of *The History of Sexuality*, trans. Robert Hurley (New York: Random House, 1990), 10; henceforth cited as *UP*.

[19] Foucault does not entirely ignore the topic of hubris. He does, however, confine his brief remarks on hubris to a discussion of the erotic relationships between men and boys of the leisure class. He notes that sexual relations between leisure-class men and boys were considered shameful unless the relation included "training for manhood, social connections for the future, or a lasting friendship" (*UP*, 224). However, Foucault's actual discussion of the tests and the training that the boy receives from his lover downplays the importance of the friendship between them. It is as though the primary aim of education is the discipline of the body and its appetites. The development of either bonds of affection or oaths of formal friendship receives too little attention.

Foucault's remarks on rape in an interview in 1977 reveal the same lack of awareness in a contemporary context. He suggests that rape could be prohibited as a crime of physical violence,

For antiquity, it is not in the body but in the social sphere that evil takes root. Hubris may involve excesses of appetites as in crimes of rape and adultery. Over-indulgence in appetite, however, is not the more invidious motive for the crime. Hubris is a crime of arrogance and social power. The surplus pleasure of this type of crime does not derive from physical pleasure or material gain but from the sense of superiority that the agent experiences through the degradation of another person (*H*, 1). Nonetheless, hubristic assault is often linked with questions of who does what work, and whether work is meaningful or socially degrading.

Greek prohibitions against hubris protected the beloved from the lover in gay sex, and prescribed rituals of hospitality or friendship on behalf of strangers and foreigners (*WE*, 21).[20] Since individuals were viewed as part of households, and the households were part of the economic and social infrastructure of the larger polis, a crime against an individual was treated as an assault against a people. The ramifications of the tragic act did not stop with its external targets (*DA*, 212).[21] An assault against friends and friendly strangers would threaten to unravel the connections that define the self.

Greek codes against hubris should not be confused with the authoritarian moral systems that Foucault rightly fears. Codes and prohibitions in the form of basic lists of human rights comprise essential tools for checking crimes of power, and allow individuals to flourish in their relationships with one another. The major source of unrestrained power in our era of globalization is white-owned capital, and this power no doubt explains the outrage of Islamic fundamentalists. In the West, we will have trouble witnessing the injustices of white capital and similar forms of domination until we learn to appreciate the individual who is vulnerable to the social force of hubris. If we are to counter cultural and economic forms of domination, then we will have to subordinate our liberal rights to the more important rights of the social person.

---

and not as a distinctly sexual act. See "Confinement, Psychiatry, Prison," in *Politics, Philosophy, Culture: Interviews and Other Writings, 1977–1984* (New York: Routledge, 1988), 200. For the Greeks, physical assault like rape was conceptualized less in terms of physical harm and bodily integrity than as an assault on one's honor. It is for this reason that the ancient Greeks included rape as well as many other forms of so-called physical assault among the crimes of hubris.

[20] On the status of rape and adultery in ancient Greek society, see Adele C. Scafuro, *The Forensic Stage: Settling Disputes in Graeco-Roman New Comedy* (Cambridge: Cambridge University Press, 1997), 232ff.

[21] See Cynthia B. Patterson, *The Family in Greek History* (Cambridge: Harvard University Press, 1998), for a full clarification of the interconnections between the family and the polis.

Charles Taylor's Politics
of Recognition and Multiculturalism

In an influential essay, "The Politics of Recognition," Charles Taylor argues that liberal theorists will need to turn to Hegel's dialectic of recognition if they are to grasp what structures human sociality.[22] Taylor traces what he describes as the monologic bent of Enlightenment liberalism back to the Stoics and the Christians, who argue that pride is not a virtue, and that how we appear in the public realm does not reflect our real worth. Stoic and Christian themes reappear in the Enlightenment philosopher Kant, who argues for the equal dignity of every citizen based on the individual's capacities to engage in rational thought. As Taylor explains, "This view understands human dignity to consist largely in autonomy, that is, in the ability of each person to determine for himself or herself a view of the good life" (M, 57).[23]

Taylor argues that the multicultural movement in the United States and Canada is challenging the Enlightenment view of the self, and he interprets the underlying thesis of this movement in Hegelian terms: "The thesis is that our identity is partly shaped by recognition or its absence, often by the misrecognition of others, and so a person or group of people can suffer real damage, real distortion, if the people or society around them mirror back to them a … contemptible picture of themselves" (M, 25). Hegel explains this need for recognition in his famous discussion of the relationship between the master and the slave in the *Phenomenology of Spirit*. Expanding upon Hegel, Taylor argues that dominant social groups need to recognize, not the actual cultural worth, but the cultural potential, of subordinate social groups. He urges us to avoid the "arrogance" of assuming that we can make judgments about the positive or negative value of another culture

[22] Taylor's essay leads off the Gutmann volume mentioned above. Taylor argues that the monological ideal "forgets how our understanding of the good things in life can be transformed by our enjoying them in common with people we love.… If some of the things that I value most are accessible to me only in relation to the person that I love, then she becomes a part of my identity" (M, 33–34). Taylor does not praise good things in life for how they might serve our amorous relationships. He praises our amorous relationships for how they might serve our enjoyment of good things. He cherishes how the beloved becomes a part of one's own identity. But he fails to mention how the lover might become a part of the identity of the beloved. There is something topsy-turvy, and finally one-sided, about his approach to love. I will return to these kinds of concerns in Chapters 5 and 9.

[23] For a richer view of the affective and temperamental dimensions of virtue in Kant, see the following by Rudolf A. Makkreel: "The Beautiful and the Sublime as Guideposts to the Human Virtues in the Early Kant," in *New Essays on Kant's Pre-Critical Writings*, ed. Tom Rockmore (Amherst, N.Y.: Humanities Press, 2001); "Reflective Judgment and the Problem of Assessing Virtue in Kant" *The Journal of Value Inquiry*, 2002; and *Imagination and Interpretation in Kant* (Chicago: University of Chicago Press, 1990), esp. chapters 6, 7, and 8.

without understanding their differences through dialogue. He argues that "real judgements of worth suppose a fused horizon of standards ... and that we have been transformed by the study of the other" (*M*, 70). We can foster the goal of "mutual recognition" and "cultural fusion" by undertaking comparative cultural studies based on the presumption of equal potential.

While Taylor's call for dialogue across cultural groups is promising, the rhetoric behind Taylor's argument may after all be arrogant. Taylor positions those individuals who represent dominant cultures as students and schoolteachers perhaps, but judges nonetheless, of weaker cultures. There is no analysis of the imbalances of power that mock the usual attempt to examine "objectively," or dialogue with, another culture. Even less is there any mention of the historical route by which these imbalances have emerged. Taylor poses the possibility that the Zulus might have developed a less valuable culture, but he does not discuss the Western destruction, and appropriation, of Zulu and other African cultures. There is, in other words, no acknowledgment of crimes committed, and economic and cultural debts owed, by European cultures. There is also no contextualization or acknowledgment of the value-making practices of colonized people who strive to overcome these assaults. The dialogue model of cultural fusion rides on the surface of deeper divisions.

Taylor's aim is to mark common ground in the multicultural debates. A symptom of his failure to establish such a ground lies in his treatment of his rivals inside and outside the circles of power. Unlike Habermas, Taylor names some of his rivals. These names include Derrida and Foucault. Taylor calls these men "Neo-Nietzscheans," and he dismisses their primary claim—that epistemological and normative claims cannot be addressed apart from issues of power—as "half-baked" (*M*, 70). It is ironic that in an essay that is meant to defend the protection of francophone culture in Anglo-dominated Canada, Taylor dismisses the arguments of men who may be counted among the leading figures in francophone philosophy. Perhaps less surprising, given the dismissal of these leading French thinkers, Taylor proceeds to construct the terms for a multicultural ethic exclusively from Anglo-American and German thought. The gesture betrays something of that will to power (or claim to high rank) that Taylor sees in his neo-Nietzschean opponents.

Europeans do not come to a dialogue without a history. This history includes wars of imperialism, justified often enough in terms of "educating" and or otherwise modernizing a people with "potential." Given this history, dialogue remains a rather superficial move in the game of power without extensive preliminary moral work. Taylor calls upon the oppressed to purge themselves of internalized images of inferiority so that dialogues across cultures might begin. He might also call our attention to the need for those of us who have enjoyed the fruits of oppression to purge ourselves, and repair friendly relations, through acts of reparation.

Third Wave Critical Theory: Social Humanism and African American Slave Narratives

Some of the most compelling narratives of freedom begin, as does Hegel, with an account of human bondage. Modern slave narratives written by Frederick Douglass (Chapter 8) and Toni Morrison (Chapter 9) support Hegel's insight into the value-creating practices of slaves. From these narratives we discover a concept of freedom that arises from the pathos and the labor of slave societies. These narratives also reflect what Hegel poses as the central irony of history: the master depends upon the slave for his identity, his culture, and his philosophy of freedom. Still, modern slavery does not accommodate Hegel's dialectical machinery.

As existential philosopher Lewis Gordon argues, modern race-based slavery differs substantially from slavery in European antiquity.[24] While Hegel's dialectic of recognition may represent the relationship between the master and slave in Europe, it does not represent this relationship in modern America. This is because Hegel's dialectical claim that the master depends upon the slave for recognition (no less than the slave depends upon the master) entails that the master see the slave as part animal but also as part human. The legitimacy of slavery depends upon the claim that in the master, the human side prevails over the animal side of the self, whereas in the slave, it is the reverse. According to the Hegelian account, the slave eventually redefines the human, giving birth to the idea of freedom in the West. Gordon points out that race perverts the dialectic between master and slave in the modern world. The black slave does not represent the mirror reversal of the white master. In other words, the black slave or colonized subaltern does not function as another (initially worse, but eventually better) self in the consciousness of the white master. The black body functions as a nonself and slips into the meaninglessness of brute existence. This is because modern race-based forms of subordination utterly dehumanize the victim. The black slave, unlike the white slave upon whom Hegel's dialectic of recognition turns, plays no role in the

[24] Lewis R. Gordon, *Existential Africana: Understanding Africana Existential Thought* (New York: Routledge, 2000), 47. See also Robert Bernasconi's important essay, "African Philosophy's Challenge to Continental Philosophy," in *Postcolonial African Philosophy*, ed. Emmanuel Chukwudi Eze (Cambridge, Mass.: Blackwell, 1997), 185.

consciousness of the white master. If I understand the implications of these claims correctly, no dialectical mediation is possible between the master and slave in the modern world. The emancipation of the oppressed in a race-torn world requires either unmediated and unrestrained violence or an ethical appeal for mercy to magical powers beyond the human realm.

These observations explain much of the dehumanizing force of modern race-based oppression. On the other hand, there is also in modern slavery and its racial aftermath a more ancient and perhaps a more perverse force. No slave narrative tells the story of this cruel and tragic force more powerfully than Toni Morrison's novel *Beloved*. From this story of American slavery emerges a dialectic of subjectivity and freedom that is not Hegelian.[25]

One of the major turns in the plot of *Beloved* occurs at the moment that the slavewoman Sethe overhears the schoolteacher (and master at Sweet Home plantation) lecture his pupils on the differences between masters and slaves. The schoolteacher divides the qualities of the African into human and subhuman functions. These words wrench apart Sethe's soul and raise disturbing questions regarding the meaning of modern subjectivity. It seems that the white slaveholder may exhibit a double consciousness when it comes to his relation with the slave. For this slaveholder, the slave is part brute but also part human. From this divided consciousness the white master derives the secret pleasures and powers of his crime. The representation of the slave as a brute masks the use of a human being as chattel in slavery, it is true. No doubt this misrepresentation eases the guilt and sets up the false consciousness of the modern slaveholder. But the representation also enacts an assault—an act of humiliation—on another human being. The surplus pleasure and social power of whiteness in the modern world depends upon this double consciousness. It is not the economic motive of racial subordination per se, but the terrifying arrogance that operates through this economic force that drives Sethe to murder her child. Sethe is a modern Medea.

I describe Sethe as a *modern* Medea because while Sethe, like Medea, reacts in justifiable rage to extreme threats on her social self, Morrison portrays these threats from a humanist and not a classical perspective.[26] Medea is the daughter of a king, and she does not question her elite status. The arrogance that she encounters in the land of her husband threatens the honor that a wife and a foreign guest would merit. She murders her children less to spare them from hubris than to have the last laugh over her husband and

[25] Toni Morrison, *Beloved* (New York: Penguin, 1987); henceforth cited as *B*.

[26] I worry about conservative, non-egalitarian, and honor-based codes of hubris that prevail among elite groups from classical times into the contemporary world. See "Arab Honor's Price: A Woman's Blood," *New York Times*, June 20, 1999, 1.

his new kingdom. Sethe is not the daughter of a king. She was born a slave. Still, like Medea, Sethe is a proud woman, and this pride drives her to extreme measures. Sethe is ready to resist at all costs the monstrous arrogance of the slave catchers. Medea's deeper motive for the murder of her daughter, however, is not the need for honor. Her deeper motive is the mother's need to be able to love and be loved by her children, and to protect that love from violation (Chapter 9). Morrison's tragic tale of hubris does not weave a plot of revenge for the sake of salvaging one's honor; this tragic tale mourns the inability to love in a world where perverse individuals and institutions threaten our intimate and ancestral relationships.

The "study" undertaken by the schoolteacher is not different in kind from the violations that his pupils commit against Sethe and her people. The lessons of the schoolteacher, perhaps no less than the theft of Sethe's milk or the beating of the Sweet Home men, constitute crimes of hubris. These crimes aim to break the spirit of the slave for economic profit but also for perverse psychic and social gain. For the Greeks, tragic crimes were affronts to the honor of their targets. For the characters in Morrison's novel, the deeper wounds are to the amorous heart.

The assaults of the schoolteacher and his students aim to dirty and humiliate or otherwise violate those whom they target. Sethe and similar characters in the novel, however, do not define themselves through the grotesque projections or arrogant fantasies of the assailants. The novel demonstrates how the victims of assault may register psychic and social damage without assuming the perspective of the agent. This moral anthropology refutes the Hegelian view of the self through its mirrorlike reflection in the consciousness of the other, and it calls into question the value of mutual recognition for freedom. In this moral anthropology, the basic drives of the emerging self are not bent on what Freudians term narcissistic wholeness (and Taylor reinterprets as cultural fusion). The basic drives of the self are more diverse, and they are originally social. The Hegelian account of sociality (based on a logic of dialectical reversal, and a metaphysics of internal relations) collapses the distinct points of view of the victim and the agent of domination into a single perspective. This account obscures the play between the individual and heterogeneous social forces. And it forecloses a multicultural dialectic of freedom.

In *Beyond Recognition*, Kelly Oliver identifies an especially virulent form of the narcissism that afflicts the use of recognition theory in postcolonial theory.[27] She questions those theorists who straightforwardly assert the need

[27] Kelly Oliver, *Beyond Recognition* (Minneapolis: University of Minnesota Press, forthcoming), chap. 1; henceforth cited as *BR*. Oliver's brilliant work has helped me significantly to

on the part of the oppressed to achieve the recognition of the oppressor. These theorists cite Frantz Fanon to support their claim, but they are wrong to do so, Oliver rightly argues. Fanon's analysis of the needs of the oppressed does not support mutual recognition as an emancipatory goal. On the contrary, his analysis diagnoses what Oliver terms the "the pathology of recognition." Those who seek recognition from the oppressor—at least in any straightforward terms—have failed to challenge the oppressor's claim to possess the measuring stick of humanity.

Of course, if recognition from the oppressor is not the answer, neither is the withdrawal of the individual from the social sphere. Hegel portrays the strength of the slave in his stoic detachment, and argues that this stoicism gives us a first glimpse into the meaning of freedom. Morrison's novel portrays Sethe's stoic retreat from her community as a wrong turn on the path toward emancipation. Withdrawal from the social sphere defers the psychic labor of working through, and, at a certain point, letting go of, the pathos from an unforgiving but deeply human past. The emotional labor of "working through" the pathos of slavery is missing entirely from the Hegelian account. This emotional labor anchors emancipation in the libidinal work of family and intimate friendships, but also in the spirited, life-affirming values that we may inherit from our culture, and in bonds of friendship across races and continents. This cathartic labor requires that we jettison the stoic rationalism in the Hegelian account of freedom, and, as I will argue in Part 2, root subjectivity in the social eroticism of the flesh.

The Soul of Justice begins with the fact of human sociality. From a philosophical anthropology that emerges out of modern slavery, I search for the deeper meaning of freedom in the contemporary world. Ancient discourses on honor and hubris strengthen the impoverished social discourses of modern theory, but these ancient discourses also legitimate inegalitarian social codes. *The Soul of Justice* experiments with the discourses on sociality by substituting for the ancient interest in honor what sociologist Patricia Hill Collins terms "eros," and defines through the value-creating practices of black women in America (Chapter 7).[28]

---

clarify the issues of my own book, including my critique of Taylor's position in the multicultural debates.

[28] Elaborating upon the intersections between Morrison's and Douglass's more literary work and the social theory of Collins among others will be aimed in part to overcome what Deborah E. McDowell analyzes as a false distinction between theory and creative writing. See McDowell's *"The Changing Same": Black Women's Literature, Criticism, and Theory* (Bloomington: Indiana University Press, 1995), esp. 170.

Philosophers typically separate the analysis of moral claims from a sociological analysis of power. These philosophers may define their task in terms of a rational reflection on moral obligations and exclude from their reflection an empirical analysis of wealth and status. Along with first-wave critical theorists, I suspect that an overly sharp distinction between ethics and politics does not help us to understand how our moral points of view may unwittingly sustain unjust political situations and false ideas about ourselves. Philosophers have come to accept that the rational mind is not entirely separable from the body and the emotions, but we must also better come to recognize how our moral judgments grow out of our social affiliations. Moral judgments made without an analysis of cultural and economic hierarchies are likely to reinforce the undemocratic distribution of power and wealth in our world. We must be alert to the fact that our moral conscience is not immune from the prejudicial images that we encounter in the media. We can also take hope in the fact that white-owned capital and other prevailing forces can bend to well-staged forms of ethical appeal. For these reasons, ethics and politics woven together constitute a better place for normative philosophy to occupy than ethics or politics alone.[29]

The ancient themes of ethics, politics, and literature pose limits for diverse sources of power across the social field, and suggest ways to shift the paradigm for democracy in a multicultural world. The Greeks extended prohibitions against hubris across cultural and political boundaries, welcoming the stranger and the foreigner as a friend (in Greek, *xenos* signifies all three meanings).[30] Following the ancient example, I would argue that formal or informal codes should establish global prohibitions against hubris without waiting for the studies of the schoolteachers or an arguably repressive fusion of cultures. Codes of humility and hospitality should accompany comparative studies, public debates, and other processes of cultural transmission, serving to guide their outcome. A synthesis of the liberal doctrine of universal rights and ancient practices of social justice brings us to see that the soul of

---

[29] On this point, I mean to avoid siding with either Aristotle, for whom politics is the master science, or Levinas, for whom ethics is first philosophy. I regard Levinas as rightly orienting our political concerns toward the poor and disenfranchised, but I do not think that the attention to oppressed subjects can begin apart from a critical understanding of material and social conditions of oppression. And I do not accept an ethics of charity in lieu of reparations and fair pay for carework or other work.

[30] Herodotus portrays the Persian attempt to expand from Asia into Europe as an arrogant response to the Athenians, who are likewise viewed as hubristic; see *The Histories*, trans. Aubrey De Selincourt (New York: Penguin, 1996), VII8b-c, and 10f. Aeschylus's *Persians* reflects the same view; see *The Persians* in *Prometheus Bound and Other Plays*, trans. Philip Vellacott (New York: Penguin, 1971), ll. 581ff. Homer portrays the abduction of Helen by the Trojans in a similar vein in *The Iliad*, trans. Robert Fagles (New York: Penguin, 1990), Bk. 2; ll. 189ff.

the individual lies in democratic relationships of love, friendship, and hospitality. For the Greek *demos*, the pathos of tragic violence does not turn on a simple error (or *hamartia* as Aristotle claims; see Chapter 7), but on the horrifying violation of basic social bonds.[31] When the social field has been devastated by crimes of hubris, individuals succumb to communal illness. The caste of honor that held together Athenian democracy lacks moral legitimacy in a modern egalitarian system, but the social vision of the citizen and the stranger as a friend does not. In response to the Greeks we might say that the person is born, not of honor, but of love. Sociality, or social eros, and not honor is the origin and the goal of the person and the positive core of freedom. The Enlightenment project of autonomy should be understood as instrumental to this end.[32]

Overview

Part 1, "A Marriage of Autonomy and Care," addresses efforts to correct the one-sidedness of the Enlightenment model of the moral and legal subject. This one-sided liberal view valorizes that mythic person whose independence from "external forces" allows for rational or self-interested decisions. This view fails to acknowledge the ways in which the rational agent depends upon carework in order to compete in the marketplace and participate in civic society. The paradigmatic case of carework is the preservative love that children receive from their mothers. While the liberal model takes either the self-interested agent of the marketplace or the disinterested rational thinker as paradigmatic of the moral subject, care ethics emphasizes the nurturing and altruistic qualities of caregivers. Philosophers, including Habermas, draw upon psychologist Carol Gilligan's research on gender differences in moral development in order to argue for a balanced conception of moral maturity. These arguments culminate in the view that the mature moral subject possesses both the traditionally male virtue of autonomy as well as the traditionally female capacity to care for others.

[31] Ober argues that the intended audience of ancient philosophical discourse was the elite, which explains its relative social conservatism in comparison with ancient drama, intended to communicate the concerns of the masses. Impoverished workers and subsistence farmers composed the bulk of the audience at the theater. See *DA*, 50.

[32] Compare Martha Nussbaum's synthesis of Greek and Enlightenment themes. She introduces an Aristotelian psychology into a neo-Kantian theory of justice, arguing for fundamental human capabilities as the basis for a liberal doctrine of moral rights. In Nussbaum's account, the social forces that define the element of human existence carry secondary importance in a list of human functions, where pride of place is given to the individual's capacity as a choice maker. See her *Sex and Social Justice* (New York: Oxford University Press, 1999), 41. See also Amartya Sen, *Development as Freedom* (New York: Alfred A. Knopf, 1999), 54–86.

Critics of care ethics, including, ironically, Carol Gilligan herself, argue that its more visionary aims are lost in the dichotomies of nineteenth-century Victorianism. I agree with these critics. It is difficult to "transvalue" (I borrow Nietzsche's term, but with some trepidation, given the topic) "caregiving" when our understanding of this term is framed by conventional oppositions between autonomy and dependency, reason and emotion, and masculinity and femininity. These dichotomies block us from fully grasping the central role of human sociality in moral development and civic society. In particular, two consequences of the conventional framework, beset as it is by the nineteenth-century dichotomies, call for more radical thinking.

First, these dichotomies sustain what has been called the paradox of freedom. According to this paradox, the individual is, as the Germans say, *frei aber einsam*. The individual is most free when he is most alone (or separated and evacuated of social, cultural, and historical sources of meaning). Many modern liberal theorists (including some care ethicists) who acknowledge this paradox argue that individuals experience a tension between the need for connection and the need for independence. I argue that this is a false dichotomy. The individual grows more spirited through desired connections with others. The meaning of freedom needs to be rethought along these lines.

Second, the conventional dichotomies support the notion that individuation requires a fundamental break from a sphere that the modernists once mythologized as "the state of nature" and continue to associate with embodiment and domesticity. According to a standard plot in modern literature and philosophy, maturation requires that the child leave home or otherwise test his independence from his family (and often, in particular, his mother). This view conceals the fact that the human being is born into a social sphere, and that an original sociality characteristic of our species shapes corporeal desires as well as family life. On the basis of these considerations, I question any theory of individuation that renders normative a separation from the mother or other libidinal attachments within or beyond the domestic sphere.

Part 2, "A Dialectic of Eros and Freedom," engages dialectical thinkers Herbert Marcuse and Luce Irigaray in an attempt to unburden care ethics of conventional dichotomies. A neo-Freudian account of drive energy and its creative sublimation developed by Marcuse and Irigaray prepares us to reinterpret care in terms of the more politically and aesthetically charged category of eros. From a critical engagement with these neo-Romantic thinkers, I argue that pro-social drives originally embedded in lyric, tactile, and rhythmic sources of meaning in infancy form the basis for mature forms of moral development and culture. The child that is not touched does not thrive. This single fact throws into question Western philosophical anthropology from Aristotle and the Stoics to Hegel and Freud, and opens the path for a dialectic of eros and freedom.

Part 3, "A Discourse of Love, A Practice of Freedom," turns to the visionary pragmatism of the African-American tradition. Such authors as Patricia Hill Collins, Frederick Douglass, and Toni Morrison expand the focus of ethics from quasi-biological instincts and their sublimation to fully human relationships. These authors do not present the individual's separation from the mother or the family as a sign of moral maturity, but as a reminder of the brutality of slavery. They do not view the mother primarily in terms of her biological function as a womb. On the contrary, the flesh and blood face of another person is the major site for ethical engagement inside and outside the family. This fact not only positions the mother as a moral agent but also challenges the prevailing assumption that separation from emotional ties is a productive stage in moral maturation and individual freedom.

In their slave narratives, Morrison and Douglass counter the stoic turn in the Enlightenment model of freedom, and project instead a dialectic of social eros that moves from family and ancestors to strangers across communities and nation-states. This dialectic carries a global call for limits against the arrogance of false needs and unchecked power. The call resonates with an ancient protest against hubris, but now spelled out in a more thoroughly egalitarian vein. Cornel West names this thorough-going egalitarianism an "ethic of love," and bell hooks brings this ethic to the heart of freedom.[33] The final chapters of my book explore the meaning of this vision, not in lists of basic capacities, rights, or primary goods, but in the more soulful weave of narrative and song.

Still, lists of basic human rights are critical for a theory of justice. Perhaps this book makes clear why such a list needs to include among central human rights the right of mothers and their children, and families more broadly defined, to significant material, cultural, and political resources;[34] the right for all workers to be free from bonded labor (which includes the right for parents along with other workers to a decent wage and social services); the right to establish limits on economic and cultural domination; the proportional representation of racial and disempowered groups in major

[33] bell hooks, "Love as a Practice of Freedom" in *Outlaw Culture: Resisting Representations* (New York: Routledge, 1994), 243–250. See Stanlie James and Abena Bousia, *Theorizing Black Feminisms: The Visionary Pragmatism of Black Women* (New York: Routledge, 1993).

[34] I fully support Eva Feder Kittay's powerful critique of Rawlsian liberalism, and her claim that a "commitment to the equality of all requires an equality that is connection-based"; see *Love's Labor* (New York: Routledge, 1999), 183.

political, cultural, and economic institutions (including the International Monetary Fund); the right to be protected from psychic violation and social humiliation;[35] the right to reparations in order to repair the damage of crimes of hubris; and most fundamentally in this era of white capital, the uncompromising priority of the needs of the social person over the protection of private property, public wealth, and social arrogance.

[35] See Martha Minow, *Between Vengeance and Forgiveness* (Boston: Beacon Press, 1998), 8.

I

A Marriage of Autonomy and Care

1
The Ethics of Care and Its Limits

Major philosophers in Europe and America are challenging the excessive rationalism of modern ethics. These philosophers, coming from diverse traditions, share the concern that reason does not suffice as the basis for understanding basic moral values. Emotions also must play a role in our moral judgments. One major impetus for this widespread interest in the emotions comes from increasing attention to realms of moral experience such as family, friendship, and romantic love. The previous neglect of these realms in modern philosophy reflects the social divisions of modern society, and in particular the separation of the public and privates spheres among the respectable middle class. The private life has been focused around the domesticity of the family, and portrayed as the sphere of women and the emotional life. This sphere was mythologized and sentimentalized but not subjected to the same norms of rational moral thinking that were valorized in the public and professional sphere. Middle-class women entering into the work force over the last few decades have brought values of emotional and interpersonal connection and styles of cognition that were previously taken to be improper for public, professional, and, so too, philosophical discourse.

Despite the revalorization of the emotions and friendship in professional and public life, however, it is not clear that there is more compassion in our political or corporate culture. Images of violence are not disappearing from popular culture. Consider the popular and critically acclaimed film *Saving Private Ryan* (Steven Spielberg, 1998). The film is remarkable in its unapologetic display of the horror of male-on-male aggression. One would think that a spectacle of war's more sickening scenes of mutilation and dismemberment would render, or at least threaten to render, the theme of war obscene. However, Spielberg's film manages to take the viewer far into the chasmic abyss of war's unbound pathos only in order to render that war's glory ever more sublime. The film salvages the value of violence by demonstrating the soldier's willingness to pass through war's horror, even accept the near-certainty of death, for the sake of male friendship and family. The rite of passage anchors the individual in social commitments within national alliances. The obligations of friendship and family do not cross over enemy lines. Could the willingness to commit wanton acts of violence actually increase with the strength of our libidinal attachments? Certainly, as the plot of the film suggests, there is no simple opposition between the capacity to love and the capacity to make war. If this was the presupposition of the cultural revolution of the late 1960s and early 1970s, it was a mistake.

In contemporary revisions of modernist philosophy, the values of love, friendship, and family move to the center of ethics. Broadly speaking, revisionist philosophies concur that significant virtues of the private sphere—virtues such as compassion, empathy, and solidarity—should be brought into the public and professional realm, and into the core of moral theory. The question is whether these diverse projects can yield a unified vision for a transcultural ethics. What is the role of domestic virtues of love and friendship in a global politics conditioned by ethnic, racial, and economic conflict?

In this chapter, I introduce the major claims of Anglo-American care ethics. Care ethics developed out of the work of Carol Gilligan in the 1980s and is now the strongest challenge to ethical theory in the analytic tradition of mainstream Anglo-American philosophy. Care ethicists argue that the modern liberal theories that focus exclusively on formal rights, abstract moral principles, and the virtue of autonomy have dissociated the cognitive component of the self from the nexus of social relationships based on nurturing and trust that make us whole persons. Gilligan's critique of the rational agent model grew out of her empirical research on gender differences in moral thinking. These differences had been occluded from view by the prevailing theory of moral development, which was developed by the American psychologist Lawrence Kohlberg from work that began in the 1950s. Kohlberg's paradigm evaluates individual moral development in terms of the ability to distance oneself from emotional responses to concrete situations, and to justify one's moral judgments though impartial and abstract principles. He argues that abstract cognitive skills measured by his theoretical apparatus test for the ability to transcend the conventions of one's culture and engage in universal moral thought. Gilligan argues that the use of Kohlberg's paradigm in order to test the moral development of research subjects is not itself impartial and universal. Her claim is that the paradigm is weighted toward the particular moral skills that are associated with the socialization of males, and is therefore not transcendent but conventional.

Anglo-American philosophers acknowledge that the historical roots of care ethics lie in a sentimental portrayal of the woman's duty in the family from middle-class Victorian and post–World War II suburban households. This portrayal confines women to the quasi-natural role of the nurturing mother, while stripping the mother's labor of any significant economic or political value. In order to avoid this truncated picture of moral identity, care ethicists argue that both reason and care should be part of the complete moral make-up of every moral person.

Missing from care ethics is a psychological theory that can explain what motivates the caring attachments that this ethics presupposes, and so too could provide an indication as to the possible limitations in our ability to care. Nel Noddings, for example, argues that care ethics transfers such "natural" and "innate" caretaking efforts as a mother's selfless devotion to her child onto other, nonrelated individuals.[1] But how does this transfer of moral affect happen? What assures a successful transfer? Noddings claims that it is proper for the moral agent to lack moral sentiments for animals and "for the starving children of Africa." This is because animals are seen as capable of very little response to our care, and the starving children of Africa demand more care than is realistic to give (*JC*, p. 15). Clearly, however, many of us find enticing possibilities for sentimental attachment and communicative response in our pets, sometimes more than in other members of

---

[1] See Nel Noddings, "Caring," in *Justice and Care: Essential Reading in Feminist Ethics*, ed. Virginia Held (Boulder, Colo.: Westview Press, 1995), esp. 9. Further references to this anthology are cited as *JC*.

our own species. Others among us find the infinite distancing of the children of Africa racially and politically suspect, especially given the intimate role of the World Bank and the IMF in transferring wealth from Africa to the United States. What explains the psychological basis for our limited ability to care? Could the virtue of care be kept pure from the distortions of such ordinary human vices as narcissistic identification, racial arrogance and greed? When and when not?

In the absence of a fully developed moral psychology, my focus in the major section of this chapter is on the object-relations psychology from which care ethics has evolved. While object-relations psychology lays out a theory of libidinal attachment, this theory does not help the project of care ethics. On the contrary, this theory poses in straightforward terms a major problem for Anglo-American care ethics. As a general project, care ethics portrays the social dimension of the self in terms that are politically and ethically underdeveloped. This project will need to draw upon resources from other traditions of culture and philosophy in order to overcome the social minimalism of American culture.

In object-relations psychology, the mother's love for her child is based on merging identities, and theorized in terms of narcissistic regression. Her moral agency is described in terms of a "primitive feeling-state."[2] The motivations for caring relationships could use a richer explanation than narcissistic identification with the cared-for object. At the same time, the use of the narcissistic mother as a model for understanding ethical relations threatens to reduce the ethical other to a dependent child or childlike creature.

The underlying problem with care ethics is not with the use of the mother-child dyad as a nodal point for conceptualizing a more general theory of ethics based in part on care. The historical configurations of the mother-child dyad reveal much about the genealogy of the person and some of the more deep-rooted desires of our species. A moral philosophy that does not analyze the genealogy of the moral person in the family misses much about what is significant in human desire. My concern is with the particular way in which the mother-child relation is figured. More often than not, the mother is portrayed in a quasi-biological role of protecting the dependent child from harm. This view of the relation misses the full drama of eros, economic labor, and social force that comes into play in the mother-child relation. As a consequence of the minimalist view of the mother-child relation, we perpetuate a minimalist view of human sociality, and so too of the mean-

[2] Nancy Chodorow, *The Reproduction of Mothering: Psychoanalysis and the Sociology of Gender* (Berkeley: University of California Press, 1978), henceforth cited as *RM*.

ing of political freedom in America. In order to address these concerns, we will need to transform the ethics of care by way of a more powerful philosophical anthropology.

Object-Relations Psychology:
The Libidinal Roots of Anglo-American Care Ethics

Anglo-American philosophers who have made exciting contributions to care ethics, including Annette Baier, Virginia Held, Diana Meyers, Sara Ruddick, and Joan Tronto, take their inspiration from Gilligan's psychological research into the male biases of Lawrence Kohlberg's neo-Kantian moral psychology.[3] Gilligan argues that Kohlberg's developmental theory of moral stages mutes an alternative moral voice, one that has culturally and historically been associated with women.[4] The philosophical interest in Gilligan's work stems from the fact that Kohlberg's theory has been used to give an empirical basis to major liberal philosophies of justice (especially those of John Rawls and Jürgen Habermas). If the neo-Kantianism of modernist philosophies privileges the insights and masks the blind spots of a male, bourgeois frame of reference, then the standard theories of justice would need in some way to be altered, according to care ethicists, in order to account for the moral experiences of women. These care ethicists more or less agree that a theory of justice based in the Kantian tradition of impartial reason must at least be supplemented by and, probably more radically, must be incorporated into an enlarged sense of justice that fully develops the moral skills of care.

Studies of the moral thinking of female subjects supports an alternative conception of moral development to that proposed by Kohlberg. Gilligan explains: "In this conception, the moral problem arises from conflicting re-

[3] Works I discuss in Chapter 1 include Annette C. Baier, *Moral Prejudices* (Cambridge: Harvard University Press, 1995), henceforth cited as *MP*; Virginia Held, *Feminist Morality: Transforming Culture, Society, and Politics* (Chicago: University of Chicago, 1993), henceforth cited as *FM*; Diana Tietjens Meyers, "Moral Reflection: Beyond Impartial Reason," in *Hypatia* 8, no. 3 (Summer 1993), 21–47 (henceforth cited as *MR*), reprinted as parts of *Subjection and Subjectivity* (New York: Routledge, 1994), henceforth cited as *S*; Joan C. Tronto, *Moral Boundaries: A Political Argument for an Ethic of Care* (New York: Routledge, 1993), henceforth cited as *MB*. Among other classics of care ethics, see Sara Ruddick, *Maternal Thinking: Toward a Politics of Peace* (New York: Beacon, 1989); and Mary Jeanne Larrabee, ed., *An Ethic of Care* (New York: Routledge, 1993), and Robin West, "Jurisprudence and Gender," in *Feminist Legal Theory*, ed. Katharine Bartlett and Rosanne Kennedy (Boulder, Colo.: Westview Press, 1991), 201–234. Much important work in care ethics has been done elsewhere, which I discuss later in the book.
[4] Carol Gilligan, *In a Different Voice: Psychological Theory and Women's Development* (Cambridge: Harvard University Press, 1982), henceforth cited as *DV*.

sponsibilities rather than from competing rights and requires for its resolution a mode of thinking that is contextual and narrative rather than formal and abstract. This conception of morality as concerned with the activity of care centers moral development around the understanding of responsibility and relationships, just as the conception of morality as fairness ties moral development to the understanding of rights and rules" (*DV,* 19).

A rights perspective emphasizes the development of inductive and deductive forms of reasoning, and relies upon the use of abstract principles in order to determine moral outcomes. Care ethics focuses instead on the need to respond to individuals who are viewed as unique and irreplaceable. Judgments about what to do in relations with particular persons in particular cases may be justified by an appeal to feelings, stories, or paradigmatic examples that grow out of local cultural traditions.

Gilligan compares the two orientations in moral judgment to a figure / - ground shift in perception: "For a justice perspective, the self as moral agent stands as the figure against a ground of social relationships, judging the conflicting claims of self and others against a standard of equality or equal respect (the Categorical Imperative, the Golden Rule). From a care perspective, the relationship becomes a figure, defining self and others."[5]

The virtue of care has been traced to the sentimentalized mother who since the industrial revolution has been represented as a haven from the marketplace, and whose sense of connectedness and empathy allow her to provide the nurturing and trust that define the conditions of the idealized family (see, e.g., Tronto, *MB*). Care ethicists are well aware of the problems of simply and uncritically reasserting this "better half" of the bourgeois patriarch in order to transform traditional liberal theory. In fact, feminists have labored to sever care ethics from its associations with self-sacrificial images of motherhood (Meyers, *S*); to reclaim authentic empathy from fantasied projections of oneness (Meyers, *MR, S*); and to salvage care from the sentimental discourse on family values that separates a private domain of feeling from the public space of praxis (esp. Tronto, *MB*, 108). Most significantly, while these theorists have all acknowledged the roots of care ethics in object-relations psychology, especially as developed in the work of Nancy Chodorow, they have also distanced themselves from the ever-suspicious neo-Freudian theory of libido that underlies Chodorow's view of the mother-child relationship by appropriating only her safest

---

[5] Carol Gilligan, "Moral Orientation and Development," in *Justice and Care: Essential Readings in Feminist Ethics,* ed. Virginia Held (Boulder, Colo.: Westview Press, 1995), 34–35.

claims. These safer and more trustworthy claims focus on the sense of connectedness that is not only essential for nurturing children but that should be developed in every citizen of a just state.

The problem with this approach to care ethics is that it fails to provide an alternative theory of libidinal attachment. For example, Diana Meyers carefully articulates the conceptual differences between the moral use of empathy from the immediate feelings of shared experience that, she explains, we sometimes call sympathy (*MR*, 25). Meyers points out that the moral use of empathy requires a highly developed reconstruction of the feelings and situation of the ethical Other. Such an imaginative reconstruction would not involve the merging of identities that defines some of the overly simple and sentimental images of mothering. Meyers's distinction between sympathy and empathy is clearly very important for ethics. However, this distinction needs more than a conceptual analysis. Care ethics lacks a full-blown moral psychology that could account for the question of with whom we can and cannot empathize. For example, if the deeper motivations of empathy trace back to libidinal relations in the nuclear family, then it would be difficult to explain how we might empathize with those who do not resemble close family members. It is also unclear what unresolved childhood problems ("ghosts in the nursery," in psychoanalytic parlance) might be lurking behind adult conceptions of who is worthy of our devoted care. Meyers aims to avoid a "speculative developmental psychology," but I think this is a mistake (*S*, 11). We need to understand the desire component of what Meyers calls empathetic thought.

The paradigmatic role of the mother-child relation in understanding the nature of care underscores the tendency for care ethicists to construe the ethical other in terms of childlike features of dependency. One of the problems with this projection of dependency onto objects of care is that it perpetuates the hubris of "infantilization." Meyers wisely combines her analysis of empathy with a call for positive refigurations of the cultural images by which we view others. Her project teaches us much about how cultural images can foster social prejudices and block empathy. However, her analysis does not address the psychic underpinnings (e.g., the narcissism or even arrogance) of our distorted views of one another. As care ethicists know, our most sophisticated texts, including the canonical texts of Western culture, reflect the fantasies and desires of their time. One of the most pervasive fantasies is the representation of the non-Western Other as needy, underdeveloped, or otherwise "like a child." This misrepresentation is used to rationalize the Western domination of those who are viewed as in need of economic or cultural development. If we are to address underlying motives for our view of ourselves in relation with others, then we will need to delve into the roots of fantasy and desire. Much of psychoanalytic theory, and object-relations psychology, reflects the fantasies and desires (for Chodorow, clearly narcissistic) of the Victorian family.

Meyers implicitly draws upon this troubling tradition of family values when her careful analysis of the emotional basis of empathy finally entrusts itself to an "attitude of concern that ... ensures that our imaginative reconstructions of other's subjectivity will be charitable, not hostile" (*MR*, 30). The final appeal to voluntary charity has a long history in Christian America. The careful use of empathy backed up by a final appeal to charity does not address the irrational roots of our libidinal responses to others. Such conceptual niceties tend instead ever so politely to cover over these unsavory experiences, keeping up appearances of good will in a Pax Americana.

Given the roots of care ethics in the sentimental tradition of family values in America, it is not surprising that so many theorists would wed empathy with autonomous judgment. Meyers terms this synthesis "empathetic thought" (*S*, 17). My fear is that the moral reflection or empathetic thought of the average citizen will not suffice to challenge large-scale patterns and long histories of domination and repression. This is why in Chapter 4, I argue that rational reflection on particular situations (Meyers's empathetic thought) or abstract rules (impartial reason) is not sufficient for augmenting our empathetic responses. Moral philosophy needs to draw upon what Fraser and Nicholson term large-scale empirical narratives of social change. Meyers wants to avoid a speculative development psychology, but she does turn to psychoanalytic feminists, including Irigaray as well as Chodorow, for countertropes of subjectivity. This is an important step toward overcoming antihumanistic distortions of our individual and cultural identity. However, I do not see how the mere posing of counterfigures can take hold in the social psyche unless these figures respond to our deepest libidinal needs. With these concerns in mind, in Chapter 6, I attempt to join large empirical narratives from Marcuse and other social theorists with Irigaray's lyrical speculations on the erotic roots of the moral subject.

Traditional psychoanalytic theory argues that moral reason develops when the child represses his erotic attachments to the mother and identifies with the Oedipal father. Chodorow does not question this view. Without an alternative genealogy than that provided by object-relations psychology, we are left by default with a notion of moral reason that owes its psychological origins to the repression of the very libidinal drives upon which care ethics seems to rely. Care ethicists who want some kind of marriage between reason and empathy need to address not only the regressive impulses of care but also the repressive dynamic of Oedipalization that lies underneath neo-Kantian models of autonomous reason.[6]

As it stands, care ethics has split the good part of object-relations psychology from the bad part. In particular, care ethics has split the conscious act of empathy from what Chodorow analyzes as its more primitive and unconscious roots in autoeroticism, narcissism, and primary love. In traditional psychoanalytic theory, these primary drives cannot be dissociated from aggression and other destructive instincts, and Chodorow does not challenge this claim. The implication is that care for the Other can hardly be separated from aggressive instincts. At the same time that care ethics has split empathy from its roots in libidinal desire, it has also split moral reason from its developmental history in Oedipalization. The splitting not only points to an uncritical faith in the caregiver's capacity for empathy, and a problematic union with a repressive model of moral reason; this splitting also perpetuates a reductive view of the erotic attachments of the family as well as of the larger social and political forces of our culture.

In particular, I worry about the reduction of the full range of pleasures and pathologies that define familial and political sociality to what care ethicists portray along a single and relatively simple dimension of human interaction. According to virtually every care ethicist, familial and political relationships should be anchored in attitudes or practices whose primary or most fundamental aim would be to establish trust (see, e.g., Baier, *BP*, 10ff.) and whose primary feeling is one of nurturing or otherwise establishing a sense of security for those who are socially vulnerable (e.g., Held, 75). Annette Baier does discuss in several of her essays the ludic and expressive aspects of the adult-child interaction (see, e.g., *MP*, 42–44, 325). However, her essays converge with those of other care ethicists in that they fall back on the view that the love ethic is primarily directed toward "helpless children," and more generally, "protect[ing] the young or the dying or the starving or any of the relatively powerless against neglect" (*MP*, 28–29) and that a moral theory that "mediates between reason and feeling," between "men's theories of obligation ... and [women's theories of] love" would be based in trust (*MP*, 10). That is, the whole of human sociality tends to be analyzed predominately, if not exclusively, in terms of the need for security.

This reductive language is not foreign to the psychoanalytic theory of Chodorow. On the contrary, even while Chodorow does not fully dissociate the experience of mothering from the complex eroticism of the

---

[6] For an extended analysis of the repressive values of Neo-Kantianism, see Andrew Cutrofello, *Discipline and Critique: Kant, Poststructuralism, and the Problem of Resistance* (Albany: State University of New York Press, 1994).

Oedipal complex, she nonetheless characterizes the experiences in the rather minimalist terms of what she calls primary love. Primary love is defined as providing emotional and physical security for the child, establishing trust, and in securing a sense of well-being and tranquility (59). It is the need for security that seems to yield the entire basis for what object-relations psychology identifies as the social bond between mother and child, and thus too the only alternative source for moral experience outside of the repressive and punitive dynamic of Oedipalization (206). While primary love seems for Chodorow to be partly associated with an autoeroticism in the child or narcissistic regression in the mother (or, as Chodorow argues, in the caregiving father; see 109), the exclusive focus of this love on securing trust and tranquility obscures ludic, symbolic, and other expressive interactions that can make up the more meaningful dimensions of the adult-child relation, as well as some of the more significant dimensions of our art, politics, and culture.

Thus, while Chodorow aims to distinguish the social bonding between caregiver and child from the routine and repetitive acts of providing physical nourishment or oral gratification for the child, she nonetheless uses terms to describe this interaction that suggest only the most minimal stage of sociality beyond the natural concern for preserving the life of the child. There is very little ascribed to primary love other than meeting the most basic emotional needs for security and trust, emotions that are fundamental to a person, and yet, as she herself admits, too primitive to constitute any of the higher functions of a self including the more significant and creative dimensions of human sociality (*RM*, 60). Given Chodorow's picture of mothering, it would seem that the emotional needs of loving the child can be fully satisfied in such stereotypical behavior as cradling and otherwise quieting the dependent child. Mothering may be a social and not a natural activity, but at least as Chodorow describes it, mothering is based on the kind of routine and repetitive interactions that according to de Beauvoir define mechanical labor and not a human identity (*RM*, 179).

Therefore, it is not surprising to find that even if care ethicists such as Tronto teach us to question the boundary between a privatized care ethics and the public space of justice, they do not sufficiently challenge other important boundaries that continue to reduce the full cultural and political force of the mother-child or the care activist–care recipient interaction to the most primitive levels of existential intersubjectivity. Tronto defines care in terms of "acceptance of some form of burden" (103), and then distinguishes care from "activities of life that do not generally constitute care … : the pursuit of pleasure, creative activity, production, destruction. To play, to fulfill a desire, to market a new product, or to create a work of art, is not care" (104). But if practices of care are to establish our most fundamental sense of justice, as Tronto argues they should, we have not advanced much beyond the kind of minimalist picture of the social self that has limited liberal theories of justice from their beginnings in eighteenth-century modernism.

As a result of the minimalist conception of sociality, discussions of human interdependence in care ethics seem to involve little more than mutual dependency. No doubt in part because this is a relatively flat conception of moral character, care ethicists such as Tronto must also reclaim individual autonomy as the highest goal of justice even as they redefine the essence of justice in terms of care (162). For example, Tronto is compelled to distinguish "smothering care" from "care that leads to autonomy" (141). Once again we have the sentimental allegory of maternal virtue preparing the way for, but not itself cultivating, more esteemed dimensions of the self. And once again, we have failed to develop a conception of sociality beyond rudimentary concerns for security.

Chodorow's object-relations psychology, unlike some care ethics, does question the boundary between empathetic concern and those unconscious drives that might form elements of the rudimentary object orientation of primary love. As Chodorow writes, "A mother's regression to early relational stances in the course of mothering activates early constituted internal object-relationships, defenses, and conflicts" (89). Still, Chodorow's description of mothering is based on the same reductive Victorian picture of the social virtues that we find a bit too often in care ethics. The mother provides a "safe and familiar refuge" (129); she is more prop than player in the drama of a social life.

Chodorow's revisions of psychoanalytic theory only more firmly secure modern stereotypes of the mother and/or other caregiver and so too the reductive modernist view of the impact of sociality on the flourishing of the self. Chodorow does not theorize the social eroticism between mother and child except in terms of regressive tendencies in the adult and the minimal consciousness of the child. The rich social and erotic expressions of our children are described by Chodorow in terms that connote little more than the need to be rocked into quiet contentment. At the same time, the mother's and potentially, as Chodorow insists, the father's ability to empathize with the child (as well as the child's deepest erotic needs) are explained solely in terms of the adult's regressive need to relive the security and comfort of infant experience.

This kind of social need is, at least implicitly, regressive for both caregiver and care recipient not only in the family but in a system of justice. If the libidinal attachments that condition care are formed within the narcissistic boundaries of the self, then it is difficult to see how we would care for anyone whom we cannot define as a dependent part of one's self. Such a theory cannot account for what would motivate care for those who are unrelated to ourselves. The simple reference to a fellow feeling for other persons does not do it. Where does this feeling stop? At the same time, a justice of care cannot easily defend itself from those conservatives who charge that liberal policies of social justice coddle or otherwise render dependent and childlike the recipients of social benefits. As we have seen, Tronto addresses this charge by subordinating the goals of a care ethics to the modernist telos of freedom in autonomy. Meyers is currently developing a procedural account of autonomy that focuses on "owning up to and owning one's ... identity."[7] While we do not want to lose the Enlightenment legacy of the rational and autonomous moral agent, we might still ask how we can generate the figure / ground shift that Gilligan envisions. Missing from modern moral theory is a normative psychology that demonstrates how the highest dimensions of subjectivity might be cultivated in social interactions, beginning with erotic sources that are not regressive or primitive, but quite sophisticated, in the adult-child relationship. As Gilligan writes, within the conventional liberal framework, the usual dichotomies between autonomy and attachment, reason and feeling, selfishness and altruism continue to prevail (*JC*, 41). Object-relations theory sustains the same oppositions, "joining separation with individuation and thus counterposing the experience of self to the experience of connection with another" (*JC*, 41). As for a care ethic, "there is no ready vocabulary in moral theory to describe its terms" (*JC*, 36). Where can we find this new vocabulary? Where can we find this new vision of humanity?

Toward a Rational Discourse of Social Life

In Chapter 2, I seek assistance for the Anglo-American project of a care ethic by turning to the discourse ethics of the post-World War II German philosopher, Jürgen Habermas. Habermas corrects the excessive individualism of liberal political theory by introducing a communicative element into the core of the moral person. For Habermas, the telos of moral maturation does not consist of the self-reflective (or even empathetic) capacities of the individual but in the discursive and democratic capacity of the individual to communicate with others.

[7] See Diana Tietjens Meyers's essay "Intersectional Identity and the Authentic Self? Opposites Attract!" in *Relational Autonomy*, ed. Catriona MacKenzie and Natalie Stoljar (New York: Oxford University Press, 2000), 151–180.

Habermas's conception of the central role of a discourse ethic constitutes a strong revision of the moral basis of modern society. Social historian Philippe Ariès provides a context in which we can better understand the import of discourse ethics. He observes that the rise of the abstract individual in public life and the nuclear family in private life displaced the sociability that brought together family, political, and professional life in pre-Enlightenment societies.[8] According to Ariès, before the "stern rationalism" of the moralist pedagogues defined the central goals of a professional education and psychological maturity in the eighteenth century, "knowing how to converse" was the central virtue (377). "Seventeenth-century society in France was made up of graded clienteles in which the little men mixed with the greatest. The formation of these groups called for a whole network of daily contacts, involving an unimaginable number of calls, conversations, meetings and exchanges." The element of sociability and civic friendship has been displaced in modern society with "the progress of domesticity" and the separation of a professional life from both the domestic and political scenes. Of course, the social virtues of the *ancien régime* are not without problems for our more enlightened times: "The main thing ... was above all to win a more honourable standing in a society whose members saw one another, heard one another and met one another nearly every day.... Hence the importance of conversation" and, I would add, a social hierarchy based on ideas about moral excellence (376–377). Habermas reintroduces the element of sociability and civic friendship into the moral core of political life without sacrificing the egalitarian impulses that take center stage with the French Revolution—or at least this is his aim.

Habermas's strategy is to bring the rationalism, along with the universalism, of the Enlightenment into his theory of discourse. The universal rationality of the human species gives discourse ethics its egalitarian base. Still, one wonders if the Enlightenment legacy of rationalism might not obscure some of the "nonrational" or other nondiscursive underpinnings of a communicative ethic. Again, the social historian gives us insight into the larger historical context of Habermas's work. Ariès characterizes the Enlightenment spirit with its "insistence on reason" as resting on a peculiar view of childhood and the life of the family. Ariès explains that the Enlightenment period replaced an earlier "concept of childhood—characterized by 'coddling'" (what Montaigne describes as the "passion for caressing new-born children") and by the social mixing of adults and children with the

[8] Philippe Ariès, *Centuries of Childhood: A Social History of the Family Life*, trans. Robert Baldick (New York: Random House, 1962), 376–377 (henceforth cited as *CC*).

view that the child possessed neither social nor erotic interest (*CC*, 132). He writes: "In the moralists and pedagogues of the seventeenth century, we see that fondness for childhood and its special nature no longer found expression in amusement and 'coddling,' but in psychological interest and moral solicitude" (*CC*, 131). This new view differed from the earlier view in that it "sprang from a source outside the family," a source that included those moralists who were "eager to ensure disciplined, rational manners. . . . In the eighteenth century, we find those . . . elements in the family, together with a new element: concern about hygiene and physical health," or the "care of the body" (*CC*, 132–133).

The dichotomy of the quasi-biological body and the autonomous, rational mind reflects a weak understanding of the origins of social life. It is this reduced view of social life from the age of the Enlightenment that continues to hinder contemporary attempts to integrate care and justice perspectives. The question is whether a discourse ethic can overcome the social minimalism of the Enlightenment era in order to develop a whole picture of moral and political life.

2

Hidden Narratives
and Discourse Ethics

Habermas's proposal for a discourse ethics goes a long way toward democratizing the practice of moral philosophy. Discourse ethics requires that oral communication, or, more precisely, what Habermas calls "communicative reasoning," replace abstract reflection and other solitary mental exercises in moral philosophy.[1] If practiced correctly, moral philosophy would be a social activity. Only through consensus reached in public debate could moral principles claim universal validity. With this in mind, Habermas cautions the lone philosopher not to preempt public debate by claiming authoritative access to visions, master narratives, or postulates for a first philosophy. Accordingly, while Habermas's rival John Rawls writes a

---

[1] Habermas distinguishes the universal claims of discourse ethics (or moral philosophy) from ethics proper, which reflects cultural and religious differences, and cannot be universalized.

grand treatise on justice, Habermas undertakes what appears to be a much more modest task.[2] As a discourse theorist, Habermas limits himself to establishing the conditions of debate, and to urging philosophers to adhere to the correct procedures for putting forth moral claims.

If moral conflicts are to be resolved in public debate, we need to examine very carefully how this debate is to be set up. For as many a savvy politician knows, the basic parameters for a debate can have much to say about the outcome. Depending upon how the debate is framed, pressing moral issues can be blocked from the public purview. What are the norms for what Habermas calls communicative reason?

In a group of essays, including most centrally the essay "Moral Consciousness and Communicative Action," Habermas draws upon a psychological theory of moral development in order to explain and justify these norms.[3] A discourse theory of ethics, Habermas notes, is "open to, indeed dependent upon, indirect validation by other theories that are consonant with it. I view the theory of the development of moral consciousness advanced by Lawrence Kohlberg and his coworkers as an example of the latter kind of validation" (*MC*, 117). This model also influences such other major liberal theorists as John Rawls.[4] Kohlberg's model posits invariant stages for the development of moral judgment. This model of human de-

---

[2] I refer to John Rawls's *A Theory of Justice* (Cambridge: Harvard University Press, 1971). Habermas has persuaded John Rawls to move away from viewing justice as a quest by impartial, rational individuals in an hypothetical thought experiment to agree upon universal transhistorical principles of justice. In his later work, *Political Liberalism* (New York: Columbia University Press, 1993), Rawls now argues that justice is not a quest for metaphysical truths about justice, but a political agreement in a particular social and historical context by people with certain shared understandings. The problem with this approach is that it does not step back to critique the material conditions (economic, technical, racial, and so on) of any particular social and historical context. This step back requires the philosopher to move beyond the limits of moral philosophy proper and engage in a critical analysis of society. In this chapter, I argue that the moral philosopher needs to borrow from the dialectical narrative of first-wave critical theory.

[3] Jürgen Habermas, *Moral Consciousness and Communicative Action*, trans. Christian Lenhardt and Shierry Weber Nicholsen (Cambridge: MIT Press, 1993), 116–194; henceforth cited as *MC*. See also Habermas's "Justice and Solidarity: On the Discussion Concerning Stage 6," in *The Moral Domain*, ed. Thomas E. Wren (Cambridge: MIT Press, 1990), 224–251; and "Lawrence Kohlberg and Neo-Aristotelianism," in *Justification and Application*, trans. Ciaran P. Cronin (Cambridge: MIT Press, 1993).

[4] See Rawls, *A Theory of Justice*, 458–479. Rawls modifies the Kohlbergian theory; however, he retains the three basic levels of moral development. While Rawls emphasizes love as an important component of the first level, he understands love to develop out of an earlier and more natural need for self-preservation (463 n. 10). This view fails (as I will argue) to acknowledge the social drives of the infant. I will explain these social drives more fully in Chapter 6. He characterizes as "the prized virtues" of level 1 "obedience, humility, and fidelity to authoritative persons" (466). He also assumes that abstract reason, rather than, for example, historical narrative or lyrical expression, constitutes the measure of moral maturity. I will argue that communicative reason needs to draw upon these alternative discursive sources.

A Marriage of Autonomy and Care

velopment counters relativists who claim that fundamental conceptions of morality vary across cultures. With Kohlberg, Habermas argues that while the content of moral judgments may indeed vary, the formal structure of moral judgment does not. Habermas notes that in fact there are formal differences in moral reasoning across cultures and among individuals. However, he believes that these differences can be mapped onto higher or lower stages of development. The stage model appears to support a relatively neutral and universal theory of moral development. Habermas argues that this neutrality is guaranteed through the theory's abstraction from the content, and detachment from the context, of moral judgments.

My concern is whether or not the formal structures of the stage model are neutral with respect to moral presuppositions, or, on the contrary, are ridden with undeclared values and invisible narratives that require substantial critique. I will argue that there are undeclared and ineradicable values that operate behind the back of the discourse ethicist. Moreover, I will argue that these values blindly perpetuate unacknowledged injustices of modernization and global development. Habermas uses a telling phrase when he interprets the logic of moral development as a "process of dichotomization and devaluation." Habermas's use of this phrase pinpoints how a universalist, formal apparatus (in this case, abstract reason) can function in the systematic exclusion and devaluation of disenfranchised social groups. It is a bold move, I think, to introduce oral performance into the practice of moral philosophy. Oral traditions of democratic debate in the assembly and the theater as well as the marketplace were central to democracy in Athens, and these oral traditions are central to disenfranchised populations today. However, Habermas's proposed norms for reason threaten to weaken communication between elite and nonelite social groups. Norms of reason or communication should not emerge from the philosophical fiat of the elite but from popular traditions of social challenge. In this chapter, I expose for critical analysis the undeclared values and hidden narratives of discourse ethics, and begin to investigate norms for alternative models of social challenge and moral development.

In order to understand how the logic of dichotomization and devaluation functions in Habermas's theory of discourse ethics, we need to inspect more closely his use of Kohlberg's moral psychology. While Habermas introduces some corrections to Kohlberg's theory, he views this empirical theory as in fundamental accord with the presuppositions of discourse ethics. According to the moral theory, there are three major levels of moral development, and each level contains two stages. The child matures by passing from preconventional to conventional, and finally to the postconventional level of moral thinking.

The *preconventional level* portrays early childhood experience as lacking any distinctly moral categories of thought or feeling. At stage 1, the child understands the difference between right and wrong in terms of obedience to rules and avoidance of punishment. The developing child then progresses to stage 2, where right and wrong depend upon what is useful to him. At the *conventional level*, the child enters stage 3, where he focuses on social roles and caring relationships. As he matures, he develops a concern for doing his duty in society (stage 4). At the *postconventional level* (stages 5 and 6), the individual breaks from his earlier conformity to social roles, and reflects upon abstract and universal principles of justice. Habermas follows Kohlberg's model up to the point of establishing the postconventional level as the goal of moral development. He disagrees with Kohlberg's interpretation of postconventional thinking.

Kohlberg distinguishes stages 5 and 6 on the basis of differences in the content of the principles. He orders the final stages and substages of moral development according to whether the individual bases his moral principles on natural right (Locke), utilitarian values (Mill), or deontological values (Kant). For Kohlberg, this peculiar evolution of thought from Locke and Mill to Kantian principles maps onto progressively higher stages of moral development. This evolution is peculiar because historical chronology would place Kant before Mill.

Habermas does not challenge the particular order of Lockean, Millian, and Kantian principles. However, he does disagree with the outcome of Kohlberg's theory. Habermas argues that there are nonempirical reasons for taking the procedural orientation of discourse ethics as a step beyond Kantian ethics and as the highest stage (stage 6) of moral maturity. Principles that have not been purged of their normative (Lockean, Millian, or Kantian) content should be relegated to stage 5 thinking.

Habermas argues that his corrections to Kohlberg's theory salvage the strict cognitivism, universalism, and formalism that a Kantian orientation to moral theory would demand but that Kantian principles cannot themselves provide. It just so happens, Habermas observes, that the necessary corrections to Kohlberg's theory can be derived directly from the two basic principles of discourse ethics. Habermas labels these two basic principles "(U)" and "(D)." The universalization principle (U) requires that a norm be accepted by all who would be affected by the norm. The discourse principle (D) locates the justification of norms in public debate with universal participation.

Habermas defines cognitivism in terms of the claim that moral judgments can be justified through the force of the better argument. The cognitivism of discourse ethics turns on whether moral issues can be decided through a style of reasoning that is defined largely by its binary opposition to emotion, or subjective will. The "reason / emotion" dichotomy is, as we will see, a deep source of trouble for discourse ethics.[5] (In Chapter 7, I examine the "metamorphosis of emotion" in moral development.)

The strict cognitivism of discourse ethics is closely tied to its formalism. The formalism of discourse ethics is defined through its opposition to a "material ethics." A material ethics is one that incorporates *any* substantial normative claims about human desires (e.g., the claim that we should desire freedom from starvation for our children or ourselves, or that this claim should define a universal human right). Habermas argues that the formalism of his moral theory follows from the fact that the universalization principle eliminates all concrete value orientations, and therefore particular values, emotions, or fantasies. An assumption is that there are no concrete values (or emotions or fantasies) that could cross race, class, or other major social divisions. I think it is fair to say that deep social conflicts will not disappear any time soon through the appeal to universal values alone. One also wonders, however, if these differences will disappear. While Habermas does not have faith in universal values, he does believe that the sheer formalism of communicative reason can produce cross-cultural, indeed universal, moral judgments. Let us see if this is in fact the case. If not, then moral philosophy and the ethical individual will have to make use of political, cultural, and legal resources beyond communicative reason alone.

Principle D requires that substantial moral principles receive justification through universalist debate. This process of debate is meant to eliminate from the agreed-upon outcome *any* remnants from a specific culture, class, or race. Habermas's claim is that Kohlberg's theory fails in this last regard because it defines stages 5 and 6 in terms of content-specific principles. These principles are considered non-universal because they are

---

[5] Thomas McCarthy argues that the line between emotion and reason is not clean, and recommends replacing Habermas's purist definition of discourse with a more pragmatic model of reasoning. See his "Practical Discourse: On the Relation of Morality to Politics," in *Ideas and Illusions: On Reconstruction and Deconstruction in Contemporary Critical Theory* (Cambridge: MIT Press, 1991), 181–199. Rawls makes a similar move in *Political Liberalism* (see note 2 above). Again, Habermas more recently takes the same course. I have two concerns with this type of proposal. First, I think that it does not take into account the significant degree to which what we call reason is inflected by symbolic and emotional norms of human behavior. This does not necessarily imply that reasoning is "subjective," but that an understanding of what is reasonable must come from a critical look at the role of both emotions and reason in the social person. Second, I join with Habermas in seeking a less conventional mode of moral thinking. McCarthy's tentative offering of a mode of reasoning, presumably contaminated by normal emotions and symbols, does not take us further from the conventions but brings us back closer to them.

derived from the cultural values of John Locke, John Stuart Mill, and finally, at stage 6, Kant. Habermas demotes traditional Kantian ethics to a substage of stage 5 thinking, and puts in its place Principle D, or discourse ethics.

Habermas's aim is to eliminate cultural imports from "traditions that hold sway primarily in England and America" by relegating all content-laden principles to stage 5 and, then, redefining the ultimate stage in terms of the cosmopolitan principle of public debate (*MC*, 173).

Habermas expresses in clear terms the need to eliminate English and American values from a strictly universalist perspective on moral philosophy. Does his effort to replace English and American values with Principle D in fact eliminate all traces of contemporary German culture? One wonders about the impact of post-World War II German cosmopolitanism (with its unacknowledged underside of economic expansionism) and the politics of "consensus capitalism" on his choice for stage 6 thinking. Neither German-led cosmopolitanism nor German-led consensus capitalism does much to correct the major economic and cultural imbalances in transnational politics. Habermas recognizes the importance of British and American styles of moral philosophy, even if he subordinates these styles to a secondary status for contemporary moral philosophy. Do the content-laden styles of disenfranchised populations (including the Turks within German borders) register at all on the Habermasian scale? Why are there British and American stages of moral evolution, but no stages derived from the Turks? What would the Turks have to do to win moral status?

According to Habermas, public debate is portrayed as a "contest," or "competition," based on the "force" of argumentation. By way of his own corrections to Kohlbergian theory, Habermas provides exacting standards for admission to the debate. Participation in debate is universal *but* regulated by a kind of moral literacy test: the stage model of moral development. This is the most substantial information that Habermas provides as to the character of the debate. The stage model accounts for how it is that those individuals who have achieved the postconventional level of moral maturity will have the capacity to engage in fair and impartial argument. The general claim is that those individuals who appeal to their own unsharable cultural beliefs, existential fantasies, or biographical experiences in argumentation need to learn to become more reflective and critical of their psychic allegiances. Only then can they debate with persons who have different backgrounds. As a general claim this would seem to be fair enough. The question is, how is readiness to engage seriously with those of different backgrounds achieved? Again, one wonders if the appeal to the abstract style of communicative reason suffices.

According to Habermas, "The shift in attitude that discourse ethics requires for the procedure it singles out as crucial, the transition to argumentation, has something unnatural about it: it marks a break ... with everyday life.... This unnaturalness is like an echo of the developmental catastrophe that historically once devalued the world of traditions and thereby provoked efforts to rebuild it at a higher level" (*MC*, 126–127). The stage model of moral maturation does not exactly mirror the historical development of modernity. If it did, then American-laden conceptions of moral theory might have to subordinate German-laden conceptions of moral theory in order to reflect the rise of American power after World War II. Kohlberg's rendition would have to win out over Habermas's corrections. However, with or without Habermas's corrections, the basic dialectic of the stage model does in fact all too suspiciously bend to recent shifts in power within modern Europe. Is this an accident? Is there a way of describing modernization without entangling its philosophical meaning in struggles for power?

Habermas claims that the decentered and alienated moral consciousness that is the outcome of modernization is uniquely capable of adopting an "outsider perspective" on moral issues. He characterizes this outsider perspective in terms of the capacity for critical reflection from a universalist orientation. Habermas proceeds to locate this outsider perspective through value-orientations from elite British, Anglo-American, and post–World War II German culture. Except for the peculiar reversal between Anglo-American and German cultures, this ordering reflects the changing patterns of cultural domination between America and Europe over the course of the last century. Are we sure that German fantasies are not involved in this formal measure of moral cognition? According to Habermas, only those individuals who achieve the modernist, outsider perspective pass the test for admission to the great debates of moral philosophy. Dare I say, this modern outsider perspective is not to be confused with the perspective of modernism's outsiders.

What becomes of the perspective of those disenfranchised outsiders who would view the aligned Euro-American forces for modernization as yet one more conventional if not savage force of human desire? From the point of view of modernism's disenfranchised outsiders, it would be hard not to see links between the philosophical-cultural and the economic-political machinery of modernization. Locke's arguments on behalf of slavery, Mill's arguments on behalf of class differences, or Kant's concept of race set forth ideas of moral universalism by way of criteria that the abstract thinkers of their time judged to be "rational." Similarly today, one wonders whether our current moral leaders obscure through blinding styles of reasoning the perpetuation of modernity's dark side. Certainly while those individuals at the lower end of the massive social pyramids continue to exhibit more or less predictable patterns of racial, cultural, gender attributes, contemporary moral theories do not make extended arguments regarding the moral or cognitive inferiority of specific social groups.[6] And yet values lurking in the theories of such important thinkers as Habermas and Kohlberg give pause for thought. Perhaps the invisible violence of modernism dwells most potently in the logic of its forms. As Charles Mills argues, post–civil rights era racism does not take shape through explicit, codified expressions of racism.[7] On the contrary, racism today works precisely through the denial of race's relevance. In what Mills calls Phase II racism, the unfair pattern of preferences is perpetuated through modernism's formal apparatus, including "objective standards" of merit. Habermas's more or less untroubled appropriation of Kohlberg's model reveals much about how Phase II racism and, as we will see, gender discrimination, occurs.

Habermas invokes the universalization principle in order to support his formalism and cognitivism. However, it is the formal cognitivism of Habermas's approach to theory that guarantees its failure to achieve universal validity, or so I argue. Consider the reported fact that Kohlberg's stage theory measures the responses of women at a lower stage of development than men, typically at stage 3, the lower stage of conventional morality. This lower stage is described as focusing moral concern on intimate relationships based on nurturing and care. Habermas draws attention to the issue of gender difference by citing Gilligan and Murphy. These psychologists, Habermas notes, "make the point that Kohlberg's criteria would put more than half of the [adult] population of the United states at some level below postconventional in terms of their moral consciousness" (*MC*, 175). Oddly enough, while Habermas openly cites this strong ammunition against his own moral theory, he then promptly turns his attention away from the evidence altogether, and once more defends his theory on abstract grounds alone. While Habermas should be reexamining how a liberal theory of moral development could produce such curiously illiberal "facts," he prefers instead to engage in an intellectual contest with rival guns. One would think that empirical anomalies might cast suspicion on prevailing scientific theories. Habermas's response implies that the formalism of his own rendition of Kohlbergian moral theory exempts him from taking any

[6] See Charles W. Mills, *Blackness Visible* (Ithaca: Cornell University Press, 1998), 1–19.
[7] Charles W. Mills, *The Racial Contract* (Ithaca: Cornell University Press, 1997), 95.

actual data seriously. In his reply to Gilligan, he simply reasserts his central claim, that his formalist theory (by definition) abstracts from cultural content, and consequently must be universalist. Habermas does not reflect upon the distinct possibility that formal structures may reflect hegemonic social forces. Is it not suspicious that Kohlbergian formalism measures the moral capacities of social groups in accordance with the usual stereotypes and prejudices of our society? This fact should make us think twice about accepting any theory that claims that an appeal to abstraction can guarantee cultural neutrality. More likely, the appeal to abstraction conceals values, and is, in this respect, duplicitous.

Gilligan rightly challenges the Kohlbergian stage model on the basis of "different voices." Her claim is that major social groups (including women) may exhibit a pattern of moral judgment that fails to register properly on the Kohlbergian scale. No doubt by associating the different voice with women in particular, Gilligan engages Kohlberg in a classic battle of the sexes, a pleasurable variation of what Habermas understands by moral contest. While Kohlberg's scale values abstract and principled considerations of right, Gilligan argues for the existence of an alternative pattern of moral thinking. The alternative scale focuses on responsible and caring relationships that emerge out of particular contexts. The claim is that a Gilligan-style postconventional stage of thinking (one that balances principles with a narrative-based understanding of special obligations) should be placed above a Kohlbergerian stage 6 as a seventh and higher stage. Gilligan terms this seventh stage "contextual relativism" (*MC*, 176). And she charges that Kohlberg's measure inappropriately records individuals (apparently, quite a few women like herself) at level 3 when in fact they merit a position just above Kohlberg's own.

If Gilligan's move sounds arbitrary or even self-promoting, it should be seen as in fact a legitimate move in a game that Kohlberg started. For, as it turns out, while Kohlberg's theory located a disproportionate number of women at stage 3, the same data reported many male adolescents as having regressed from stage 4 thinking to the kind of instrumentalism and relativism that is characteristic of stage 2 thinking (*MC*, 175). It could not be that men regress to a stage lower than women. Faced with this discomforting fact, Kohlberg modified the theory so as to insert a stage 4 ½ for those otherwise mature fellows who have not found their way out of the skepticism of adolescence (*MC*, 184). Why should Gilligan not make a similar move?

It seems that certain facts are troubling enough to alter a theory, and others are not. How is it that Kohlberg can alter a theory on behalf of male adolescents but not on behalf of women? What about the masses who register well below stage 5 thinking? How far has modern theory advanced beyond the Aristotelian thesis of democracy for those who possess the requisite intelligence and various degrees of disenfranchised servitude for others?

This would all appear to be a very comic and quite enjoyable battle of the sexes except for the fact that the terms of the debate continue to reflect the same old social realities. Habermas's response to Gilligan stands in disrespect for the curious "facts" produced by the Kohlbergian theory. Instead of facing these disturbing "facts," Habermas prefers to engage in a top-down debate over first principles for the sake of protecting his claim. The claim is that only a formal cognitivism can effectively oppose cultural bias and other sources of relativism. He repeats this claim again and again, despite hard facts that suggest that the formal cognitivism of liberalism may be replicating the gender bias of modern social systems. One wonders if something more personal is at stake.

According to Habermas, Gilligan's concerns do not touch moral theory per se. Her concerns have to do with the application of moral principles. He argues that a formal cognitive theory can provide the basis for dealing with concrete issues (embedded in specific contexts) by developing universalist methods of interpretation.

Moreover, he argues, his concept of cognition is flexible enough to allow for the moral use of the emotion of care in empathetic understanding. His contention is that care has moral relevance only after it has been purified of biographical, cultural, and other special ties or particular biases and develops into a universalistic "agape." Moral consciousness plus or minus care achieves its cognitive advantage only when it generates "demotivated solutions to decontextualized issues."

Habermas's insistence on moral reasoning as principled understanding severed from context blinds him (and that type of consciousness that measures high on his scale of reasoning) to the ways in which principled thinking can perpetuate the social inequities of modernism. Understanding the relation between so-called objective criteria of moral cognition (or other measures of human progress) and large-scale patterns of social inequity requires a context-based, narrative style of critical thinking. Habermas consigns social issues of development to secondary matters of application and context, and then forgets them altogether. His reduction of large-scale social inequities to secondary matters in the application of principles joins with his glorification of moral emotion to an almost fantasmatic, godlike agape.

This synthesis of decontextualized reason and glorified care reproduces a monstrous force in modern development and globalization. Behind that force is the ideology of the disciplined and stoic manager of governmental or corporate resources, whose care about the world is all too demotivated and decontextualized, at least in relation to the objects of care.

Habermas insists that the moral point of view centers on a contest of cognition that is carried by the "force of argument." He counters Gilligan's attack by confiscating her conception of care, and adding it to the general artillery available in that contest called discourse. How in the world the force of contest bends to the emotion of agape is not in the least bit clear. The relation between agape and intellect remains totally untheorized. I can only hypothesize that if we understand Habermas's use of the research on care by way of his own account of the moral point of view as "decentered" and "alienated," then the kind of emotion that he has in mind must be a strangely disconnected and disembodied form of libido. What kind of psychological theory could account for this type of libido? In reality, the libido of the modernized subject is often geared toward a consumer frenzy bent on pleasure or minor middleclass skirmishes over status. How does a disembodied libido disconnect itself from the force of these drives?

It is not clear that there is any empirical evidence or moral psychology that could explain the development of what Habermas calls agape. For that matter, there is not even any sound empirical evidence for what Habermas analyzes as stage 6 moral thinking. Habermas himself notes this curious fact in the course of his essay. Longitudinal studies do not provide evidence for a stage of thinking higher than stage 5. There is not even evidence that moral subjects can make any real progress toward this godlike status. Given these facts, the claim to occupy such a position smacks of sheer hubris. Habermas believes that the lack of evidence for the natural development of a moral stage that, as he puts it, must be unnatural only means that the argument for the necessity of this stage must stem from philosophy and not psychology (*MC*, 173). At the point that Habermas detaches himself from empirical evidence and social realities, he also stops doing critical theory and regresses toward precritical metaphysics. Habermas knows there is no evidence for the existence of stage 6 thinking. Suppose we call a global debate on the principles of justice. Who would qualify to come?

Still the data produced by Kohlberg's theory does register participants at the lower-level of postconventional thinking, stage 5. One might think that the existence of subjects at this postconventional level of thought is sufficient for moral theory to proceed in a public forum. In recent efforts to respond to the multicultural movement, Habermas, like Rawls, retreats to this more pragmatic claim (see Prologue). The problem with this retreat is that even the interpretation of stage 5 thinking as "postconventional" fails to deal with the implications of the fact that utilitarian or other principled styles are in fact reflecting, to quote Habermas, a "particular culturally specific substantive manifestation of principled moral judgment" (*MC*, 173). Meanwhile, Kohlbergian moral theory escapes the charge of relativism only by capping biased stages of development with a stage devoid of existential meaning and empirical reference. Unfortunately, this empty subject position does perform a crucial function in the ideology of modernization. Those who make the claim to have advanced further on this ladder of moral and cognitive success can also claim to represent the true moral viewpoint on behalf of those who lack their advantages. All the while, the service workers and nonprofessionals who do not make it up the steps of an English, American, and German education must labor to support those very same people who will represent them in the moral and public spheres.

It is curious that Habermas fails to cast a suspicious eye on the fact that more than half of the population of the United States (and who knows how much of the rest of the world) has failed to register that "shift of attitude that ... has something unnatural about it" (*MC*, 127). Kohlberg's apparently objective, universalistic, and formal criteria continue to position women, minorities, members of lower classes, and non-Western cultures at developmental stages that are lower than the Western elite.[8] These hierarchical stages are structured by dichotomies. Underdeveloped man or woman is to nature as modern man is to reason. A conventional formula for oppression turns up in high-modern guise.

It is more than curious that exactly those individuals who are most on the institutional margins of Western power, and most in need of articulating their demands for justice, are relegated by the formal tests of discourse ethics to a lower moral and cognitive status. Could it turn out to be an unfortunate "fact" that those very individuals who are most exploited are least competent to represent their own claims to injustice? Could it be that they will have to depend upon the moral advocacy and educational leadership of those individuals who are in the compromising position of profiting from their labor? Could it be that they will have to rely specifically on those

[8] See Sandra Harding, "The Curious Coincidence of Feminine and African Moralities," in *Women and Moral Theory*, ed. Eva Kittay and Diana Meyers (Totowa, N.J.: Rowman and Littlefield, 1987); Elizabeth Spelman, "Theories of Race and Gender: The Erasure of Black Women," in *Introduction to Ethics*, ed. Gary Percesepe (Englewood Cliffs, N.J.: Prentice Hall, 1995); and Carol Stack, "The Culture of Gender: Women and Men of Color," *Signs* 11, no. 2 (Winter): 321–324. Joan Tronto explains that the success of Kohlberg's theory has less to do with its truth value and more to do with its power consequences: "Kohlberg's theory ... risks nothing in the current configurations of power ... being relatively well off and well schooled seems to be a necessary ... condition to achieve the highest stages of morality." See her *Moral Boundaries* (New York: Routledge, 1993), 76. Thanks much to Dawn Jakubowski for helping me to locate these important sources.

people whose very ideas of development and competence assure that they do not belong in positions of power? Or might it be that the formal cognitivism of modernist theory is just another literacy test for the disenfranchisement of the many and democracy for the few at the top of the pyramids of power? Criteria of excellence derived from an elite style of cultural expression are used to verify the superior development of those who occupy the positions of privilege. I fear this is a logic of hegemony, not democracy.

Habermas himself points out that prejudicial attitudes such as racism, homophobia, or conceptions of entitlement to excessive amounts of wealth cannot be either attacked or identified through argument alone. Dealing with these attitudes requires an existential address to the emotive core of the moral individual.[9] In a world where most people (in fact, all of us by Habermas's own admission) are constitutionally incapable of living up to standards of impartial reason, existential appeal must take a central and not a peripheral place in moral philosophy. Both humor and tragic pathos may be needed in order to extend communicative competencies; as Martin Matustik explains, "Democratic theory needs to realize that humans bring bodies, attitudes, and motives into discursive debates."[10] Under conditions in which invisible forces shape the forms of modern social structures and the fantasies of moral individuals, the ideal of rational discourse functions conservatively. Moral discourse must articulate the secret desires and invisible narratives of modern life.

Habermas claims that moral theory cannot detach itself entirely from empirical testing. He argues that an empirical theory such as Kohlberg's offers an "indirect" test for his moral theory. However, neither Habermas nor Kohlberg reflects on the social context and invisible narratives behind Kohlberg's empirical theory. Suppose that we construct the missing narrative connections between the three moments of moral development in Kohlberg's theory. If we interpret these connections in terms of the historical context in which Kohlberg was working, we find in idealized and abstract form the story of the nuclear family in Cold War America. (His original data was based on male Harvard students from the 1950s.) In this Cold War picture, the ideal family is composed of a disciplining but principled father, a nurturing mother,

[9] Along the same lines, Patricia Huntington argues that discourse ethics must include as a key moment a critique of fantasy. See her "Asymmetrical Reciprocity and Practical Agency: Contemporary Dilemmas of Feminist Theory in Benhabib, Young, and Kristeva" (forthcoming). And David Ingram argues that "the task which Habermas sets for critical theory cannot succeed without the help of aesthetic imagination," in *Critical Theory and Philosophy* (New York: Paragon House, 1990), 177.

[10] Martin J. Beck Matustik, *Specters of Liberation* (Albany: State University of New York Press, 1998), 22.

and a dependent child. Kohlberg's story of family life unfolds from the point of view of the father. The parent-outsider would view the young child as an authoritarian and/or quasi-biological creature moved only by pleasure and pain or instrumental values. The idealized Cold War mother would view the child in more sentimental terms. Kohlberg's failure to render care equal to discipline in the story of individual development opens the door for a mother's perspective on moral development. This second perspective leaves the underlying picture of the Cold War family intact.

According to a basic picture shared by Gilligan and Kohlberg, the child leaves the quasi-natural state of the family (in suburban America) and enters a second major step of development as he enters school. At school, he learns social roles (apparently, he had not already been helping out around the house) and develops friendships and relationships based on care and trust (which also apparently did not happen earlier, in the family). At the next stage of development, the child develops a sense of group loyalty (an especially salient virtue during the Cold War, but apparently one not understood by small children playing war games). Finally, the child enters adulthood through a difficult stage of adolescence where he learns, apparently for the first time, how to think critically (these model children had never before challenged their parents' or teachers' rules). At this final step, the child begins to separate himself from his family and the particular institutions in which he developed loyalty and trust. The culmination of moral growth is the liberal individual who governs him or herself according to principles (stages 5 or 6) that may or may not be balanced by care (or Gilligan's stage 7). The historical narrative that informs this picture of maturation is not a general modernist view of coming of age. Its context is circa-1950s America.

This retro stage model reenacts in abstract form the elements of a specific genre of cultural expression. As I interpret the Kohlberg/Habermas model, it borrows its structure, or "plot," from the quest narrative (especially popular in Hollywood Westerns of the 1950s, such as John Ford's 1956 *The Searchers*). The quest narrative celebrates heroic individuals who undertake some superhuman or "unnatural" feat. This genre differs from romantic, tragic, and comic tales of love or friendship. In these tales, coming-of-age plots focus on romantic relationships, friendships, or community life.[11] The unbound and "unnatural" feats of the heroic quest narrative in America translate into acts of hubris against social taboos for audiences of

[11] I discuss this point more fully in "Hollywood Comedy and Aristotelian Ethics," in *Sexual Politics and Popular Culture*, ed. Diane Raymond (Bowling Green, Ohio: Bowling Green State University Popular Press, 1990), 15–24. On the history of narrative, see Jill Ker Conway, *When Memory Speaks* (New York: Alfred A. Knopf, 1998).

classical drama (see Chapter 7). Philosophers as diverse as Aristotle and Hegel have given the quest narrative less attention than tragic drama. Hegel explains that the contests in action-oriented quest narratives emphasize plot to the point of missing the ethical development of character, and on this I would agree.[12]

My concern regarding the invisible narrative woven by Kohlberg and Habermas is not simply with its duplicitous partiality. I question whether their joint project does not perpetuate multiple weaves of oppression. The notion that maturation requires a separation from the mother, or an onto-logical break with family and community involvement, and the commu-nicative resources that these social groups may possess, functions to weaken these popular sources of resistance against colonization and patriarchal domination. Empirically and ethically more convincing narratives of moral development begin with what may be too easily missed by decontextualized and decentered caregivers: from the first kick in the womb, the child is so-cially responsive and spirited.[13] The fact that the infant who is deprived of social interaction develops major psychological problems cannot be ex-plained by any philosophical theory that assumes that the human being be-gins life as the preconventional primitive. According to this traditional the-ory, the primitive human being is driven by pleasure and pain or instrumental values alone. This myth of the child as a primitive serves to legitimate the modern dichotomization and devaluation of caregiving. In the modern world, caregiving is not treated as valued labor.

Habermas underestimates the willfulness and creativity of young chil-dren when he supposes that the "hypothetical attitude" comes only much later, apparently in adolescence. He falls into mythic daydreaming when he fancies middle childhood as an Edenic "horizon of life world certainties" unmarked by alienation. The home may be for some a social haven from the antisocial marketplace, the dream of Victorian culture that was rein-voked after the Second World War. However, the home may also be torn by struggle and turmoil. In Chapter 8, we view the other side of the Victo-rian dream through Toni Morrison's novel *Beloved*. Inside or outside the Victorian home, the child does not passively assimilate values. The child actively interprets and responds to social meanings. While the Cold War

---

[12] Hegel argues that characters are only externally related in epics, and that as a consequence, epic misses the subjective development of character. Drama brings together the subjective mo-ment of lyric with the objective moment of epic. See *Hegel: On the Arts* (New York: Frederick Ungar, 1979), 146–147.

[13] Cynthia Willett, *Maternal Ethics and Other Slave Moralities* (New York: Routledge, 1995), chap. 2, 31–47.

family might suppress internal conflict and communicative reasoning, post-1970s norms emphasize communicative and cognitive skills in young children. Perhaps economic pressures for middle-class women to enter the official labor force make clear to middle-class parents today what middle-class parents in the 1950s might not have seen: economic and political forces can make or break family life. In fact, the private bubble of family life in the 1950s was subsidized by massive social and economic programs from the federal government.[14] The recent development of educative programs for infants, and the view of the daycare worker as a teacher rather than a passive babysitter, acknowledge a more active and communicative child. Gone is the passive and dependent child that we find in the quasi-natural or conventional stages of Kohlbergian theory. The skilled daycare worker today does not, as did the mythic father and mother from the suburbs in the 1950s, discipline or care for a dependent child. The daycare teacher communicates with a responsive child according to diverse narratives of social norms.

Anthropologist Meredith Small points out that the new field of ethnopediatrics (opened up in 1995 with a series of papers introduced by Carol Worthman) directly challenges the view that normal, modern children advance through universal developmental stages.[15] Ethnopediatrics owes much of its theory to Russian psychologist Lev Vygotsky, who insisted that "child development was inseparable from society and culture" (*OB*, 63). Even biological processes of attunement between children and adults are now viewed as bearing social significance. As Small notes, "Data suggests that babies and their caretakers are intertwined in a homeostatic relationship." The synchronization of basic physiological processes (including heart rate) suggests that infants and adults are "partners in an interactive social dance in which they jointly regulate each other, and this dance is essential for ... social and psychological development" (*OB*, 37).

Generalizations about a universal human nature are virtually impossible to make based on data from a modern industrial society, Small adds. For 1.5 million years, until the agricultural and industrial revolutions, human beings lived as hunters and gatherers. An investigation of these societies (her example are the !Kung) reveals a society in which adults work two or three days a week gathering food, and group relations are based on reciprocal exchange rather than on an economy of ownership. "The switch to a settled

[14] Sylvia Ann Hewlett and Cornel West, *The War Against Parents* (Boston: Houghton Mifflin, 1998), 88–124.

[15] Meredith F. Small, *Our Babies, Ourselves: How Biology and Culture Shape the Way We Parent* (New York: Doubleday, 1998), xi; henceforth cited as *OB*.

life means, by definition, ownership of goods, which in turn promotes privacy and results in monetary-based work to acquire those owned goods. Ownership also means a loss of the routes of necessity of gift exchange, the disintegration of sharing, and a need for social and physical privacy" (*OB*, 84). Productive work for profit and pleasure diminishes and even overturns the need to cultivate social relationships.

Would transformation of the modern, Western subject require dismantling the capitalist system? Small argues that the example of Japan demonstrates that even a modern industrialized political economy can develop from narratives and practices of childrearing that are fundamentally at odds with those of the West. The sense of group belonging that prevails over individualism "simply applies the values of a small hunting-and-gathering group to a national level." Children are viewed as "pure spirit, essentially good by design, and in need of being incorporated into the maternal self." The Japanese view directly contradicts the American view of the child as dependent and self-centered. The Japanese do not socialize the child toward independence and separation from the family. She explains that mothers view a strong connection with their children as an "indicator of a good and healthy bond that fosters emotional security, rather than something pathological that has to be 'dealt with,' ended, severed" (*OB*, 102).

The cultivation of adult forms of emotional or cognitive expression do not require an ontological break with childhood experience. Social and critical traits may mature and alter their shape through development, but they are not introduced to an otherwise asocial or passive child.

For Habermas, the critical standpoint of the adult emerges in the turmoil of adolescence. The adolescent undergoes a process that is like a second birth but, unlike the first birth, generates a transcendent moral standpoint. One would think that this standpoint would be saturated with the hormones and social posturing of adolescence. In order to avoid clouding the moral standpoint with adolescent sexuality and social embarrassment, Habermas attempts to explain its emergence in terms of a funny metaphysics of a "gap": "The post-conventional disengagement of morality from ethical life signifies a loss of congruence between fundamental moral conceptions ... and the certainties of the life world in general.... The resulting gap between moral judgments and moral actions needs to be compensated for by a system of internal behavior controls that is triggered by principled moral judgment ... and that makes self-governance possible" (*MC*, 183). This mythic gap yields an individual who transcends existing social institutions and relationships, and can act according to pure principle alone. Wow!

If one wanted to invoke non-Western humor, one might suggest that at the existential core of this alienated creature lies what Eastern European Slavoj Žižek discerns as the modern vertigo of the big "empty nothing."[16] For Žižek, the big empty nothing motivates moral irony, not clarity of thought, in the modern subject. Other psychologists might see in Habermas's metaphysis the symptoms of traumatic loss. Still other theorists might trace this metaphysical subject to the diminished sociability or to the general malaise of modern Western culture. Could one become postconventional without passing through some kind of an emotional trauma? Should emotional trauma function as a normal stage in the maturation of the moral subject? If childhood experience already exhibits moral emotions and cognitive thought, then perhaps the mythic break into adulthood functions less as a conversion to the moral point of view than as a suppression of the spirited social world into which we are born.

These suppressive measures cohere with Habermas's interpretation of the logic of moral development in terms of a "process of dichotomization and devaluation." According to Habermas, the logic of dichotomization and devaluation accounts for the development of autonomy: "The more complex concepts of normative validity and autonomy emerge from the simpler concepts of an imperative will and personal loyalty, or pleasure-pain orientations. What happens in each of these cases is that the central semantic component of the more elementary concept is decontextualized and thus thrown into sharper relief, which allows the higher-level concept to stylize the superseded concept as a counterconcept.... To cite an ... example, ... pleasure-pain orientations become *mere* inclinations sharply set off from duties.... A similar process of dichotomization and devaluation takes place with the transition from a concept of externally imposed punishment to the concept of shame and guilt" (*MC*, 169).

Habermas's formulation of this logic highlights what a critic of the hegemonic processes of modernization could expect from modernity's dehumanizing procedures—both at home and abroad. A logic of dichotomization and devaluation guarantees that the so-called more developed stages emerge only through a systematic forgetting or dismantling of the context and complexity of earlier "primitive stages" of human experience. What from a "higher stage" of Habermasian reflection appears to be *mere* inclination may in fact turn out to be much more than mere pleasure and pain.

---

[16] Slavoj Žižek, *Looking Awry: An Introduction to Jacques Lacan through Popular Culture* (Cambridge: MIT Press, 1991), 87.

The normative definition of maturity as a dichotomization and devaluation of maternal or "conventional" sources of values—the view that maturity requires a break from ties that are viewed as quasi-biological or unreflective—conceals the social eros of the domestic realm. The various stages of dichotomization and devaluation that according to Habermas / Kohlberg mark the major tests of maturation (e.g., the development of manipulative or strategic behavior, and the balancing of this development with social duty or rational obligation) may very well appear to the less detached caregiver as symptoms of the breakdown in social ethics. This social ethics does not emerge from a quasi-biological childhood. It is already there in the infant who smiles in response to touch.

The logic of development reinscribes the gender dichotomies of modern thought. It does so in a way that devalues not only the social eros at the core of person, but also the kind of symbolic, erotic, and societal work that the child demands. The work of "nurturing" is misread through a logic of "dichotomization and devaluation" that renders it menial labor fit for little pay or social recognition. Those who raise children are devalued in a society where the material and abstract products (Coca-Cola, theorems, moral principles) of the autonomous individual (developed through stoic breaks from human relationships) are valued over the existential achievement of defining who we are in relation to one another.

Habermas thinks that he can distinguish the metaphysical break that defines the autonomous individual from the existential crises that may also rock the adolescent. While the autonomous individual distances him or herself from social forces in calm reflection, the existential individual cannot alienate himself or herself from these forces without experiencing emotional turmoil. That is because these social forces form essential aspects of personal identity. One wonders, however, how deep critical reflection can in fact go if it is not to shake the existential roots of the person.

The first wave of critical theorists believed that the art of the outsider provokes turmoil in the conventional bourgeois consciousness. By analogy, I would argue that the most relevant *test* for an authentic moral encounter under conditions of domination (i.e., in this world as we will ever know it) is the experience of existential turmoil. This turmoil may provoke a life crisis, but also give rise to forces for social renewal. As long as social identities are formed in systems of oppression, oppression cannot be successfully challenged unless we target those existential roots. The test for a transformative social ethics cannot be formal; it must be existential.

The abstract picture of cognitive development fails to deal with the field of social forces that define modern life. An overweening pride in individual or intellectual achievements can blind one to the forces that make us feel alive and connected in the world. Philosophical argument or social debate that leaves intact the modern logic of dichotomization and devaluation cannot have adequately challenged the larger unseen narratives that inform our individual moral ideals. The narrative of self-governance for those who have earned it legitimates serious social divisions. These divisions are the outcome of an oppressive system that sublates its opposition but does not hear it. If what is called critical reflection is not to block access to those larger historical narratives, then so too it must not block access to the existential individual. Justice begins as we transform the existential roots and historical conditions of our lives, making it possible that we might be happy together.

3

Joining Together Reason and Care

Habermas does not address head-on the challenges posed by the emergence of women's voices in the public sphere. He postulates a metaphysical gap that separates moral consciousness from the embodied self that makes ethical decisions in everyday life. Only such a gap could guarantee the independence of an autonomous individual from "the external pressure of an existing recognized legitimate order."[1] This gap also separates moral discourse from an ethics of care. Seyla Benhabib questions the strict separation of moral and ethical spheres.[2] Against Habermas, she contends that the two spheres

[1] Jürgen Habermas, *Moral Consciousness and Communicative Action*, trans. Christian Lenhard and Shierry Weber Nicholson (Cambridge: MIT Press, 1993), 183.
[2] Seyla Benhabib, *Situating the Self: Gender, Community and Postmodernism in Contemporary Ethics* (New York: Routledge, 1992), 169–170; henceforth cited as *SS*. For further

are poles of one continuum of moral issues. And in place of Habermas's funny gap, she proposes a "synthesis of autonomous justice thinking and empathetic care."

As Benhabib explains, Habermas locates the moral perspective exclusively in terms of the rights and duties of the public realm. Excluded from this perspective are those concerns of friendship and family that garner greater moral attention for most individuals. Benhabib writes: "There is something profoundly odd in [Habermas's] insistence that these issues are 'personal' as opposed to 'moral'; in fact, this claim runs just as contrary to our moral intuitions as Kohlberg's assertion that 'the spheres of kinship, love, friendship and sex that elicit considerations of care are usually understood to be spheres of personal decision-making....' Even in highly rationalized modern societies where most of us are wage-earners and political citizens, the moral issues which preoccupy us most and which touch us most deeply derive ... from the quality of our relations with others" (SS, 184).

Benhabib's wise remarks call into question the funny metaphysics of the gap between moral consciousness and lived experience. Against such a metaphysics, she argues that moral consciousness is necessarily "embodied and embedded" in concrete situations. She allows for individuals to use personal narrative as well as moral principles to invoke the empathetic response of others. Nonetheless, she insists, the moral perspective must not degenerate into what she portrays rather colorfully as a "tribalism." In order to avoid tribalism, the "different voice" that Carol Gilligan's research introduces into moral discourse must yield to the universal principles that emerge from the perspective of the "generalized other." This generalized perspective requires a hypothetical attitude toward social conventions and personal desires. Still, for Benhabib, this postconventional appeal to reason does not call for a detached mind. While the postconventional thinker is in some sense in exile, a lone moral heroine who "like Antigone" is heard from "beyond the walls of the city," Benhabib acknowledges that the place beyond the city is situated inside another social reality (SS, 206, 226).

While Benhabib's introduction of a woman's perspective shifts the paradigm of liberal moral theory, this shift nonetheless leaves the basic principles of modernism intact. Benhabib's reconstructed modernism

---

contributions toward this project, see Johanna Meehan, ed., *Feminists Read Habermas: Gendering the Subject of Discourse* (New York: Routledge, 1995); Mechthild Nagel, "Critical Theory Meets the Ethics of Care: Engendering Social Justice and Social Identities," *Social Theory and Practice* 23, 2 (Summer 1997): 307–326; and Patricia Huntington, "Asymmetrical Reciprocity and Practical Agency: Contemporary Dilemmas of Feminist Theory in Benhabib, Young, and Kristeva," forthcoming.

salvages the "cognitive kernel" in discourse ethics while acknowledging that the autonomous ego is embedded in a network of relationships and immersed in the libidinal drives of an embodied creature. Benhabib rejects the sharp dualism of Habermasian discourse ethics, but she also insists that universalizable moral principles "trump" the ethical considerations that grow out of personal narrative and affect-based connections. Her rejection of dualism in favor of a continuum between the particular concerns and life history of the existential individual and the formal cognitivism of moral consciousness prompts her to reject as well the demand that debate issue in consensus. Her plea is for a debate where process is more important than outcome. The goal of debate is not total consensus but "mutual understanding."

The shared social reality, or "horizon," for this "mutual understanding" is modernism. Benhabib argues that Habermas is right to adopt a version of the stage model of moral development from Kohlberg. However, she argues, critics are also right to point out that it is not possible to deduce or otherwise legislate the correct formula for the final stage of postconventional thinking on any kind of transcendental or psychological grounds. Any specification of postconventional reason is subject to challenge in debate. The normative principles of discourse theory, which include universal respect and reciprocal recognition, follow from the shared meanings of modernism. Indeed, in response to multicultural and postmodern critics, Habermas backs away from his funny metaphysics, and takes a turn toward the kind of proposal that Benhabib makes (see Prologue).

However, while Habermas hesitates to commit discourse ethics to a doctrine of rights, Benhabib argues that the norms of universal moral respect and egalitarian reciprocity constitute basic moral rights that are universal.[3] These two basic rights function to guarantee qualified individuals the right to participate in discourse ethics on equal terms with everyone else. Benhabib is content to leave all other moral rights open to debate, and this worries me.

The question remains as to whether Benhabib can sustain the claims of discourse ethics (and, in particular, its formalism, cognitivism, and universalism) once she has denied the metaphysical break between moral consciousness and the lived self; or, if the introduction of the situated individual into the moral realm demands a more dramatic shift in moral consciousness than discourse theory can sustain.

[3] Seyla Benhabib, "Toward a Deliberative Model of Democratic Legitimacy," in *Democracy and Difference: Contesting the Boundaries of the Political*, ed. Seyla Benhabib (Princeton: Princeton University Press, 1996), 78; henceforth cited as *DD*.

At the root of the question lies the issue of what is meant by the shared meanings of modernity. For Benhabib, this shared horizon of modernity replaces Habermas's transcendental definition of postconventional thinking. Benhabib rejects specific definitions of postconventional judgment on the grounds that these definitions are arbitrary if simply asserted by the moral expert. However, one wonders if the same argument might not also apply to the definition of modernity. As we have seen in Chapter 2, conflicting interpretations of postconventional reason trace back to the diverging cultural backgrounds of the theorists. Similarly, one would think that interpretations of modernism might reflect the larger social divisions that modernization perpetuates. It is unlikely that the perspectives of those who witness the economic, cultural, and environmental devastation of modernism would converge with the perspectives of those who enjoy economic prosperity and democracy. This would certainly be unlikely if it were known that prosperity for all is not possible under such high rates of consumption as we have now in the American or European middle class.

Benhabib seems to believe that divergent interpretations of modernization can be resolved by a "process of 'reflective equilibrium,'... whereby one, as a philosopher, analyzes, refines and judges culturally defined moral intuitions.... What one arrives at the end of such a process ... is a 'thick description' of the moral presuppositions of the cultural horizon of modernity" (SS, 30). Again one wonders what could guarantee that the philosopher's description is not "embodied and embedded" (to use her wonderful phrase) in the hegemonic culture of globalization. The (melodramatic?) trope of the moral thinker as an exiled Antigone avoids the question of what social position characterizes some specific philosopher. If modern liberal theory is not to preempt communication across social positions, it will need to shift its focus from the perspective of the lone individual to the relationships that sustain conflicting points of view.

Benhabib locates the cause of social conflict in "tribalism" and argues that tribalism is overcome in the process of "modernization and rationalization." The thick description of premodern conflict in terms of tribalism disguises the deep cultural and economic conflicts that modernization itself perpetuates. For those who are not exiled outside of the centers of power by choice, the so-called modernists may represent yet one more tribe. Consider the experience of Native American children who were stripped of their families, community, and language in the early part of the twentieth century. These children were sent away to white schools or convents for modernization by their European conquerors. As Toni Morrison portrays the experience in her novel *Paradise*, the separation of children from the "tribe" did not lead to cognitive break-through. It led to psychological and social breakdown.

Morrison tells the story of native children as part of a larger dialectic, a trilogy of novels, on love and conflict in America (see Chapter 9). This trilogy of narratives gives us a sense for how intuitions and principles that define the prevailing norms of modernization and rationalization might appear to those who reside on the other side of the social divides. Racialized distortions of social space can so easily transform principled moral practice into crimes of humiliation. Without a genealogical critique of moral consciousness, moral theory blocks from our view an understanding of how intuitions and principles may take root in the social perversions of the modern landscape. The modern subject who owes his or her culture to a history of crime (slavery, colonialism, and neocolonialism) wants to believe in the link between modernization and moral progress. But nothing in the horizon of modernism guarantees that moral development does not stagnate or even wither in savage ruin, while cognitive, technical, and productive forces march on.

One reason to think twice about the moral progress of mainstream modern philosophy is its weak conception of human relationships. In fact, it is Benhabib's concern for precisely this issue that motivates her to undertake the project of reconstructing modernism. She argues that the overemphasis on the rational capacities of the autonomous individual slights the female domain of experience, which she does not hesitate to characterize in terms of nurturing and care: "At the beginning of modern moral and political philosophy stands a powerful metaphor: the 'state of nature.'" This metaphor is used to represent the split between the public and the domestic domains. While the public realm is circumscribed by principles of reason, the private realm is understood as a matter of nonrational choice. "This metaphor [of the state of nature] is at times said to be fact.... At other times it is acknowledged as fiction.... [The Kantian] transforms the 'state of nature' from an empirical fact into a transcendental concept. The state of nature comes to represent the idea of *Privatrecht*, under which are subsumed the right of property and 'thinglike rights of a personal nature,'... which the male head of a household exercises over his wife, children and servants" (*SS*, 155). Benhabib argues that "the varying content of this metaphor is less significant than its simple and profound message: in the beginning man was alone." "The denial of being born of woman frees the male ego from the most natural and basic bond of dependence" (*SS*, 156).

It is by acknowledging the bond of dependence that Benhabib aims to correct the major problem of universalist moral theories in unreconstructed modernism: "The universalism [traditional modernists] defend is defined surreptitiously by identifying the experiences of a specific group of subjects as the paradigmatic case of the human as such. These subjects are invariably white, male adults who are propertied or at least professional" (*SS*, 153). The question is how far Benhabib's theory of moral reason goes toward challenging the bias of propertied, or professional, white, male experience, and the modern myth of nature as dreamed up by our European forebears.

Benhabib argues that the universalist norms of respect and egalitarian reciprocity in modernism contrast sharply with the tribalism, or group-oriented respect, of premodern societies (*SS*, 32). The dismissal of tribalism is not based on a respectful and reciprocal engagement with nonmodern (or non-Western?) peoples, or at least not from what I can see. It seems to be based on a denial of their relevance to globalization. Does not this dismissal, in effect, consign these people to the state of nature? The Western arrogance of dismissing the moral relevance of non-Western peoples is perhaps more easily seen today than it was in the 1980s when Benhabib began writing her major essays. Still, Benhabib's reconstructed modernism needs to do more to challenge the arrogant dismissal of whole groups of people as underdeveloped. Whole societies have been represented as lacking the cognitive and moral tools necessary for leaving behind a quasi-natural social condition. The mandate is for Western intervention. We need to supplement Benhabib's project with an analysis of the underlying conflicts that might compromise the postconventional situatedness of the modern elite.

For there is more than one formula for oppression. Inegalitarian theories of the polis in premodern Athens divided individuals into natural kinds. According to Plato and Aristotle, class-based divisions are based on differences in rational or moral capacities. These differences were said to justify social hierarchies. High modernism (e.g., Locke, Kant, and Mill) also locates man in terms of various definitions of reason, and then establishes universal human rights based on the simple presence or absence of the relevant type of reason. Kohlberg's theory of moral development has aspects of both hierarchial and exclusionary logics. As Habermas argues, the ontological break between conventional and postconventional forms of thinking lends the theory its decidedly modernist import (Chapter 2). The modern measurement of reason functions in a starkly dualistic logic in which only those who test positive count as moral subjects. Those who defend the logic argue that modernization, unlike "premodern" tribalism, aims for universal inclusion. However, the practices of exclusion trace back to the definitions of the human. For those who have been dismissed from universal discourse, the problem is clear: the "definitions belonged to the definers—not to the defined."[4]

For example, John Locke conceptualized rationality in terms of the English middle-class appreciation for the market value of productive labor and property.[5] The middle class was suspicious of the leisure class and its idol games, which, I think, is a good thing to be. However, when these middle-class merchants interpreted native Americans engaged in forms of work (e.g., hunting) that did not accumulate property or "improve" nature, they saw wild tribes of subhuman animals lacking reason and culture.[6] On the other hand, for native peoples, modernization means subordinating the social and symbolic exchanges that define community life to the production of exchange commodities. This is not a humanizing process.

Habermas draws a sharp line between those who possess the cognitive skills for moral discourse and those who do not. Benhabib complicates the model by replacing Habermas's dualist logic with a continuum model of moral reason. She opens discourse ethics to universal participation, and allows for participants to challenge the basic parameters of the debate itself. Modernism's dualist logic resurfaces, however, when Benhabib remarks that, at some point, certain types of people are going to reveal that they lack the "requisite" reason to continue to debate. Her choice of example, unfortunately loaded with ethnocentrism, gives a glimpse into an invisible weave of oppression that inhabits the cognitive core of modernism.

"The Mormon" or "the Arab," Benhabib speculates, will defend moral claims with an appeal to an authority or a doctrine that cannot be universalized: "Now, as a defender of communicative ethics, I know that those who adhere to a conventional morality have a cognitive barrier beyond which they will not argue; that they will invoke certain kinds of reasons which will divide the participants of the moral conversation into insiders and outsiders." (SS, 43). The cognitive weakness of the Mormon or Arab is set in stark contrast with "the traditional attributes of the philosophical subject of the West, like self-reflexivity, the capacity for acting on principles, rational accountability for one's actions and the ability to project a life-plan into the future, in short, some form of autonomy and rationality"; of course, Benhabib reminds us, the modern doctrine of rational autonomy needs to

[4] Toni Morrison, *Beloved* (New York: Alfred A. Knopf, 1987), 190.

[5] John Locke, "An Essay Concerning the True Original Extent and End of Civil Government (1690)," in *Two Treatises of Government*, ed. Peter Laslett (Cambridge: Cambridge University Press, 1960).

[6] Carolyn Merchant, *Ecological Revolutions* (Chapel Hill: University of North Carolina Press, 1989), 163.

be "reformulated by taking account of the radical situatedness of the subject" (SS, 214). But I wonder if the situatedness of the philosophical subject of the West, perhaps like that of the Mormon or Arab, would not mess with his or her cognitive core.

On the basis of their moral maturity, the Western subject is allowed to decide who does and does not possess what Benhabib describes as a "deficit" of moral reason. In an era where unreconstructed capitalist philosophies of wealth and development prevail, one wonders if the relevant questions are not as much economic as moral. From the point of view of the non-Western nation striving to deal with Western arrogance, the cognitive surplus of the Western subject may mask moral blindness. Meanwhile, for their own peace of mind, Western powers may find that claims of moral and cognitive superiority serve well to justify economic policies that render nations rich in natural resources (such as oil) their dependents.

Benhabib formulates a "thick description" of the moral presuppositions of the cultural horizon of modernity. She lays out six steps that lead to the "establishment of the norms of universal moral respect and egalitarian reciprocity" (SS, 30–31). Those steps begin with the need to justify moral judgments, and proceed to locate the meaning of justification in terms of "a fair debate." Strangely enough, Benhabib's interest in promoting a narrative ethics of care drops out of this formalized schema of moral discourse. Again and again, Benhabib's corrections of discourse ethics point toward a larger and disavowed narrative. The larger story behind the six steps of modernization and rationalization reinforces the cultural biases of the modern professional, and silences altogether the storytelling other.[7]

This cognitive approach to moral discourse misses dimensions of human encounter that are cultivated in narrative or other genres of communicative reason. This approach blocks these dimensions from our modern point of view by portraying what I would call the ethics of friendly relationships through images that resonate with the modern metaphor of the state of nature. Benhabib represents non-Western subjects (apparently the Mormon and the Arab) as quasi-natural tribal thinkers. She reinvokes the conventional role of the "helpmates," or wives, of professional men, and interprets the impact of women's voices in moral discourse in terms of quasi-natural images of nurturing and care. The claim that "Gilligan or Chodorow or

---

[7] Benhabib responds to similar charges made by Iris Young. For Young's critique see "Communication and the Other: Beyond Deliberative Democracy," in DD, 120–135. For Benhabib's response, see her essay in DD, 83. The response is that discursive reason appeals to principles commonly shared unlike storytelling and rhetoric. Here again, however, she fails to deal with the genealogy (the larger narrative) of these principles.

Sarah Ruddick (or for that matter Julia Kristeva) only articulate the sensitivities of white, middle-class, affluent, first world, heterosexual women *may* be true," Benhabib writes; and, yet, she continues, "what are we ready to offer in their place: as a project of an ethics which should guide us in the future are we able to offer a better vision than the synthesis of autonomous justice thinking and empathetic care?" (*SS*, 230; italics added). The question is, who is included in the "we"? Benhabib's marriage of reason and care subordinates what she describes as the ethical perspective of the wives of bourgeois men, and excludes altogether much of the rest of the world as morally underdeveloped. This double gesture is a troubling reminder of the arrogance of any claim to own reason.

Benhabib restricts her interest in noncognitive styles of moral expression to narrative, and then narrows the narrative function to a sentimental style geared toward invoking empathy and care. The exclusive focus on this genre of narrative virtually guarantees the privileged entry of a perspective associated with middle-class wives into a moral discourse dominated by the argumentative style of male-dominated professions. Benhabib explains that women have been "more attuned to the 'narrative structure of action' and the 'standpoint of the concrete other.' Since they have had to deal with concrete individuals with their needs, endowments, wants and abilities … women in their capacities as primary caregivers have had to exercise insight into the claims of the particular. In a sense the art of the particular has been their domain, as has the 'web of stories'" (*SS*, 14). This view of the moral voice of women restricts both caregiver and her art to secondary tasks in a universalist doctrine of reason. As Nancy Fraser has remarked, "In stratified societies, unequally empowered social groups tend to develop unequally valued cultural styles."[8] There is in effect a glass ceiling that limits the significance of the moral voice of women.

Indeed, if women did nothing more than weave local narratives about particular others, then these arts might need to be sheltered in a larger and more abstract moral framework. Benhabib's view of narrative and care contrasts with the narrative techniques and moral perspective of authors like Morrison. Morrison uses cognitive disjunction (the "rememories" of Sethe in *Beloved*) and aggressive provocation (e.g., the first sentence of *Paradise*: "They shoot the white girl first.") in order to reconstruct the classic role of pathos and catharsis in modern narrative. Such terms as "mutual understanding" and "empathetic care" barely touch the surface of the existential

[8] Nancy Fraser, *Justice Interrruptus: Critical Reflections on the "Postsocialist" Condition* (New York: Routledge, 1997), 79.

turmoil that her narrative style provokes. My suspicion is that this is for good reason.

Benhabib argues that narrative captures the embedded and embodied subject (*SS*, 5–6). She does not treat other forms of art that might also express social dimensions of our ethical lives. Some critical theorists, including Angela Davis, contend that it is through the disjunctive musical phrases of jazz that the inner soul of the moral subject might be reached. Citing Langston Hughes, she writes of jazz as "a potent social catalyst that could awaken to consciousness slumbering black intellectuals.... 'Let the blare of Negro jazz bands and the bellowing voice of Bessie Smith singing Blues penetrate the closed ears of the colored near-intellectuals until they listen and perhaps understand.'"[9] Acts of resistance and emancipatory visions may not accommodate the narrative or professional styles that are privileged by discourse ethics.

Benhabib speculates that cultures might be assigned a position on the three-level model of moral development that she borrows from Kohlberg. She does not give an example of a culture at a preconventional level. Of course, how could one "measure" some cultures at a preconventional level of moral development without representing entire groups of individuals as subhuman? Benhabib teaches us to question the modern metaphor of the state of nature. This metaphor conceals social bonds that precede the entry of the individual into the modern market economy and continue to have an impact on the exiled moral thinker. But Benhabib should not cut short the critical force of her vital insight. The dualist lens of modern moral theory (its cognitivism, universalism, and formalism and their rigidly opposed alternatives) does not perceive the individual who lives and dies in the social sphere.

Benhabib uses the term "high culture" to describe the "hypothetical attitude" that characterizes modernism. This valorization seems destined to reinforce prejudices of the elite, who may question various cultural traditions but who do not question their own class and race bias. Certainly such canonical works of high modern art as Joseph Conrad's *Heart of Darkness* (1898) or D. W. Griffith's *Birth of a Nation* (1915) have hardly freed themselves from the fantasies of whiteness and class privilege that proliferate in modern societies.

On the other hand, critical views or hypothetical attitudes missed by high culture may thrive in low culture. Historian Julie Willett explains that working-class films produced for the nickelodeons in the United States beginning in 1905 documented oppression in the workplace and challenged middle-class conceptions of virtue as self-control, at least until subject to

[9] Angela Davis, *Women, Race, and Class* (New York: Random House, 1983), 151.

censorship from the high-brow bourgeoisie.[10] Groups of trade unionists and socialists protested these moral campaigns, arguing that progressive efforts to "uplift public morals" mask middle-class control over working-class culture. These films disturb middle-class audiences because they failed to fulfill Victorian ideas about virtue. The films portrayed women who were "driven by carnal desires," and who did not even strive to fit the modest and "passionless" ideal of "true womanhood." Similarly "indecent" displays of male physicality (e.g., in the boxing ring) mocked middle-class norms of respectability and self-control. While the working class viewed their films as expressive of moral values and political concerns, the censorship advocates denounced these films as "wholly devoid of moral and educational values." Willett points toward the underlying economic interests of these moral campaigns: "Much to the delight of reformers, *Birth of a Nation* helped bring middle-class patrons out of nickel theaters and into lavish [and more expensive] movie palaces." Of course, this exemplary modern film commemorates the role of the Ku Klux Klan in the formation of a modern nation.

Benhabib sees the values of the narrative voice in terms of its capacity to elicit empathy for a concrete individual whose moral concerns reflect a particular life-history. But this narrative function is characteristic of sentimental novels, and reflects the diminished sociality of the modern middle class. Benhabib locates a second significant function of narrative. She explains that narrative "integrates what 'I' can do, have done and will accomplish with what you expect of 'me'" (*SS*, 5). The explanation of narrative in terms of what "I can do" in relation to "what you expect of me" weaves a threadbare account of human relationships into a larger story of individual accomplishment. Narrative genres that develop perspectives in terms of a broader understanding of human conflict and social engagement drop away.

Jill Ker Conway explains genres of narrative in relation to persistent patterns of gender difference.[11] "For men, the overarching pattern for life comes from adaptations of the story of the epic hero in classical antiquity. Life is an odyssey, a journey through many trials and tests, which the hero must surmount alone through courage, endurance, cunning and moral strength.... His achievement comes about through his own agency, and his successful rite of passage leaves him master of his fortunes" (*RA*, 7). In contrast, "the archetypal form for bourgeois female history came in the early nineteenth century from the secularized romance, the life plot linking the

---

[10] Julie Willett, "The Prudes, the Public, and the Motion Pictures," *Gateway Heritage* 15, no. 4 (Spring 1995): 43.

[11] Jill Ker Conway, *When Memory Speaks: Reflections on Autobiography* (New York: Knopf, 1998); henceforth cited as *RA*.

erotic quest for the ideal mate with property and social mobility" (*RA*, 13). The modern novel cast the white female heroine in a passive and sentimental role. However, the modern literary scene also allowed for "a new kind of woman autobiographer, ... the escaped female slave who could ignore the social taboos" (*RA*, 14–15). The voices of a new kind of woman writer calls to mind the limits of the modern marriage of reason and care. The analysis of narrative function, in terms of ego unity plus care, modifies modern moral theory only so the ego function that the Victorian era associated with bourgeois men could be complemented with the caring persona associated with their wives.

The Victorian portrait of the white, middle-class family changes in the early part of the twentieth century. The moral role of the Victorian mother gives way to the mother as disciplinarian who is to be guided by the new class of scientific experts and health care professionals. These experts instructed the mother to place an over-demanding infant on strict feeding and sleeping schedules, and to resist the temptation to caress the infant in order to soothe its cries. This view began to change again after World War II. My hypothesis is that the introduction of household appliances into the suburban home challenged the picture of the mother as a disciplining machine. The appliances relieved the housewife from many of the mechanical tasks of domestic work, and allowed her to reinterpret her role in more sentimental terms. Psychologist Harry Harlow's experiments with infant rhesus monkeys in the 1960s brought these more sentimental terms to the experts.

Harlow demonstrated that an infant monkey deprived of its mother would prefer the substitute comfort of a wire and wood figure wrapped in terry cloth over a machine that delivers milk.[12] Meredith Small explains his contribution: "Harlow thus documented that whereas young primates need to nurse, they are even more driven to find comfort" (*OB*, 18). The stark biological picture of the infant as organism driven solely by the need for self-preservation would have to be modified in order to account for the minimal social need for comfort. This Cold War discovery of the importance of "a basic security system" in early childhood prepares the way for women to reclaim from their Victorian forebears the moral role of empathy and care. Of course, the monkey's preference under conditions of stress for the figure that offers security over nourishment depicts the main virtue of the mother in terms of a very minimal social presence. In the new imaginary, this basic love was dissociated from menial labor (which would be reduced by household

---

[12] Meredith F. Small, *Our Babies, Ourselves* (New York: Doubleday, 1998), 17, henceforth cited as *OB*.

appliances and paid caregivers). It was also dissociated from the ultimate goal of moral education, that is, initiating the child into the mature responsibilities of adulthood.

Benhabib's analysis of the moral person would leaves these middle-class categories of domestic life unchallenged. The "I can do" narrative function focuses around cognitive activity. The supplementary narrative function of care associates sociality with "dependence" and "vulnerability," life in the "home," and a quasi-biological need for "nurturing," "security," and "trust" (SS, 50, 156, 158, 162, 188–189, 58–59 n. 30). In either view of narrative function, the strong and valued side of the individual remains the independent, autonomous "I can do" public citizen carried over from the professional demeanor of the educated middle class. While the "I can do" person is not disembodied and disembedded, his aim is to be less embodied and embedded. The telos of development from Kohlberg and Habermas to Benhabib has not changed.

Benhabib translates the full libidinal range of what Kohlberg describes as "'the spheres of kinship, love, friendship, and sex'" into sentimental narratives of "nurture, reproduction, love and care," and then dismisses these narratives altogether in favor of narratives that report what "I can do" (SS, 153, 155, 5). The human drive to relate to another person is viewed through the quasi-natural metaphor of nurturing, and autonomy is reclaimed as the proper measure of human development.

This evaluation of human worth conspires with the elevation of capital production over the labor of friendship, or so I believe. The impact of mothering is exaggerated and diminished as unconditional love at the same time that it is dissociated from measures of economic growth.

This dissociation not only blinds us to the productive labor of mothers; it also blinds us to the economic realities of immigrant women who must leave their families in order to care for the families of others, and of those workers who have few options to poorly paid carework. As Benhabib envisions the complete moral person, we are first of all wage earners and citizens and secondly caregivers (SS, 184). In fact, the middle-class family with young children today is likely to include not only one or two wage earners and caregivers but also a nanny who is not a citizen. Cheap forms of labor (including low-paid service workers and cheap products from low-paid workers in the underdeveloped world) support the average family and demand moral virtues not addressed in the marriage of reason and care. Again, I wonder if joining together reason and care assures a glass ceiling on the relevance of "care issues" in the economic and political realm.

For those who dwell outside the walls of modernization, the conditions of intimate love no less than of public discourse may include terror.

Benhabib observes: "Of course, our moral and political world is more characterized by struggles unto death among moral opponents than by a conversation among them. This admission reveals the fragility of the moral point of view in a world of power and violence, but this is not an admission of irrelevance.... As a critical social theorist, the philosopher is concerned with the unmasking of such mechanisms of continuing political ideology and cultural hegemony; as a moral theorist, the philosophy has one central task: to clarify and justify those normative standards in light of which such social criticism is exercised" (SS, 33).

The question is whether one should strive to separate the moral and the critical tasks of philosophy in a world where struggles for power prevail. Benhabib explains that she is "committed to the position that the discursive procedure alone and not some additional moral principles of utility or human well-being define the validity of general moral norms" (SS, 188). This is a mistake. Without a counternarrative of justice, moral discourse returns by default to the conventional intuitions and principles of the professional man or woman. The professional who perceives himself or herself as engaged in moral conversation may appear to others inside and outside the walls of the city as engaged in a game of power.

Benhabib believes that the norms of universal respect and egalitarian reciprocity can assure that moral debate does not turn into politics. She explains "the intuitive idea behind the norms of universal respect is ancient and corresponds to the 'golden rule' of the tradition—'Do unto others as you would have others do unto you.' Universalizability enjoins us to reverse perspectives among members of a 'moral community' and judge from the point of view of other(s). Such reversibility is essential to the ties of reciprocity that bind human communities together" (SS, 32). If reversibility is required in order to participate in moral discourse, and if the exchange is *situated* in a world structured by the harsh realities of social conflict, then mutual understanding cannot happen without artful provocation and existential turmoil. Moreover, if this exchange is to communicate experiences of traumatic loss, mutual understanding may require the use of disjunctive narrative. It is premature to appeal to standards of impartial reason in a world (is there any other?) where painful loss and struggles for power are part of everyday reality.

The reversibility requirement systematically eliminates from discourse those moral claims that issue from nonreversible experiences. It is not clear that experiences of traumatic loss (e.g., the Holocaust,) could be shared with those who have not lived through them. Even more, the bystander's claim to understand others' experiences of terrible loss may constitute an insult to those who have survived them.

Benhabib believes that she has made three contributions to moral philosophy. However, each of these contributions raises new questions. First, Benhabib argues for reconstructing the core modern concepts of reason and autonomy through discourse ethics. She defines the discourse ethicist as committed to the position that discursive procedures alone and not some additional insights into human nature define the validity of general moral norms. In fact these procedures rely upon a specific psychological theory of moral development. This theory of moral development subordinates the drama of social life to the more austere Western values of autonomy and reason. What happens to these austere values when we recognize that we live and die as social creatures?

Second, Benhabib aims to incorporate into discourse ethics the moral perspective of caregivers in the domestic sphere. However, the characterization of women's "different voice" in terms of quasi-natural virtues of nurturing and care condemns this alternative moral perspective to serve a secondary role in the development of the modern subject. How might a thicker description of the labor of love shift the ground for the modern subject?

Third, Benhabib responds to feminist and postmodernist attacks on modernism by acknowledging the relevance of personal narrative for understanding the context of moral issues. However, Benhabib does not locate personal narratives within larger, historical patterns of economic or political conflict. These larger conflicts can block the capacity for mutual understanding. She gestures toward the larger context with her claim that mutual understanding requires a shared horizon of modernism. The problem with this claim is that there are no shared meanings of modernism. These meanings conflict along lines of power. In order to expose the lines of power, normative philosophy will have to rejoin critical theory.

Nancy Fraser and Linda Nicholson examine the massive inequities of modern systems, and conclude that the larger, empirical narratives of critical theory must take priority over normative philosophy.[13] Fraser argues as well that the modern liberal conception of the citizen-worker does not adequately respect the value of carework. She urges us to replace the liberal definition of the citizen with a universal caregiver model of the citizen. In Chapter 4, we will examine what it might mean to reconstruct modern liberalism through the emancipatory narrative of the universal caregiver.

[13] Nancy Fraser and Linda Nicholson, "Social Criticism without Philosophy: An Encounter between Feminism and Postmodernism," in *Theory, Culture and Society* (London: Sage, 1988), 5: 380.

4

The Outsider Within

A Model of the Citizen as Worker and Friend

The cognitive core of modern moral theory is designed to safeguard moral principles from reflecting the point of view of a particular social class. This aim is lost in the failure to scrutinize the entrenchment of thought and discourse in invisible networks of power. In order to counter the bourgeois perspective of discourse ethics, Fraser returns critical theory to its roots in Marxism. As she states in an essay on Habermas, "To my mind, no one has yet improved on Marx's 1843 definition of critical theory as 'the self-clarification of the struggles and wishes of the age.'... A critical social theory frames its research program and its conceptual framework with an eye to the aims and activities of those oppositional social movements with which it has a partisan, though not uncritical, identification."[1] With Linda Nicholson, Fraser calls for the replacement of philosophy with "immanent social critique."[2]

In this last respect, Fraser may go too far. Seyla Benhabib asks whether immanent critique could adjudicate between conflicting social norms or judge social systems that are thoroughly evil.[3] Benhabib's position is that "criticism presupposes a necessary distanciation of oneself from one's everyday certitudes, [and]... to this extent the social critic is more like the vocation of the social exile and expatriate than the vocation of the one who never left home" (SS, 227). Benhabib's image of the philosopher as the one who leaves home is troubling because of its symbolic alignment with androcentric views of moral maturation. Fraser's immanent critique of modern liberalism brings us back home from the perspective of the social exile, offering in its place a strong philosophical defense of a universal caregiver model of the citizen.[4]

Fraser's proposal adjudicates between the concerns of feminists in the United States, who are primarily interested in gaining equal treatment for women, and European feminists, who seek recognition for the differences between male and female culture. The way that Fraser frames her proposal anticipates its strengths as well as its weaknesses. The caregiver model of the citizen does an excellent job of opening up a middle ground between egalitarian liberalism and cultural feminism in the United States and Europe. Less clear is whether this proposal coheres with another concern that Fraser voices, and that is the need for social theorists to move issues of race, class, and sexuality from the margins to the center of their theories. Fraser explains that white, middle-class debates over feminism lack a framework "for mediating various struggles over 'multiple intersecting differences,' hence for linking various social movements" (JI, 181). Given these concerns, it is important to determine to what extent the universal caregiver model breaks out of the middle-class orientation of academic debates, and to what extent it represents a view of social roles immanent in the white, middle-class home.

I argue that Fraser's methodology along with her concrete proposal for a universal caregiver model of citizenship would benefit from an encounter with what sociologist Patricia Hill Collins terms the "outsider-within"

---

[1] Nancy Fraser, *Unruly Practices: Power, Discourse and Gender in Contemporary Social Theory* (Minneapolis: University of Minnesota Press, 1989), 113; henceforth cited as *UP*.

[2] Nancy Fraser and Linda Nicholson, "Social Criticism without Philosophy: An Encounter between Feminism and Postmodernism," in *Theory, Culture and Society* (London: Sage, 1988), 5: 373–394.

[3] Seyla Benhabib, *Situating the Self"* (New York: Routledge, 1992), 226; henceforth cited as *SS*.

[4] See "After the Family Wage: A Postindustrial Thought Experiment," in Nancy Fraser, *Justice Interruptus: Critical Reflections on the "Postsocialist" Condition* (New York: Routledge, 1997), 41–66; the book is henceforth cited as *JI*.

perspective.[5] The outsider-within perspective contrasts with that of the social exile or the immanent critic. Collins defines this critical perspective through the example of the nonwhite domestic servant. The nonwhite domestic servant occupies a position of both insider and outsider in the white household. From this vantage point, the critical theorist neither romanticizes the perspective outside the home; nor does the theorist focus on the caregiver-citizen inside the home. This third-wave critical theory perspective focuses its critical narrative through humanist voices at the margins of modern society.

From the outsider-within perspective, I seek a model of the citizen that contests both the cognitive (Habermas) as well as the caregiver models (Fraser). The alternative model emerges from a long history of exploited household labor, and from soul-wrenching experiences of child rearing. From this enlarged narrative of labor and care, I would question the restricted categories of work and leisure in the modern nation-state. In place of cognitive and caregiving models of citizenship, I urge that we view the cosmopolitan citizen of the global economy as the worker and the lover or the friend.

Let us begin by examining more carefully some of Fraser's vital contributions to critical theory. One major impetus for many of Fraser's central essays is to mediate differences between modernists and postmodernists. Often the basis for the mediation turns on issues of gender. In "Social Criticism without Philosophy," Fraser and Nicholson argue that postmodernists such as Lyotard are right "to claim that philosophy, and, by extension, theory more generally, can no longer function to *ground* politics and social criticism" (375). These postmodernists are wrong, however, to infer "the illegitimacy of large historical stories, normative theories of justice and social-theoretical accounts of macrostructures which institutionalize inequality" (379). Feminist social theorists make the opposite mistake. While feminist theories may "purport to be empirical," they "tacitly presuppose... essentialist assumptions about the nature of human beings....They are insufficiently attentive to historical and cultural diversity" (382).

Among these modern feminists, Fraser and Nicholson mention the names of Nancy Chodorow and Carol Gilligan. As they explain, Chodorow locates female identity in a concern for relationships but fails to see how her concept of relationship (intimacy, friendship, and love) is tied to modern western societies. Similarly, Fraser and Nicholson observe, Gilligan's

---

[5] Patricia Hill Collins, *Black Feminist Thought: Knowledge, Consciousness, and the Politics of Empowerment* (New York: Routledge, 1990), 194; henceforth cited as *BF.*

alternative 'feminine' model of moral development fails to attend to which women, under which specific historical circumstances the theory of care ethics might have in mind. Fraser and Nicholson conclude by calling for a "robust, postmodern feminist paradigm of social criticism without philosophy." Such a theory would be "comparativist rather than universalizing," and "look more like a tapestry composed of threads of many different hues than one woven in a single colour" (391).

Fraser shifts her position in those more recent essays collected in *Justice Interruptus*. The "tapestry" model of critique now sounds too close to what Fraser associates with "mainstream multiculturalism." Fraser reclaims a stronger normative role for critical theory in order to adjudicate between conflicting demands from the "tapestry" of opposition groups in diverse societies. She charges multiculturalists, radical democrats, and postmodernists (who are now associated with feminists such as Judith Butler rather than with Lyotard) with having failed to answer such questions as "Which kinds of differences ... should a democratic society seek to promote? And which, on the contrary, should it aim to abolish?" (*JI*, 174). Moreover, she goes a long way toward giving these questions a philosophical answer. According to Fraser, the answer to these questions requires mediating demands for recognition of cultural differences with the modern struggle for social equality. "A promising rallying cry for this project," Fraser suggests, "is 'No recognition without redistribution!'" (*JI*, 187).

Fraser locates multicultural concerns as part of the third stage of recent feminist history. These stages begin with the emphasis on social equality in the 1960s and 1970s, turn in the 1980s toward the demand for the recognition of women's differences, and expand in the 1990s to a "multiple intersection of differences" that cross gender with race, sexuality, and class (*JI*, 180–181). She calls for theorists to mediate these emerging differences on the basis of social equality.

This call returns us to serious questions with regard to basic questions of justice. As I would state these questions, they include: What is it that makes human beings equal to one another? And, how does the demand for social equality interface with ever more evident cultural, social, and individual differences? Fraser takes some steps toward answering these questions with her proposal for a universal model for citizenship. My concern is that Fraser's model borrows more than it needs to from white feminist ideas about equality from the 1960s. It could express more strongly the multicultural concerns that, according to Fraser's historical narrative, begin in the 1990s but in fact were already voiced in the 1960s. By bringing diverse voices earlier into the story, they might contribute more to Fraser's own project.

The proposal for a universal caregiver model of citizenship appears in the second chapter of *Justice Interruptus*. The first chapter, "From Redistribution to Recognition?" sets up some of the larger normative issues that lead to the proposal. Fraser explains how the new politics "centered on notions of 'identity,' 'difference,' 'cultural domination,' and 'recognition' has displaced a socialist politics "centered on terms such as 'interest,' 'exploitation,' and 'redistribution'" (11). This is a problem, she argues. What we need is a "critical theory of recognition," which she defines as "one ... that can be coherently combined with the social politics of equality" (12). As she points out, at first glance, these two kinds of demands seem to clash and to clash badly. Leftist demands for redistribution focus on class-based inequalities. Their aim is to eliminate the economic basis for group differentiation. In contrast, multicultural movements work for the cultural recognition of marginalized social groups; the aim of these movements is to promote group differentiation. While class warfare exemplifies the need for equality, the gay rights movement exemplifies the need to recognize difference. Some group movements (e.g., those that focus on race or gender politics) typically involve both economic and cultural demands. What should we do? Work to overcome differences among us? Or allow these differences to achieve greater legitimacy in our social system? Grand style liberal philosophy from the 1960s and piecemeal identity politics from the 1980s and 1990s have yet to find common ground.

For Fraser the clash takes the form of what she calls the "recognition-redistribution dilemma"—and it is a dilemma that she thinks we can resolve. The trick turns on a distinction between "affirmative" and "transformative" remedies for injustice. Affirmative remedies aim to correct "inequitable outcomes of social arrangements without disturbing the underlying framework that generates them." Transformative remedies target the generative framework of injustice. Fraser then aligns affirmative remedies with mainstream multiculturalism and transformative justice with deconstruction. "By destabilizing existing group identities ... , [transformative remedies] would not only raise the self-esteem of members of currently disrespected groups; they could change everyone's sense of self" (*JI*, 24). Her paradigmatic example is "queer politics which, in contrast [to gay-identity politics], treats homosexuality as a constructed and devalued correlate of heterosexuality.... The transformative aim is not to solidify a gay identity but to deconstruct the homo-hetero dichotomy so as to destabilize all fixed sexual identities. The point is not to dissolve all sexual difference in a single, universal human identity; it is, rather, to sustain a sexual field of multiple, debinarized, fluid, ever-shifting differences" (24). The categories of race, class, and gender require similar deconstructive transformation. Fraser leaves the concerns of ethnicity out of her analysis, although in a later essay she suggests that the deconstruction of race, at least in the case of African Americans, might mean the "transformation of a subordinate racialized caste into an ethnic group" (*JI*, 102).

Fraser's assumption is that categories such as race, gender, sexuality, and class form reactive and pathological identities with no positive remainder beyond their troubling histories. Other categories, such as some ethnic or cultural differences, might be affirmed as positive sources of identity, but not race, gender, or sexuality. The guiding principle is the demand for social equality. Fraser's aim is to locate a transformative basis for social equality via the deconstruction of racial, gender, class, and sexual politics. As she sees it, the unfortunate obstacle is that deconstructive projects are "far removed from the immediate interests and identities of most people ... , [at least] as these are currently culturally constructed" (31).

We need to understand why people would resist "deconstructing" identities such as blackness, femaleness, or gayness even though these identities cause varying kinds of alienation from the larger culture. One thought is that these dimensions of our identities might rather need reconstructing than deconstructing given the fact that we are embodied creatures with distinct experiences of our erotic drives and physical appearance. For example, the mere fact that in a heterosexist culture one might have strong impulses toward same-sex encounters means that we need to find ways to cultivate and not overcome sexual differences.

A second problem with the demand for a brave new world of social identities concerns the transition phase. It is one thing to project an ideal society. It is another thing getting there from here. Any number of philosophical ideals may be nice if we could leap into their pictures of a perfect future. The problem is that most of history (all of history?) can be little more than the process of transformation. So more important than the ideal is understanding and evaluating the process of change that the project entails.

Fraser's proposal is a bit vague. It is not clear what it would mean to live one's life in the process of deconstructing major dimensions of one's identity. Fraser's appeal to Marx anchors her project in 1960s social movements and the radicalization of liberal thought. From this point of view, the proposal for a deconstructed subject bears some of the same advantages and disadvantages as the proposal for the disembedded and disembodied subject that originates in Enlightenment philosophies. The deconstructed subject shares with the abstract, universal subject of the Enlightenment the imperative to uproot oneself from ingrained social meanings and libidinal loyalties. The idea is that the de-eroticized and detached subject enters into the public sphere as an equal to all others. New interests would develop out of addressing contemporary problems in an all new present rather than carrying around old meanings from irrational and alienating sources of difference.

However, I do not see how existing populations can make the transition toward this brave new world without a passage through the dark side of modernization. If history is any guide, empowered groups will experience this transition differently than disempowered groups. This is because empowered groups in modern social systems already view themselves less as the expression of specific cultural or social traditions, and more as the transcendent norm. Native Americans and other colonized people know the dark side of modernization along these transcendent lines quite well. The reeducation of native persons in American schools stripped them bare of native speech, family, and community traditions for the sake of their white European correlates. The result of modernization has not been citizenship upon an equal basis but social nightmare. We have hardly yet to heal from the consequences of "educational" policies that are a century old.

Contemporary liberal and leftist theorists do not aim to put resistant populations through this trauma. Certainly, Fraser does not. Deconstructive policies, like other strategies for modernization, aim to unweave personal and social narratives of race, sex, and gender for us all equally. Deconstructive policies would erase core domains of our divisive social identities, and allow for the proliferation of multiple new identities.

However, it is not clear how actual policies of deconstruction would work. I think it makes sense to use deconstructive policies to attack the center for the sake of those people located at the margins of power—although I would argue that the salutary aim might be to establish limits on the power of social groups, rather than to eradicate identities. Of course, this is not what Fraser has in mind. She argues that marginal and center groups (all identities) require total deconstruction. My fear is that this massive strategy of deconstruction would risk the opposite effect of what it intends, given the ineradicable realities of social power. Less empowered targets are more likely to budge than those targets fully entrenched in the prevailing regimes. If this is true, those people who feel least bound by their social positions would feel the least pressure to change. Blackness would be deconstructed before whiteness, femaleness before maleness, gay identity before straight identity, and so on. The deconstruction of social identities risks reenforcing existing distributions of race-, sex-, and gender-based power rather than restraining them.

It is not clear that deconstructive philosophies would work better than discourse ethics at countering the realities of social power. These realities are not going away anytime soon (and they probably never will). We do not need social policies that pretend they can eliminate these realities; we need policies that counter these realities on a continual basis. Those very people who feel least bound by their social position need most to be reminded of their limits. They do not need to be encouraged to view themselves as having transcended them. It is premature to construct rules for a world where sources of inequality would be gone. That world is just too far away. Basic laws need to check unequal sources of power, rather than assume these unequal sources of power are on their way out.

Most, if not all, of history is what we might as well call a transition; at the least, there is no endpoint in sight. A progressive project that requires too much or too little in the way of transformation can turn into a nightmare. Fraser's proposal for the massive deconstruction of gender, race, and sex threatens to strip us of orienting sources of erotic desire without offering an alternative source of identity. The total deconstruction of identity is likely to have more effect on those groups that have less power than on those that have more power. Blackness is more easily deconstructed in a white hegemonic system than is whiteness. Of course, our past identities and relationships are never going to be wiped out in total. This means that the deconstruction of gender is more likely to reinforce a multiplicity of new gender meanings built around universal maleness than around femaleness. Whether the de-eroticization and detachment of the subject from sedimented sources of identity is implemented on a partial or a total basis, it may not be justice. It may be *justice interruptus*.

In the end, the deconstructive model of identity reiterates much of the same abstract universalism that we were left with in the liberal theory of the 1960s. In the real world of entrenched power relationships and social stereotypes, this bare abstraction does not always help. Fraser's call for a *universal* caregiver model of citizenship as an example of a *deconstruction* of gender dichotomy underscores my concerns.

In "After the Family Wage: A Postindustrial Thought Experiment," Fraser again constructs a narrative around a central axis of conflict. This conflict sets in motion differences between U.S. feminists, characterized as liberals, and European feminists, characterized as social democrats. She argues that these two groups each attempt with only partial success to provide a normative picture of gender in postindustrial society. Fraser's strategy is to mediate by way of a third alternative.

U.S. feminists are identified as demanding that the "breadwinner model of the citizen" include women on an equal basis with men. The aim would be to "reorient women's aspirations away from domesticity toward employment" so that women could emulate the same model of citizen-worker that men have enjoyed. Fraser notes that this model "is far removed" from present realities where there are very few jobs for breadwinners and many for "disposable workers," and where some of these disposable workers include immigrants and other marginalized workers who perform poorly paid carework. Still, she argues, we might imagine for the sake of a thought experiment that "its condition of possibility could be met" (53). She proceeds to evaluate the universal breadwinner model, finding that it registers poorly in categories of leisure-time equality and anti-androcentrism. These women have changed their identities in order to fit the historically male model. However, since they are also doing much of the carework, they are often exhausted. Of course, if we count as a third issue the default dependency of this model on disposable workers (immigrant nannies, daycare workers, fast-food chain employees, even overseas toy and clothing makers), this model registers even more poorly.

She then turns to consider European feminism. These feminists express more interest in what Fraser calls the "caregiver-parity model of citizenship," which aims to provide compensation for child care and housework. Rather than evaluating an ideal version of this model (as she did for the breadwinner model), Fraser examines the Nordic experience. She concludes that the model is at least as problematic as the breadwinner model. The "caregiver-parity" model institutes a "mommy track" in employment, which prevents income equality, and it perpetuates the political and economic marginalization of women.

Fraser constructs her dialectic through the views of white, middle-class feminist movements in the United States and Europe. Fraser acknowledges the fact that women of color and immigrants perform much of the caregiving work, but she does not focalize her discussion from the perspectives of these women. She does not include the issue of immigrant labor or disposable workers among her focal criteria for the evaluation of models of citizenship. Both models are stipulated as "good" on measures of anti-exploitation.

It is this issue of labor, however, that reveals where we might improve on her dialectic. A full consideration of the issue of disposable workers (including those in the growing service economy) urges us to reevaluate the two models of citizenship that Fraser offers. Moreover, the perspective of the disposable care worker also calls into question some of the dichotomies that Fraser's framework employs. Patricia Hill Collins observes that standard dichotomies (e.g., public vs. private, or economic and political vs. religious, cultural, and domestic divides) that structure white middle-class societies do not reflect the greater divides as experienced by

African-American people. For African-American communities, the divide between the races has been and continues to be salient; the divide between public and private has not and in some communities is still not as salient as it is for whites. The perspective of what Collins terms the "outsider-within" white culture, and exemplifies in terms of the black domestic maid, does not quite fit into the framework that Fraser articulates. The universal caregiver model reflects its starting point in a white middle-class feminism in the United States and its less idealized engagement with a similarly positioned feminism in Europe.

The dialectic that Fraser unfolds turns on the issue of care and its relation to work. Fraser proposes to resolve the difference between European and American feminist movements with what she calls the "universal caregiver model of the citizen." She defines the model through its primary advantage, which is that it "values female-associated practices enough to ask men to do them too." Fraser explains that the first two models aim either to make women more like men or leave gender difference intact. The universal caregiver model would assume that all workers are also caregivers, and therefore require shorter work weeks and various employment-enabling services. A division of labor that has for hundreds of thousands of years defined the salient difference between men and women would once and for all disappear.

Fraser claims that the advantage of her model is that it deconstructs gender. In the previous chapter, she linked deconstruction with the multiplication of fluid identities. In discussing that chapter's proposals, I argued that the deconstructed subject seems to return to the same abstract and universal model of identity of traditional modernism. This second chapter of *Justice Interruptus* takes us even more directly to this point. The deconstruction of gender means its elimination in favor of a universal model of identity. The intersection of multiple differences that Fraser argues defines third-wave feminism yields a conception of the universal citizen. This conception of the citizen is borne at the intersection of two conventional identities: the breadwinner and the caregiver of the white, middle-class, and probably American family. The problems with this marriage of the conventional breadwinner and the conventional caregiver in a universal model of citizenship are multifold.

First, the model of the universal caregiver relies on the homogeneous and abstract measures of the human that develop out of the enlightenment (Locke, Kant, Mill), and return in more radical egalitarian projects (Rousseau, Marx, Maoism). The model of the citizen purports to measure the significance of the person in relation to the larger society. Modern definitions of citizenship rights focus on the contribution of those who create value through labor, serve the country through the military, or conduct their lives according to reasonable principles (e.g., what Habermas calls discourse and Fraser unmasks as bourgeois thinking). As Fraser points out, these traditional models do not make a place for the distinctive contributions of the caregiver to society. At this point, Fraser could have argued that caregiving should qualify as a significant and distinct source of skilled labor. Instead, she claims that carework is a universal activity, and that all citizens should be expected to do it. If she had gone the other route, and recognized care as a distinct source of labor and value in our society, then a more encompassing vision of justice might be possible.

In fact, I propose that the entry into citizenship for the immigrant careworker should parallel the entry for African-American men via the military service. This would mean that any immigrant who works as a caregiver for citizens qualifies as a citizen in our expanding democracy.

The major issue here is that we need to deal head-on with the fact that many caregivers in the United States are not now (and historically were not) citizens. Fraser tends to focus more on the conventional middle-class family (minus the disenfranchised nanny). She argues that both mother and father are to be expected to do two kinds of work, production and caregiving. Not only does this model relegate that domestic servant (Collins's "outsider-within") a bit too much outside the family; it also assumes that there is only one path toward citizenship, and that everyone must perform the same basic range of functions in society. The problem that I see is that individual skills and preferences cannot be easily reconstructed around a single norm of a socially useful person. No cultural revolution can make us all the same, or at least not in the respects that Fraser has in mind.

From the beginning of philosophical modernism, social theorists have attempted to find some common capacity (or list of functions) that defines humanity in order to defend social, political, or economic equality. Marx expanded the Enlightenment vision of human equality through his dream of a society without borders. In this beautiful society, we would conduct the work and leisure of our lives in unison. This beautiful society opens up on the other side of the sublime warfare and extreme conflict that, according to Hegel, blocks our way to a more cosmopolitan world. *The German Ideology* paints a picture of a society where we would "hunt in the morning, fish in the afternoon, rear cattle in the evening, criticize after dinner."[6] Of course, the several personae for so many of our dreams often turn out to be multiple projections of a single self. So too, the Marxian dream did not go

[6] David McLellan, ed., *Karl Marx: Selected Writings* (Oxford: Oxford University Press, 1977), 169.

far enough from the ideal selves of its author. No only did this beautiful dream assume that we all possess the same natural talents and interests; the dream did not include those who raise the children and manage the home.[7]

Fraser rounds out the dream by bringing caregiving into our species being. However, this remedy to the ills of modern social theory does not go quite far enough. The age-old problems reoccur. The underlying assumption is that we can be equal only by exercising the same range of special talents and interests, now including caregiving. This is a first problem with Fraser's model. If caregiving is a special talent and a distinct skill, then it cannot be included as a universal human capacity. Obviously, it was too special of a skill for Marx to imagine for himself. Second, like Marx's model of man, Fraser's model of the citizen leaves out of the picture whole groups of people who prop up the dreams of the modern theorist. If Marx forgets to reserve a part of the day for the raising of children (although he remembers the cattle), Fraser's proposal marginalizes the work of the disposable worker. From disenfranchised populations emerges another view of care and work, as well as an enlarged measure of the human. This alternative model turns on the simple fact that for those who dwell on the other side of the bourgeois family, care is not leisure; it is undervalued and underpaid labor.

Fraser's model of the citizen as worker plus caregiver does not come fully to terms with this fact. The model grants to citizens a shorter work week only in order to consign caregiving to a second task of citizenship and / or to a peripheral job in the larger economy. In fact, caregiving is a major source of "productive" value in the larger service economy. It involves material concerns of survival and symbolic issues that enable children to develop socially, cognitively, and emotionally. Its labor is not leisurely but intensive and skilled. Even the "natural function" of breast-feeding requires education and practice. Not everyone possesses the talents and capacities to perform the labor of care. Could older people stand the all-night hours and the backbreaking labor of nurturing young children? Could childless individuals with no informal or formal training in cognitive development or early sociality and emotional growth communicate significant cultural symbols to children in appropriate ways? Daycare workers are more and more expected to train for their jobs through relevant courses and workshops, but still they are paid as though their jobs were passive caregivers.[8] Modern parents who are missing the informal training from extended kin and midwives turn to courses and manuals from experts on everything from

[7] Ann Ferguson, *Blood at the Root* (London: Pandora Press, 1989), 209–218.

[8] My remarks here have benefited much from conversations with daycare workers at Clifton Child Care Center in Atlanta, and especially with Christi Cameron, from fall 1997 to spring 1999.

physical development to discipline problems. The horrors of institutional-
ized care, especially in the former Soviet Union, have alerted us to a simple
fact: infants and young children require vital symbolic resources as well as
human contact. Passive caretaking is not enough. Without social exchange,
the soul of the child does not grow.

The work of care is not adequately recognized until it is viewed as on
par with any historically male occupation. This means that it cannot be legislated as a citizen duty; it should be well-compensated labor. For market
economies that treat this service as duty and not productive work, carework
functions as a form of bonded labor. The market takes advantage of unpaid
labor through the maldistribution of profits and resources. Profits from the
marketplace trickle down on some but not all of our children in this nation
of plenty. My concern here is no more complex that this: Where markets
contribute toward major social inequalities, they need to be regulated by
those individuals who are affected. In a global era, this demand entails an expanded conception of citizenship.

Acknowledgment of the specific skills and interests that are necessary for
caregiving as well as its productive value in the larger economy is sorely
needed in modern liberal theory. The failure to view care as skilled labor on
par with other kinds of work traces back to public/private and gender
dichotomies that carry over from eighteenth- and nineteenth-century processes of modernization. Modern conceptions of gender difference reflect
the separation of productive labor performed for pay in the public sphere
from unpaid work done in the home. While the former type of work was
viewed as requiring various degrees of talent, training, and interest, the latter work was viewed as a quasi-natural duty or low-level task to be performed in the private realm. The idea was that anyone, or at least any
woman, could do it. While Fraser aims to deconstruct modern gender-
and-work dichotomies, her consignment of the work of caregiving to a universal task of citizenship reinforces the old categories. Day-care workers,
parents, and the informal economy of care workers have not yet sufficiently
brought out into public knowledge what it is not in the public's economic
interest to know: that care is not a quasi-natural, semi-passive, or unskilled
labor. It is mentally, emotionally, and physically draining labor. It can be a
source of alienation. It can also be a source of meaningful connection. In any
case, as Simone de Beauvoir has well argued, the rewards of this labor cannot be guaranteed by some mysterious force of nature.[9] Fraser's model of the

[9] Oddly, while Simone de Beauvoir continues to treat parenting as a quasi-natural and almost
animal function rather than a human identity, she is quite informative at explaining the

universal caregiver needs to come to full terms with the underlying blind spot of modern social theory and practice: caregiving is a significant source of economic as well as cultural labor that some individuals may choose to pursue as a primary occupation.

Fraser's deconstructive project for transformation tends to revert to a universalist, modernist project reminiscent of the projects of the feminists she defines as "first." The universal caregiver model marries male and female components of work only in order to leave standing the historically male model of work. It is only for this historically male model of work that we are to be compensated in terms of social and material resources (in a market economy, this means money and status). Meanwhile, it is expected that all citizens adopt the same mold of worker (defined in historically male terms) plus caregiver.

This leads one to wonder if the caregiver parity model of citizenship might not better reflect the diversity of lifestyle choices and the importance of recognizing care as a type of work. While Fraser poses the model in its real rather than ideal form, she offers very good reasons to conclude that the model reinforces oppressive views of gender identity. Fraser argues that the caregiver parity model marginalizes women. For Fraser, the implication is that women should enter into other forms of labor. I would agree that women might enter into various forms of labor, especially given the various degrees of work involved in care through our lives. However, I would also argue that the issue of marginalization needs to be addressed head on. The caregiver parity model marginalizes women and those who assist them in raising their children because it does not problematize the line drawn between the domestic and public spheres. This line reinforces conventional associations of care with a quasi-natural function and with subhuman dependency, and separates carework from economic productivity and civic status. Power is dissociated from care, and care is disempowered. This split between private and public affairs intersects with another axis: the separation of power (or political and economic activity) from art (or cultural, religious, and artistic expression). These two axes obscure the point at which they collapse: it is the point that is called care.

Or at least this is the blind spot for the dichotomies that frame conventional white narratives of work and personhood. For, as Fraser herself notes in another context, these dichotomies do not bear the same force in African-American communities.

---

social conditions that render this work utterly alienating and uninspiring. See *The Second Sex* (New York: Vintage Press, 1989), 484–527.

Fraser mentions this fact in the essay on Habermas (referred to above), drawing from alternative experiences of modernism in order to explain exactly why conventional dichotomies of gender and work are misconceived. Habermas articulates the conventional dichotomies in terms of the satisfaction of two fundamental needs in society. He explains these two kinds of needs as material and symbolic. Material needs are satisfied by what he terms economic productivity, which we would now expand to include the service economy. Symbolic needs for reproduction grow out of women's work in the domestic sphere, and include socialization and cultural transmission. Fraser's contention against Habermas is that both child rearing and economic activity are what she terms "dual aspect" activities; both involve material issues of survival and symbolic construction of social identities (*UP*, 116). This is a very helpful point. The separation of child rearing from paid work, she adds, is a linchpin of modern forms of women's subordination. This separation blocks our understanding of the ways in which the family is an unpaid or underpaid site of economic activity.

The value of household labor grows ever more apparent as we shift our focus away from the conventional home of the professional middle class and toward larger historical and anthropological studies of the family and social life. Social histories of the family from ancient Greece through early modern times locate child rearing as an essential part of the domestic economy, and the household as an integral part of the larger political economy.[10] Anthropological studies view child rearing along side hunting, gathering, and farming as contributing toward the labor required by nonindustrial societies.[11]

Fraser's philosophical analysis provides a powerful understanding of the meaning of work in modern and nonmodern societies. Fraser points out that all work involves material and symbolic dimensions. She also argues that the "symbolic norms of cooperation and equality" should prevail over "strategic and hierarchical forms of interaction." Joining together these two claims, I would argue that the definition of work should focus first and foremost on its contribution to the nexus of relationships that make us human. Measured in these terms, caregiving counts as highly skilled and valuable labor. Therefore, my first revision of Fraser's model is to include carework as paid labor that might or might not be performed by any particular citizen.

[10] Cynthia B. Patterson, *The Family in Greek History* (Cambridge: Harvard University Press, 1998); and Philippe Ariès, *Centuries of Childhood: A Social History of Family Life*, trans. Robert Baldick (New York: Random House, 1962).

[11] See Walter L. Williams, "The Relationship Between Male-Male Friendship and Male-Female Marriage," in *Men's Friendships*, ed. Peter M. Nardi (London: Sage, 1993), 190; essay henceforth cited as *MM*.

The dual-aspect definition of work needs to be brought into our understanding of citizenship. This is a more difficult task. We can begin by understanding how the androcentric view of "women's work" as deskilled and passive misses not only its value in satisfying material needs; it also misses how dimensions of child rearing (including the creation of symbols) play into the civic sphere. In this sphere, subtexts of meaning operate all too often behind the back of rational decision-making processes without ever being named. The result is the perpetuation of unimaginative and oppressive symbols that do not receive the critical, public attention that they deserve. From these symbols come the usual maldistributions of power and recognition based far too much on race, sex, and gender. These symbols need to be addressed already in the education and socialization of young children. Cultural work is important for a well-functioning society.

In order to redistribute power and recognition around the issue of care, we must do more than expand our concept of work and citizenship. We must also redesign public spaces in order to make them more accessible to children and their caregivers. Buildings and sidewalks can accommodate those who move in wheelchairs to the point of virtually eliminating some forms of disability and minimizing others. So too civic, commercial, and professional spaces can accommodate in appropriate ways children and their families. One consequence of deconstructing the divide between family and work worlds may be to bring some of the social concerns of the family into the production and consumption of products and services, and into the heart of public policy.

Fraser mentions that in African-American culture, the church has been taken as a primary site for political activity and discussion. The practices of the institution assisted in bringing together domestic and political concerns by making provisions for children. Moreover, the African-American church was not the only significant institution to stand outside mainstream dichotomies. Historian Julie Willett describes how the beauty shop has performed a similar role in African-American communities.[12] The black-owned beauty shop has been a center of community involvement, serving multiple functions. This was a place where loans were worked out and civil rights battles were planned. Female hairdressers could earn an income while raising their children. As sites of public discourse, the church and the beauty shop empowered women not only because they admitted a "women's view" but also because these were public spaces that were accessible to children and their caregivers.

[12] Julie Willett, *Permanent Waves: The Making of the American Beauty Shop* (New York: New York University Press, 2000).

Of course, in the larger market economy, many of these women were not paid or were paid poorly for their actual services as caregivers and domestic maids. In order to overcome the larger issues of distribution and recognition in our society, it does not suffice to reconstruct public space along lines of the beauty shop and the church in the African-American community. As Collins writes, "In contrast to the cult of true womanhood, in which work is defined as being in opposition to and incompatible with motherhood, work for Black women has been an important valued dimension of Afrocentric definitions of Black motherhood" (*BF*, 124). In a just social system, carework would be recognized as socially significant and would be compensated as valued labor.

In Chapter 7, I examine Sylvia Hewlett and Cornel West's call for a parents' bill of rights. As I point out, the compensation for carework cannot come at the expense of making the caregiver dependent upon an independent breadwinner. The labor of care needs to be compensated through government taxes on corporate profits. In this sense, the compensation of caregiving should, as Hewlet and West recommend, parallel our policy for rewarding those who perform military service. If we sever carework from paid work, then so too we sever recognition from issues of redistribution. Perhaps, then, we might revise Fraser's inspiring slogan, "No recognition without redistribution!" and call instead for "No separation of recognition from redistribution!"

The recognition of care as real work, and the definition of work in terms of its symbolic and social functions, prepares us to rethink our models for citizenship. From Fraser's critique of Habermas, we learn to develop further what discourse theory begins to teach us: symbolic and social functions are more vital to human well being than rational or productive capacities per se. It is not a far step to argue that both rational and productive activities need to be evaluated and rewarded on the basis of their contributions to our social selves. But then, what model of citizenship might reflect this more augmented conception of the individual?

Fraser's proposal takes us far toward understanding what an alternative model might entail. According to Fraser, our private and public institutions need to support the expectation that every citizen engages in carework by reducing the work week. We can alter her proposal appropriately by bringing into consideration the two claims that (1) care is skilled labor, and that (2) all work bears some symbolic and social value. While not everyone possesses the talents and interest to take on the work of care, everyone needs to engage in a sphere of meaningful human relationships. A social system that measures its productivity in strategic terms only misses the importance of the larger social meanings of our lives. The fact that the social milieu of our existence is ever more threatened is evident from the longer work weeks for high-income professionals as well as low-wage earners since the 1970s. The lengthening work week diminishes community involvement for those not performing carework; it makes it impossible for those of us who do un-paid carework plus paid labor. Fraser's proposal is that we set limits on the work week. These limits make time for the work of care. If, however, we see care as skilled labor requiring suitable compensation, then the social functions that Fraser restricts to dependency work might be expanded to include political, intellectual, and artistic modes of social interaction.

On this basis, I would advocate that we reduce the work week to thirty-five or thirty-six hours, as in Europe. (This proposal would require clear limits for the amount of work expected for promotion and raises, as well as the unionization and citizenship for all service workers). Parents of preschool age children should be compensated for carework via corporate taxes. If we were also to add one or two hours to the average American school day, then parents of school age children could participate with their families in leisure-time activities. Meanwhile, the skills and services of well-paid carework should count as experience toward other forms of employ-ment, and allow for greater movement between child rearing and corpo-rate or professional life.

With care work receiving recognition as a form of labor, the social and symbolic activities that exceed work-related duties would come to the fore as having special significance for the individual and the society. Anthro-pologist Walter Williams argues that American men experience alienation from the absence of the close friendships that flourish in non-Western so-cieties and for much of our history as a species.[13] In many societies, friend-ships are recognized as the center of one's emotional life. Formal ceremonies or rituals render these relationships official parts of public life. In main-stream America, intimate male-male friendships survive in attenuated form in athletic (and, I would think, nonathletic) contests as "team loyalty, com-petition, and success" (*MM*, 189). After noticing the sharp contrast between mainstream American and non-Western societies, Williams notes the lack of ritual for celebrating close friendships in Protestant churches and the dis-couragement of intimate friendships among the clergy in the Catholic church. As he states it, "The question is, are there other alternatives to the

---

[13] Williams draws many of the insights for his study of friendship in American Indian and Asian societies from Robert Brain's study of friendship in African societies. See Brain's *Friends and Lovers* (New York: Basic Books, 1976).

patriarchal nuclear family that will help to prevent an increasing sense of alienation in the lifestyle of the twenty-first century?" (*MM*, 193).

Several centuries before Christianity, Aristotle reflected on the significance of Athenian democracy and defined the citizen as the friend. The ancient Greek people viewed the capacity for friendship in diverse terms, ranging from *philia* (friendship) and *xenos* (stranger, foreigner, and friend) to *eros* (or love). I will return to a discussion of the significance of friendly relationships for democracy in later chapters. Here it is important to see that the capacity for friendship may establish a meaningful basis for citizenship as well as an alternative basis for modern views on equality and human rights.

As human beings we do not possess skills of reasoning or productivity on an equal basis with one another. What Habermas calls communicative rationality is not a universal capacity, but, as Fraser argues, a bourgeois style. Many of us are mentally or physically incapacitated for a sizable portion of our lives. As Eva Feder Kittay underscores in her inspiring critique of mainstream models of liberalism, this incapacitation means that many of us are unable to work on an equal basis with others.[14] I would add that many also will not be able to engage in caregiving. As a skilled labor, caregiving cannot be legislated as a universal duty. On the other hand, caregiving generates symbolic practices for human freedom. At the core of these practices are the vital communicative resources sought by a more egalitarian discourse ethics. For these reasons and others, I wonder if Fraser's proposal for a universal caregiver does not open us toward a more expansive conception of the citizen as the lover or the friend. The last major male philosopher to make such a proposal was Herbert Marcuse. Marcuse found the center of man in his erotic desire, and from the need to liberate eros, he called for a global revolution. I will examine his contributions to critical theory in the next chapter.

---

[14] Eva Feder Kittay makes the point that liberal theories of justice require the fiction that most people in society for most of their lives are not living in various states of dependency. She points out that this assumption is far from true, introducing what she calls the "dependency critique" of justice theory. See *Love's Labor: Essays on Women, Equality, and Dependency* (New York: Routledge, 1999).

II

A Dialectic
of Eros
and Freedom

5

The Erotic Soul
of Existential Marxism

Marcuse

After 1968, philosophical writers began a retreat from social visions based on what Herbert Marcuse called a "new type of man."[1] Modernist dreams of a more enlightened world dimmed into everyday scenes of abject poverty and political oppression. The emerging generation of postmodern writers responded to the entrenchment of power by refusing the dream. It would seem that revolution was, to borrow from Sartre's definition of man, a "useless passion." While postmodernist writers have constructed literary techniques that privilege irony, and its disruption of narrative unity,

Special thanks to Walter Adamson and Kent Durning for very helpful comments on an earlier version of this chapter. A version of this chapter is to appear in Kelly Oliver and Steve Edwin, eds., *Between the Psychic and the Social* (forthcoming).

[1] Herbert Marcuse, *An Essay on Liberation* (Boston: Beacon, 1969), 19; henceforth cited as *EL*.

postmodern theorists have exposed the irrational core of human experience. But if postmodernists have avoided direct normative statements, they have also claimed that their transgressions against meaning and thought are not wholly without moral and political significance. They have claimed that their strategies were both moral and political, even leftist, in underlying orientation. Derrida, for one, claims to draw moral force by appealing to an alterity that lurks in the margins of Western culture.

However, it is this claim to think from the unknown place of the "Other" that also reveals the limits of postmodernism. The vague appeal to alterity barely made contact with any specific social groups in struggle. Postmodern allegories of the "Other" turned out to be little more than narcissistic fantasies of the "Same." Again, classical deconstruction provides a clear example of the problem. The occasional use of feminine tropes in order to deconstruct the phallocentrism of reason did not express female subjectivity but unrepressed male pleasure, perhaps at the expense of female subjects.[2] While postmodernism would claim to undermine the master narratives, the pleasure of transgression would reveal little more than the dark side of those same masters. It is true that reform movements benefit from the destabilization and ironization of power. However, as Martin Matustik argues in *Specters of Liberation*, leftists and liberals will have to break out of the narcissistic projections of postmodernism if they are to recognize the "faces in the margins" of power.[3] As I reinterpret the claim, social theorists will have to move past deconstructing, reconstructing, or otherwise reiterating history's "master narratives," and turn to the narratives of history's "slaves." It is not enough, however, to proliferate narratives of resistance at the margins of power. As Matustik also argues, fragmented narratives and local strategies of resistance are too easily appropriated in the global expansion of unchecked capital. The final aim must be to mediate situated histories of oppression toward a global politics of freedom.

In *Specters*, Matustik reinvokes the spirit of Marcuse and the political fervor of the 1960s in order to offer some fundamental statements for the contemporary left. Most significant among these theses, Matustik argues that the left must expand its communicative competencies in order to respond to the diversity of those who are struggling on the margins. This means that we cannot afford to relive old leftist mistakes of identifying from among the many struggling groups a single standpoint or particular social group to

---

[2] Gayatri Chakravorty Spivak makes this argument in "French Feminism in an International Frame," in *In Other Worlds: Essays in Cultural Politics* (New York: Routledge, 1988), 134–153.

[3] Martin J. Beck Matustik, *Specters of Liberation: Great Refusals in the New World Order* (Albany: State University of New York Press, 1998).

represent the universal cause of justice. Struggles for freedom will wither away before the growing onslaught of unrestrained conservatism unless social groups forge paths of communication *and* dissent across lines of conflict. Identity politics needs to give way to a dialectic of multiple origins.

bell hooks expresses the same wise concern in different terms. In "Love as the Practice of Freedom," hooks writes, "There is no powerful discourse on love emerging either from politically progressive radicals or from the Left. The absence ... arises from a collective failure to acknowledge the needs of the spirit and an overdetermined emphasis on material concerns."[4] "To heal our body politic we must reaffirm our commitment to ... where true liberation leads us. It leads us beyond resistance to transformation... .[It leads us] to the beloved community" (*OC*, 250).

It is bell hooks's call for "love as a practice of freedom" and Matustik's vision of a multidimensional dialectic that has made me wonder if we might turn once again to Marcuse's dialectic of eros and freedom. Marcuse's psychoanalytic view of libidinal man and moral freedom contrasts sharply with the stoic rationalism in modern liberal views. These modern liberal definitions vary from left to right but they cluster around ideas about taking ownership of oneself through rational principles, enlightened self-interest, or existential choice. In a competitive, self-achieving society, these notions translate into the development of individual capacities for making decisions about one's own life. Marcuse does not question self-control, individual achievement, or existential choice as ultimate goals. He does argue, however, that in a society dedicated to capital production, and not individual erotic expression, the individual has absorbed the values of capitalist production into his rational capacities and existential choices. The American worker does not know himself.

Much has not changed about capitalist society and liberal theory since Marcuse's time. Classic bourgeois liberal theory (and especially Locke) rose up to combat state tyranny, the major source of unrestrained power several hundred years ago. Marcuse understood the limits of this liberal tradition. The state has not been the sole or even the major source of unchecked power over the last two centuries. On the contrary, the double liberal focus on state power and individual rights plays into the invisible hands of larger economic and technological forces that roll through both individuals and nation states and wrap the globe. These forces sink nations into the black hole of economic debt and ruin individual lives at will. Within liberal states

---

[4] See bell hooks, "Love as a Practice of Freedom," in *Outlaw Culture: Resisting Representations* (New York: Routledge, 1994), 243; henceforth cited as *OC*.

and international organizations, the myopic defense of bourgeois rights conspires with superindividual economic forces that divide us into classes, and abandon massive numbers of children to misery.

At the end of the twentieth century, these forces are growing. Major first-world governments are relinquishing their role in promoting egalitarian social policies, and serving instead as venders for corporate interests and private wealth. The facts are more dire as we expand our focus across the global "community." The United Nations Human Development Report estimates that the "richest fifth of the world's people consumes 86 percent of all goods and services while the poorest fifth consumes just 1.3 percent." According to the same report, "The additional cost of achieving and maintaining access to basic education for all, basic health care for all, reproductive health care for all women, adequate food for all and clean water and safe sewers for all is roughly $40 billions a year—or less than 4 percent of the combined wealth of the 225 richest people of the world."[5]

There is, however, no political will to undertake small changes in wealth redistribution that would result in deeply humanizing consequences. The bourgeois-based individualism of liberal theory predisposes the average citizen of a modern democracy to think that redistribution is a matter of individual choice or social charity but not a matter of right. The liberal hope is that modernization in American terms will overcome the worse social ills, but this hope is naive. The United States has 6 percent of the world's population and yet consumes 40 percent of the world's natural resources. We cannot universalize the American style of freedom without risking the ruin of the planet. If modernization does not also entail lowering high standards of living among the middle-class elite, then massive numbers of individuals are doomed to slave-status at the periphery of power.[6]

Liberal freedoms based on bourgeois autonomy overemphasize the virtues of self-control, rationality, and individual choice at the expense of libidinal connections that we make with one another. These freedoms do not encourage the average citizen of a liberal democracy to think about the ways in which we depend upon one another inside and outside national borders for our economic well-being. It is too easy to use bourgeois freedoms in order to prop up national and international policies based on arrogance and greed.

---

[5] For synopsis of the United Nations Human Development Report, see "Kofi Annan's Astonishing Facts," *New York Times*, September 27, 1998, 16.

[6] For the United Nations Office for Drug Control and Crime Prevention Report on slavery, see "U.N. Warns that Trafficking in Human Beings Is Growing," *New York Times*, June 25, 2000, 9. The report estimates the increasing number of people who are now involved in sexual, economic, and classic slavery to far exceed the 11.5 million Africans in the Middle Passage.

The growing recognition of our interdependency points to significant changes in productive relations (i.e., the economy) since Marcuse's time. The basis for wealth has shifted from individual accumulation and local management toward flexible capital and overseas production. As historian George Lipsitz observes, high-tech capitalism is not fueled by the bourgeois drive to control and possess, but by expanding socioeconomic connections: "For more than a hundred years, struggles for social justice and equality have been waged as battles over the control of places—countries, cities, factories, and neighborhoods....[But] new technologies that separate management from production, flexible forms of capital accumulation that discourage investments in infrastructure, and increased emphasis on consumption rather than on production ... all increasingly make urban identity a matter of connections between places."[7]

These changes in productive relations require that we rethink the basis for Marcuse's critique of capitalism. The corporate culture that Marcuse critiqued in the 1950s and 1960s secured lonely workers in feudal hierarchies where uniformity guaranteed efficiency. Marcuse argued that this type of culture breeds fake individuals with pseudo-autonomy. The individual is socialized into believing that he acts on his own desires when in fact his desires represent the values of capital. He desires to work for the company, and feels guilty when he does not, because he has internalized the repressive work demands of a society whose basic interests are economic. Leisure recreates the energy necessary for work but does not stimulate any dreams for a more meaningful life. Marcuse dares the ersatz individual to rebel against the societal authorities and reclaim his true individuality by exploring erotic drives that are left unsatisfied in repressive modern life.

The ethos of the high-tech corporation in Silicon Valley does not resemble the repressive atmosphere of the quasi-feudal institutions of Marcuse's time.[8] The progressive corporation encourages its employees to think of themselves as part of a creative team of sexually charged and self-expressive individuals without bosses. Where high standards of living do not suffice for reconciling employees with their lives, the corporate community provides the necessary libidinal cathexis for a new type of family. Social skills are now viewed by prospective employers and educators as essential for making the

[7] George Lipsitz, *Dangerous Crossroads: Popular Music, Postmodernism and the Poetics of Place* (New York: Verso, 1994), 6; henceforth cited as *DC*. For progressive dimensions of commercialized leisure within the United States, see Randy D. McBee, *Dance Hall Days: Intimacy and Leisure among Working-Class Immigrants in the United States* (New York: New York University Press, 2000).

[8] Nina Munk, "The Price of Freedom," *New York Times Magazine*, March 5, 2000, p. 50.

right kind of connections in the new corporate world. Employees are made to feel more comfortable with their "family" at work than their dysfunctional family at home. Things are not, however, what they seem. The ersatz family at work is based on the interests of capital production, and is a displacement and substitute for authentic social life. Employees are not valued as irreplaceable individuals with long-term connections to the corporation or each other. Corporations claim to represent the interests of their employees, but do not. They give employees more freedom through flex-time to be with their families at home, which is good. But the fax machine and the computer also make the home an extension of the workplace and an occasion for extending the workday. Corporations claim that workers gain more free time and control over their work with temporary or part-time positions. But what this really means is that a growing number of permanent, full-time positions with benefits have been transformed into jobs with few or no benefits. Corporations reward their employees not only with high salaries but also with stock options and partial control over the company. But what this really means is that corporate loyalty to employees has been replaced with the constant threat of downsizing in order to increase profits for shareholders.

Meanwhile, the new urban identity of the professional worker does not automatically lead to either cooperation or assimilation with those poorly paid service workers or foreign laborers at the periphery of power. The standard claim that a global "mass culture" will normalize a docile body of workers and consumers across ethnic and economic divisions fails to heed evidence to the contrary. Disenfranchised populations are not ignorant of the fact that their natural resources and cheap labor prop up the American dream. The mass media, and especially the Hollywood film industry, is thought to play a primary role in the process of homogenization. While Hollywood films may encourage American audiences to imagine that they can make peace with the past and present terror of American imperialism, the same films are used for the subversion of American values by anti-American groups. As Lipsitz notes, "Hollywood films intended to assuage the effects of the American defeat in Vietnam become icons for anti-American militia fighters in Beirut" (*DC*, 6). These opposition groups take films mourning the American involvement in Vietnam as inadequate substitutes for the political reckoning needed to redress decades of oppression.

Behind the visible screens of first world prosperity lie invisible battlefields of struggle. U.S. corporations cross borders into third-world countries in order to make the cost of labor virtually disappear. But those low-skilled workers who labor for next to nothing in order to serve the global marketplace do not necessarily assimilate American values. Many of these laborers resist through such democratic worker organizations as the Mexican *Frente Auten-tico del Trabajo*.[9] The vision of modernization that combines Americanization with rationalization conceals a painful truth: the American style of freedom depends upon the bonded labor of disenfranchised populations across the globe. We know this is true. But we cannot bring this dire fact into the heart of liberal discourse without altering the paradigm—or, establishing a new Gestalt, as Carol Gilligan argues—of modern freedom (Chapter 1).

The sharp double focus on the individual versus the state blinds the average citizen of the modern liberal democracy to the ways in which networks of capital and technopower cross national borders and seal individual fates. Atomistic moral psychologies focus on an individual's personal moral ideals, underemphasizing the vast impact of cross-continental historical, cultural, and environmental forces on our psychic well being. The deep sources of human meaning, the capacity for alienation and outrage as well as joyful recognition, lie in libidinal forces of human connection. Social forces make up the air that we breathe. Without these forces, we diminish as human beings. If these forces work against us, we lose energy and direction. Classical writers including Plato and Aristotle placed *eros*, *philia*, and *xenos* at the center of their political philosophies. But then why would mainstream liberal writers since the time of Locke downplay the social and libidinal core of our human existence?

The Stoic Origins of Modern Freedom

In the *Phenomenology of Spirit*, Hegel traces the modern notion of freedom to the rise of Stoicism during the time of slavery in the Roman Empire.[10] This modern concept, Hegel argues, had to originate under conditions of "universal" bondage (sec. 199). As I interpret the *Phenomenology*, the trauma of slavery in the Roman Empire brought to each man the realization that death was his true master, and this realization transformed the essence of man's identity. Fear in the hands of death purged man of his libidinal attachments, and turned his thoughts toward a more abstract plane of existence. Stoic practices of self-discipline and inner peace provide a therapy for coping with the trauma that bondage occasions. Work, which Hegel defines in terms of the capacities to overcome libidinal desire and to

---

[9] For reports on FAT and Chiapas from Fred Evans, Patricia Huntington, and Martin Matustik, among others, see current issues of *Radical Philosophy Newsletter*.

[10] G. W. F. Hegel, *Phenomenology of Spirit*, trans. A. V. Miller (Oxford: Oxford University Press, 1977), secs. 194–201.

shape and control objects, develops in the self-consciousness of the slave and marks the "beginning of wisdom" (sec. 195).

In classical Greek culture, according to Hegel, there was no capacity for genuine thought: "In thinking, the object does not present itself in picture-thoughts but in Notions [or Concepts]" (sec. 197). The ability to think in concepts requires that one abstract from immature forms of knowledge. Conceptual thinking abstracts from the literary images and dramatic staging that compose the dialectic in Plato's dialogues. Conceptual thinking abstracts also from the social relationships that lay the basis for what Aristotle calls practical judgment. These pre-philosophical modes of knowledge fail to grasp the world as a construction of my *own*. "In thinking, I am free ... because I remain simply and solely in communion with myself" (sec. 197).

The Stoic break from modes of thought that are embedded within social praxis and emotive forms of understanding marks a problematic response to the trauma of slavery and a wrong turn for modern philosophy.[11] It prepares the rising middle class to accept productive values of capitalist growth over the social values of hospitality and friendship. Prominent slave narratives written in modern America avoid the stoic turn. These narratives respond to the terror of slavery and its aftermath through a wisdom that is rooted in an expressive, humanist culture. Like Hollywood's conventional war movie, Hegel's phenomenology leaves out of the dialectic what the Stoic philosopher does in fact seem to deny: the real life turmoil of pathos. This pathos comes of losses that are not abstract and general but specific and overwhelming. These are losses of family, friends, cultures, and place. These losses do not heal via the path of social withdrawal and inner retreat. They require emotional engagement and political struggle.[12]

Marcuse's Theory of Eros and Freedom

Marcuse aimed to account for the erotic soul that is absent from modern consciousness and necessary for political struggle. He argued that the repressive stoicism of modern consciousness fuels capitalism by alienating the individual from his deepest erotic drives. Alienated students, oppressed blacks, and exploited workers share an aversion to capitalism that is instinctive, he claimed. It is this quasi-biological libidinal force that would gener-

[11] Cynthia Willett, *Maternal Ethics and Other Slave Moralities* (New York: Routledge, 1995), 97–104.

[12] Leonard Harris, ed., *Philosophy Born of Struggle: Anthology of Afro-American Philosophy from 1917* (Daybook, Ia.: Candle / Hunt Publishing Company, 1983).

ate the basis for political solidarity across diverse populations.[13] At the same time, Marcuse's exposure of our unconscious erotic drives opened a path for appealing to unhappy professionals, technicians, and corporate executives. Beneficiaries of capitalist wealth would seem to be content with the system that rewards their productivity. In fact, the mirroring facades of high-rise towers reflect less the pleasure than the narcissistic emptiness of productivity and success. Marcuse discerned in this emptiness the source of a distinctly modern cultural syndrome, which he termed "one-dimensional man."[14] The excessive demands of the economy under capitalist systems drain the high-powered worker of his erotic energy and dull his creative powers. The empty narcissism of modern life skims over the surface of man's deeper needs for autonomous reflection, aesthetic cultivation, or communion with nature.

Marcuse's diagnosis of the false consciousness of the middle class or wealthy elite was based on his philosophical reinterpretation of Freud's theory of basic human drives.[15] For Marcuse, three of Freud's claims are especially significant for understanding modern society.

First, Marcuse reinterprets Freud's concept of Eros as the fundamental instinct of biological man. This notion is much more interesting to Marcuse than Freud's earlier, more narrowly focused theory of sexuality, which emphasized the antagonism between instincts of sex (or libido) and those of ego (or self-preservation), and then defined the libido in terms of oral, anal, and genital stages of sexuality. Marcuse argued that Freud's discovery of *infantile narcissism* radically expanded his conception of erotic drives. According to this new thesis, the infant is born into an experience of diffuse and unlimited libidinal connections with the world around it. For Marcuse, "the discovery of infantile sexuality and of the all but unlimited erotogenic zones of the body" means that the infant's first experience of the world is of a peaceful, solitary, and pleasurable sense of connection, or even womb-like submersion with the world (*EC*, 23). He adds that "the introduction of narcissism into psychoanalysis marked a turning point in the development of the instinct theory: the assumption of independent ego instincts (self-preservation

---

[13] C. Fred Alford argues that Marcuse's theory of eros solves the political problem of who might become the agency of revolution "now that the proletariat had so clearly failed its historical task....The answer is not a social class but a biological dimension within us all." See "Marx, Marcuse, and Psychoanalysis" in *Marcuse: From the New Left to the Next Left*, ed. John Bokina and Timothy J. Lukes (Lawrence: University of Kansas Press, 1994), 133.

[14] Herbert Marcuse, *One-Dimensional Man: Studies in the Ideology of Advanced Industrial Society* (Boston: Beacon Press, 1964), esp. 12; hereafter cited as *OD*.

[15] Herbert Marcuse, *Eros and Civilization* (Boston: Beacon Press, 1966), 159–172, henceforth cited as *EC*.

instincts) was shaken and replaced by the notion of an undifferentiated, unified libido prior to the division into ego and external objects....Primary narcissism is more than autoeroticism; it engulfs the 'environment,' integrating the narcissistic ego with the object world ... as 'limitless extension and oneness with the universe' (oceanic feeling)" (*EC*, 168).

A second point concerns the telos (or goal) of human existence. Freud replaces his earlier interest in the conflict between the sexual instincts (the pleasure principle) and self-preservation (reality principle) with the antagonism between what he terms Eros (life drives) and Thanatos (a drive toward death or destruction). Freud's convoluted remarks on this antagonism between life and death instincts seem to suggest that both drives stem from a single impulsive drive toward "Nirvana," and that "Nirvana" is yet another name for death. Marcuse reinterprets this final impulsive drive in terms that support his belief in moral progress. According to Marcuse, the Nirvana impulse ultimately signifies nothing more mysterious than man's desire to avoid pain or an early death (*EC*, 207, 235).

The third point concerns the source of man's unhappiness. According to Marcuse, Freud rightly points toward a general social malaise that accompanies modernization and rationalization. As Freud explained, the malaise that characterizes the affluent society reflects the conflict between pleasure drives and the need to work (or the reality principle). Marcuse admits with Freud that the need to work will require some repression of drives bent on immediate gratification. Freud is wrong, however, to think that civilized man is doomed to be unhappy. According to Marcuse, our highly productive society demands too much work from us, and is based on what he terms "*surplus-repression*" (*EC*, 35). In modern society, we conspire against ourselves and each other, inducing in one another fear and guilt to propel excessively high rates of productivity, and absorbing ever more of our identity into our status as worker. From early childhood education, the social value of the person is measured in terms of standardized skills and qualities of adjustment (*EC*, 96).[16] Marcuse terms the specific sociohistorical form of the reality principle that describes what drives the competitive individual in capitalist societies the "*performance principle*" (*EC*, 35). He argues that moral conscience developed under these conditions "seems to skip the stage of individualization: the generic atom becomes directly a social atom" as corporate culture and mass media transmit the moral values that were once the province of the family (*EC*, 97).

[16] Kate Zernike, "When Testing Upstages Teaching," *New York Times*, June 18, 2000, sec. 4, p. 6.

Corporate-sponsored pleasures distract the exhausted worker from more deeply rooted desires and lure him into an almost seamless identification with the cycles of production and consumption that measure material prosperity. Almost seamless—for Marcuse aimed to train our eyes to see the oppressive guilt that lies behind the obsessive-compulsive worker and the empty narcissism of consumer pleasure. The accomplished man whose freedom is celebrated by mainstream, middle-class liberal culture turns out to be enslaved by the cramped impulses of a fetishistic consumerism and a workaholic psychology.

For, according to Marcuse, those men who occupy positions of economic and managerial power are the privileged sites, but slaves nonetheless, of the economic forces that they serve. "This is the pure form of servitude: to exist as an instrument" (OD, 33). The exploited worker and the lofty executive are the tools of capital growth. This mutual dependence of the worker and the executive is not "the dialectical relationship between Master and Servant ... but rather a vicious circle which encloses both the Master and the Servant" as the nature of domination changes to abstract relations based on administrative rationality (OD, 33).

Marcuse calls for a "Great Refusal," which is a protest against unnecessary repression. "Liberation of the instinctual needs for peace and quiet, of the 'asocial' autonomous Eros presupposes liberation from repressive affluence: a reversal in the direction for progress" (EC, xiv). "'Polymorphous sexuality' was the term which I used to indicate that the new direction of progress would depend completely on the opportunity to activate repressed or arrested organic, biological needs: to make the human body an instrument of pleasure rather than labor" (EC, xv). While our innermost desires and ambitions have been trained by the demands of the performance principle, our fantasies bear memories of the erotic freedom of infancy. Marcuse does not by any means advocate that we return to a quasi-mythical past. But he does believe we should attend to our repressed instinctual needs.

Finally, and rather belatedly, Marcuse calls upon the "social instincts" (EC, 207). He tentatively traces these instincts back to "aim-inhibited sexual instincts." According to Freud, aim-inhibited sexual desires are rooted in an incestuous relationship between the little boy and his mother. These sexual desires will have to be severely prohibited (by the little boy's father) and eventually displaced onto a spouse (who reminds the grown man of his mother). Freud's "Oedipal theory" of sexuality does not encourage erotic revolution; it rationalizes the need for the father and other social authorities to repress our original sensuality so that we might conform to society's needs. Therefore, it is not surprising that Marcuse does not further discuss these sexual instincts, but returns instead to the thesis of infantile narcissism. For Marcuse, it is the oceanic oneness, or polymorphous libidinous ties of early childhood, that makes possible a "civilization evolving from and sustained by free libidinal relations."

To what extent does Marcuse's theory of eros offer a plausible theory of human desire today? Can we harness this erotic synergy in order to struggle in solidarity along the multiple fronts of global oppression?

Maternal Utopia without Mothers

With the rise of the health industry and the shift of the life sciences away from the Freudian language of instinct and asocial drive, Marcuse's call for the liberation of libidinal man sounds arcane. Even worse, his language is insulting to those "outsiders" (the black and the poor) who were supposed to exhibit this premodern, unrepressed, "primitive erotic force." Still there is, I think, something of Marcuse's critical project that reverberates with late postmodern life. Just as Marcuse saw in the psychosomatic syndrome of "one-dimensional man" something absent from the modern values of production and consumption, so over the past decades there has been a growing apprehension of the psychic and social costs of unchecked corporate growth. Excessive demands of production are thought to correlate with stress, and with related physical and emotional ailments. Open-ended schedules of work, transient social life, and distracting levels of infotainment produce in well-positioned individuals symptoms of a malaise similar to what Marcuse identified in the 1950s and early 1960s as a significant social crisis.

There are differences too. The response to this contemporary malaise has yet to produce a progressive political or cultural movement across social groups. Moreover, this malaise has less to do with the sexually repressive climate of the 1950s and early 1960s than with the need to reconstruct a more satisfying social infrastructure. One symptom of this malaise is what a *New York Times* article reports as "a wide trend": the resignation of career politicians, corporate executives, and sports stars from high-status and well-paying jobs. Interviews with "baby boomers giving up the grind" turn up a common complaint: eighty-hour-plus work weeks weaken family connections.[17] Well into the twentieth century, at least according to historian Philippe Ariès, the nuclear family provided a safety valve for cultivating social needs that were repressed in productive spheres. Ariès claimed that "the

---

[17] Jill Abramson, "For Political Quitters, It's the Family, Stupid," *New York Times*, April 12, 1998, sec. 4, p. 4.

family has advanced in proportion as sociability has retreated. It is as if the modern family had sought to take the place of old social relationships (as these gradually defaulted), in order to preserve mankind from an unbearable moral solitude."[18] However, over the last few decades, the liberal policies that have opened up paths for women in economic and political institutions have also put new pressures on the family, and have not addressed the social vacuum of modern life. The expansion of corporate life yields by default a middle-class nostalgia for the nuclear family of the 1950s and early 1960s.

The social life of the family did not especially excite Marcuse. On the contrary, Marcuse saw the patriarchal and monogamous family of the 1950s and 1960s as a source of repression. Marcuse believed that the way out of social repression lies in the individual's cultivation of erotic fantasies in high art and poetic thought. The modern consumer tries to stimulate his dulled sensitivity through pleasures sponsored by the entertainment industry but fails. The "desublimated repression," or uncultivated pleasure, offered by this industry falls short of the creative power of "authentic art" to expand the sensibility. Only "authentic art," which is necessarily free of economic motives, could cultivate the "needs of a new type of man" (*EL*, 19). Like pretechnological culture, high art expresses "alienation from the entire sphere of business and industry, from its calculable and profitable order" (*OD*, 58–59). And like primitive man, the new man would "have the good conscience of being human, tender, sensuous." His sense of morality would not be grounded in some secret shame, or some failure to measure up, before the unseen god of capital. His morality would be grounded in a childlike yearning of erotic life to overflow borders and expand into the "infinite womb" of the "cosmos." Authentic art symbolizes the purity of this original craving. At the same time, this art mobilizes the contemplative soul to break out of "false consciousness" and rebel against social forces that threaten individual autonomy.

Marcuse characterizes the differences between high culture and commercial culture in terms of their effects on the erotic appetite of the male viewer. The super sexy images and especially, Marcuse notes, the sexy stars mass-marketed by Hollywood stimulate the hunger of one-dimensional man. However, these commercial images of female beauty cannot nourish the soul (*OD*, 77). The authentic image of beauty (Marcuse's example is a prostitute who appears in a novel by a high modernist writer) hints at a sensuality that is innocent and diffuse, but also, I would add, devoid of

---

[18] Philippe Ariès, *Centuries of Childhood: A Social History of Family Life*, trans. Robert Baldick (New York: Vintage, 1962), 406.

subjectivity and power: "Hers is a tenderness which blossoms only in infinity" (*OD*, 59; cf. 78).

Marcuse had hoped that student intellectuals and artists would lead racial minorities and the third-world proletariat to demand that moral and political limits be placed on the tyranny of unregulated economic power in the name of his aesthetic man. The traditionally patriarchal but increasingly bureaucratic machinery of capital would yield to erotic sources of renewed humanity. These are sources that, according to Marcuse, were cultivated "once upon a time" in matriarchal societies, and might be glimpsed again in a utopia that Jessica Benjamin aptly and ironically describes as "maternal."[19]

Marcuse's mythological fantasy of the new man may be less matriarchal, however, than classical in origin. The idea that the highest type of man would pursue the kind of intellectual or artistic pursuits made possible in a life devoted to leisure owes its clearest philosophical expression to Aristotle. This valorization of the pleasures of friendship and leisure contrasts sharply with the work ethic that develops in modern philosophy. For Aristotle it is clear that the highest class of man must have little to do with work, and that in order to have a class of men who could devote themselves to the arts of leisure, these men would require slaves, servants, and wives to do their work and raise their children.

Marcuse attempts to subvert the slave economy that underlies the classical conception of the highest man by replacing our insatiable need for third-world workers with the labor-saving devices of modern technology. The result is a utopian society of minimal work and maximal freedom on prelapsarian grounds. There is, however, something missing in Marcuse's maternal dream. The dream fails to encounter the one worker who cannot minimize her labor without destroying her product. That worker is the mother.

When Marcuse lists those marginal subjects who make for revolutionary forces, he carefully sets aside the housewife. Apparently the labor of the housewife, unlike that of the exploited worker or the racialized outcast, lies beyond redemption. Having praised the sublime image of the whore in the modern novel, Marcuse turns disapprovingly to the housewives of his generation. These women are not "images of another way of life but rather freaks ... of the same life, serving as an affirmation rather than negation of the established order," Marcuse remarks (*OD*, 59). Indeed the mother was the one subject who was nowhere to be found in Marcuse's maternal utopia.

---

[19] Jessica Benjamin, *The Bonds of Love: Psychoanalysis, Feminism, and the Problem of Domination* (New York: Pantheon, 1988), 177ff.

The narcissistic enjoyment of the body of the mother by her child and the subtle evocation of the all-giving-body of the mother in the sublimated erotics of high art strips the mother of the multiple dimensions of her subjectivity. Marcuse's analysis of the housewife consigns her once and for all to a female species of one-dimensional man. Her care for the child is not viewed as intelligent labor but as passive instinct, her tenderness is only vaguely sexual and certainly non-intentional, and her protests against society or home life are dismissed as neurotic complaint.

Marcuse elaborates upon the Freudian thesis of infantile narcissism in order to envision a future society of self-contained thinkers and childlike artists untainted by the marketplace. He expands upon the Freudian thesis by tracing back the origins of consciousness to Greek sources. He argues that Plato in the *Symposium* defines philosophy as the highest form of erotic love, and that Western philosophy has since yielded Plato's seductive form to the desiccated abstractions of stoic reason. And it is from Plato that Marcuse sees even more clearly how cosmic love may grow out of a physical passion that is originally narcissistic. In the *Symposium*, Plato unfolds a dialectic of eros that begins with a physical attraction to bodies and culminates in transcendent yearnings for cosmic union. Plato writes, "Every one of us, no matter what he does is longing for endless fame ... and the nobler he is, the greater his ambition, because he is in love with the eternal....Those whose procreancy is of the body turn to woman as the object of their love, and raise a family....But those whose procreancy is of the spirit rather than the flesh ... conceive and bear the things of the spirit. And what are they? you ask. Wisdom and all her sister virtues; it is the office of every poet to beget them, and of every artist whom we may call creative."[20] The dialogue appropriates the image of physical procreation in order to illuminate intellectual and artistic creation in communion with the cosmos. Neither in Plato nor Marcuse's dialectic of love is there an original erotic interest in another person.[21] A woman, a child, a brother—those relations serve as metaphors for a more noble and infinitely more distant object of love, a love that would prefer even the tiniest star to the bonds of friendship and family.

[20] *Symposium*, in *The Collected Dialogues of Plato*, ed. Edith Hamilton and Huntington Cairns (Princeton: Princeton University Press, 1973); sec. 208d–209a.
[21] See Martha C. Nussbaum's powerful critique of Plato in "The Speech of Alcibiades: A Reading of the *Symposium*," in *The Fragility of Goodness* (New York: Cambridge University Press, 1989), 165–199.

The Contradictions of Motherhood

If Marcuse would have listened more carefully to the "neurotic complaints" of housewives against narcissistic conceptions of male identity, he might have seen through Plato's appropriation of erotic human capacities for the sake of some relatively abstract and impersonal truths. So too he might have seen in the domestic sphere a site of struggle that could provide a basis for dialectical change and authentic erotic love. Sociologist Sharon Hays has collected significant data in a study involving extensive interviews with mothers from diverse social and racial groups in the United States in her book *The Cultural Contradictions of Motherhood*. The book opens with a case of an outraged mother whose daughter has been hospitalized for an illness. The woman's employer refuses to excuse her from an important assignment at a time when she needs to care for her sick child. According to the study, the mother expresses typical sentiments of parents who perceive employers to be indifferent to the needs of the family. Hays explains, "[It] is clear to [this mother] that her child is far more important than any work assignment, and she believes that everyone *should* understand that."[22] This incident frames the argument of the book. Hays claims that there is strong evidence for a fact that is surprising given the incentives of the American economic system. While the economy rewards the "individualistic, calculating, and competitive pursuit of personal gain," mothers are putting ever greater resources and more intensive efforts into the economically unrewarding task of raising children. When mothers are asked to explain why they do so, an even more curious fact turns up: If the logic of the marketplace teaches the virtues of instrumental rationality and profit maximalization, mothers are holding fast to a "logic requiring a moral commitment to unremunerated relationships grounded in affection" (*CC*, 152). Hays concludes: "It becomes clear that the beliefs of today's mothers and the cultural contradictions of motherhood point to a persistent, widespread, and irreducible cultural ambivalence about a social world based on the motive of individual gain, the impersonality of bureaucracies and market relations, and the calculating behavior of *homo economicus*....The ideology of intensive mothering must ... be understood as one form of a larger cultural opposition to the ideology of rationalized market societies" (154).

Values based on friendship or love may invert dominant social values based on economic incentives and individual self-interest. The question is whether or not there is any reason to see in this inversion a catalyst for

[22] Sharon Hays, *The Cultural Contradictions of Motherhood* (New Haven: Yale University Press, 1996), 1; hereafter cited as *CC*.

social transformation. Hays argues that "one of the few sources for making the world a better place seems to be grounded in the ethic of maternal love and unselfishness and in children's apparent innocence, purity, and goodness" (CC, 174). But she also notes that this love is focused narrowly in the private realm and away from larger social demands. Peta Bowden has pointed out that the experience of maternal selflessness may be less a privileged source of moral feeling than the result of the lack of public recognition and sheer exhaustion.[23] While some ethicists believe that maternal love can be transformed into universal compassion, there are problems with any easy translation of this private passion into a basis for wide-scale social change.

Still, the contradictions of motherhood do not make for a fully stable system. On the contrary, perhaps more so than friendship, the inversion of values in mothering conceals a persistent source of trouble in our societies. Our societies sentimentalize the relation between mothers and children while failing to recognize caregiving as skilled labor. The contradictions between the sentimental conception of mothering and economic realities pressure women to rely upon cheaply run day cares while experiencing guilt for pursuing more lucrative work. The only forthcoming solution to the pressure on women to work outside the home is the "double shift." And the only available solution for easing the burden of double shifts on mothers is more cheap day care or poorly paid immigrant nannies. As Hays points out, clearly this approach to the problem leads to greater economic inequality, which manifests itself in growing class divisions between women who work in the care profession and women who pursue higher paying careers traditionally associated with men. The Labor Department estimates that about 95 percent of the 2.3 million child-care workers in the United States are women. Seventy percent of these workers earn poverty-level wages.[24]

The sentimental image of the mother cradling the infant conceals the labor-intensiveness of child rearing. Representing the complex social and ethical dimensions of child rearing in terms of selfless nurturing plus exhausting physical labor blocks our understanding of how cultural meanings and ethical scenarios are developed in interactions with our children. Our association of high class cultural practices or moral thought with alienation from labor obscures the fact that the production of social and cultural values is itself a significant form of skilled labor. Our myopic view of the

[23] Peta Bowden, *Caring: Gender Sensitive Ethics* (New York: Routledge, 1997), 55.
[24] These facts are reported in Rosemary Jordano and Marie Oates, "Viewpoint: Invest in Workers for Best Child Care," *New York Times*, June 21, 1998, sec. 3, p. 13.

ethical, social, and cultural capacities of children closes off possibilities for understanding how we might cultivate new sensibilities. Perhaps these new sensibilities could bear some kinship with the expanded aesthetic capacities that Marcuse envisaged. But the contradictions of motherhood cannot support the kind of revolution that Marcuse has in mind.

Following Marxist traditions, Marcuse calls for the "distribution of the necessities of life regardless of work performance, reduction of working time to a minimum, [and] universal all-sided education toward exchangeability of functions" as "the preconditions ... of self-determination" (*OD*, 44). Missing from this call for the "exchangeability of functions" is a discussion of the "'biology'" of the mother. The intimacy that comes with pregnancy and breast-feeding cannot be exchanged with other adults without loss of their "erotic" (and I do not mean sexual or narcissistic, as I will explain below) import. Scientific and anthropological research suggests that "the hormones we once thought were important only for pregnancy, lactation and sexual drive have profound effects on just about *every organ* in the body. In fact the reproductive organs, which from a biologist's perspective are our only reason for existing, control and contribute to everything from mood to how cholesterol is used in the body."[25] Clearly, also, hormonal differences are more complex than what could be rigidly categorized as normal male or female patterns. And clearly, too, human identity, including the ability to bond with children, cannot be reduced to hormones. For while the ability of some mammals to bond with their young correlates with presence of "female" hormones or simple experiences of imprinting, there is no evidence that attachment works so simply for the human species (*OB*, 29). But these hormones can also not be dismissed as irrelevant to self-identity.

Marcuse believed that we could tap a polymorphic sexuality in infantile narcissism as theorized by Freud in order to support revolutionary claims. However, as Luce Irigaray has argued, the Freudian theory of the libido is hardly so polymorphic as to contain even the "'biological' instincts" of women (Chapter 6). A philosophy of freedom that is propelled by eros cannot claim to understand oppression until it deals with diverse experiences of libidinal energy—experiences that expand our conceptions of gender, work, and pleasure.

One of the crucial distinctions missed by philosophers from Plato to Freud and Marcuse is that the distinction between sexuality (viewed as a quasi-biological appetite) and original erotic needs for emotional, physical, and cognitive intimacy with another person. As a consequence of this distortion,

[25] Dorion Sagan, "Gender Specifics: Why Women Aren't Men," *New York Times*, June 21, 1998, sec. 15, p. 1.

philosophers reduce the social meanings of sensual pleasure (including the pleasures of touch, smell, rhythm, and tone) to a sexual or quasi-sexual context. (As Freud argues, affection is nothing more than aim-inhibited sexual drive.) These theorists perceive the need for sensual pleasure as kind of asocial appetite or antisocial drive. This quasi-biological dynamic of appetite or drive does not offer an adequate interpretation of the sensuality of children, or of our pre-subjective consciousness. Playful attunements and violent dissonance weave and unweave social bonds from generation to generation and across cultures and animal species.

Marcuse celebrates the great philosophical and artist rebel who would affect a "conscious methodical alienation from the entire sphere" of labor (*OD*, 58). Those of us who raise children perform significant, time-consuming work in society. We cannot alienate ourselves from the "entire sphere" of labor without experiencing a corresponding alienation from our reproductive bodies or from the children that we raise. I do not know if manufacturing and service work could ever be replaced, or substantially reduced, by machines in some utopian future. But I do know that the work of child rearing cannot be minimalized without harm to our children and ourselves.

Marcuse envisions a society of artists and intellectuals at play. He is right to see in playfulness a significant sign of human flourishing. Indeed, leftist dreams of an aesthetic type of man encourage us to imagine alternatives to bourgeois models of personal identity and individual freedom. But these leftist dreams of a new type of man have yet to yield an image of a new type of woman. An interview in the Hays study illustrates the absence of this vital activity of play in the relationship between mothers and their children, due to the sheer exhaustion of the mother's work: "I wouldn't know how to play with [my daughter], but I know how to take care of her when she's sick"; it is the husband who plays with the child, or as another mother remarks, "introduces all the fun and spontaneity" (*CC*, 106).

Marcuse invites us into the aristocratic charms and aesthetic liberation of a quasi-mythic past. He imagines this past would pace itself in accordance with "the rhythm of those who wander or ride in carriages, who have the time and the pleasure to think, contemplate, feel and narrate" (*OD*, 59). But was there or could there ever have been a time when we would not have had to wonder who drives us in those carriages? Who bears us in those wombs?

The Cultural Revolution that followed Marcuse's teachings has since been critiqued for its narcissism. Conservative critics have located the problem of a generation in the absence of strong fathers who would support the autonomy of their sons, and eventually too of their daughters, by providing standards of self-discipline and moral responsibility. For second- and third-wave feminists, the analysis is entirely different. These bold thinkers have urged us instead to reconsider the maternal sources of moral development and individualization. Some of the alternative conceptions threaten to resubmerge the mother / child relationship in narcissistic fantasies. This, I think, is the problem with Hays's suggestion that a better world might unfold from the ethic of "maternal un-selfishness and children's apparent innocence." The fact that "maternal utopias" and other visions of paradise have in the past not included women, at least not as full subjects, takes us to some fundamental questions for philosophy: How might we understand the meaning of humanity if we were to establish once and for all that our maternal origin is not a body but a subject? that this body is not primarily a zone of pleasure or tie of dependency but a site of social contact? What then would be the relationship between eros and freedom?

Social Eros and Freedom

We can begin to respond to these questions by introducing some classic psychoanalytic distinctions that are missing in the writings of Marcuse.[26] In *Civilization and Its Discontents*, Freud distinguishes between an erotic drive that is oriented outward toward another person and a narcissistic drive that is autoerotic and asocial. He then proceeds to categorize human beings according to whether their prevailing temperament is erotic, narcissistic, or driven by ego needs to control. Freud writes: "There is no golden rule which applies to everyone: every man must find out for himself in what particular fashion he can be saved....It is a question of how much real satisfaction he can expect to get from the external world, how far he is led to make himself independent from it, and finally, how much strength he feels he has for altering the world to suit his wishes. In this, his psychical constitution will play a decisive part, irrespectively of the external circumstances. The man who is predominantly erotic will give first preference to his emotional relationships to other people; the narcissistic man, who inclines to be self-sufficient, will seek his main satisfactions in his internal mental

[26] See Douglas Kellner's call for a new critical theory of socialization in *Herbert Marcuse and the Crisis of Marxism* (Berkeley: University of California Press, 1984), 159. See also Gad Horowitz's discussion of the contributions of Nancy Chodorow and Jessica Benjamin to psychoanalytic theory in "Psychoanalytic Feminism in the Wake of Marcuse" in *Marcuse*, 118–130. He argues that Benjamin's reframing of the infant / adult relation in terms of mutual recognition corrects the psychoanalytic view of the "'limitless narcissism' of the babe at the breast who does not recognize the mother's, or anyone else's, equal subjectivity" (cited by Horowitz, 119). Horowitz agues that Benjamin's position needs in turn to be supplemented by a theory of sexuality, or drive for bodily pleasure. While Horowitz's reduction of infant and adult sensuality to elaborations of sexual drive is too narrow a conception of bodily pleasure, his arguments move us in the right direction.

processes; the man of action will never give up the external world on which he can try out his strength."[27] I find this threefold distinction significant for differentiating three very general approaches to political liberty.

Marcuse bases his vision of human freedom on the prevalence of narcissistic drives in the human psyche. He rejects the drive for control, or mastery, as a significant source of self-expression. He does not believe that human beings have a drive for control, or mastery, that is independent of the narcissistic drive for pleasure (or Eros). Labor that is not inherently playful is necessarily for him always alienating, and never gratifying. For this reason, he rejects the possessive individualism of bourgeois liberalism as a basis for defining freedom. At the same time, Marcuse blurs the distinction between social drives and narcissistic, sexual drives at the expense of the former, and so too a third route for conceptualizing individual freedom. Following Freud, I would accept that erotic, narcissistic, and possessive drives would all need to factor into a more complete picture of human nature. Given the inevitability that work will consume much of our lives, I would urge us to reshape the drive to mastery in view of a transformed work ethic. Productivity should (as I argued in Chapter 4) be measured primarily in terms of its contribution to individual and social meaning rather than in terms of economic prosperity. Marcuse does not help us to understand the positive intersubjective meanings of work or pleasure. Finally, I would argue that erotic connection, and not narcissistic drives for pleasure or egoistic drives for control and mastery, should define the core of the individual in a democracy.

The difference between narcissistic drives for pleasure and erotic drives for intimacy lie at the center of Irigaray's moral vision. She challenges directly the image of the mother as a quasi-biological container for the child, and the thesis of infantile narcissism to which this image gives rise. She suggests that we replace the image of the womb with the image of the umbilical cord and placenta in order to symbolize what she richly portrays as the "quasi-ethical" link between mother and child.

Irigaray gives us deep insights into human needs for intimacy. However, she stops short of acknowledging how our fleshy connections might be scarred by wounds from past relationships or weighed down by the politics of skin. African Americans who write out of the legacy of slavery expand our sense of connection beyond the organic links of the family that are celebrated by Irigaray. In her aforementioned essay on freedom, bell hooks cites Cornel West as an important source for the reemergence of an ethic

---

[27] *Civilization and Its Discontents*, in *The Freud Reader*, ed. Peter Gay (New York: Norton, 1989), 34.

of love in the African-American tradition. Like Marcuse, West argues that European societies have been driven by capitalism and white supremacy into nihilism. This nihilism will not be "overcome by arguments or analyses." Like any disease of the soul," "it is tamed by love and care." "A love ethic," West adds, "has nothing to do with sentimental feelings or tribal connections. Rather it is a last attempt at generating a sense of agency among a downtrodden people. The best exemplar of this love ethic is depicted ... in Toni Morrison's great novel *Beloved*."[28]

It is finally to Morrison that we must turn in order to complete Irigaray's project. Morrison gives her deepest insight into the meaning of freedom in a passage from *Beloved* in which the ex-slave Sethe expresses to her lover, Paul D, her joy in having escaped with her children from slavery in Kentucky. As he listens, Paul D recalls his own escape from a prison camp in Alfred, Georgia. "Listening to the doves in Alfred, Georgia, and having neither the right nor the permission to enjoy it because in that place ... everything belonged to the men who had guns....So you protected yourself and loved small. Picked the tiniest stars out of the sky to own....Anything bigger wouldn't do. A woman, a child, a brother—a big love like that would split you wide open in Alfred, Georgia. He knew exactly what she meant: to get to a place where you could love anything you chose—not to need permission for desire—well now, *that* was freedom."[29]

Marcuse invokes classical mythology and projects the fantasy of a maternal utopia without mothers. What happens if we rewrite his erotic vision of freedom by joining together a new type of man with a new type of woman?

[28] Cornel West, *Race Matters* (Boston: Beacon Press, 1993), 29.
[29] Toni Morrison, *Beloved* (New York: Penguin, 1987), 162.

6

This Poem That Is My Body

Irigaray

We need a "new type of man," Herbert Marcuse told his students in the 1950s and 1960s. Under the reign of Capital, the individual has been overrun by obsessive drives to perform for the symbols of status and power. These drives to produce and consume may seem to benefit human society. But in fact, Marcuse pointed out, these drives serve corporations, sustain

Thanks much to Alia Al-Saji, Amy Coplan, Julie Piering, Amy Story, and Lissa Skitol for their engaging ideas in and outside of class. Thanks also to Richard Rojcewicz, Fred Evans, Leonard Lawlor, Edward Casey, and Lewis Gordon for their discussion of this chapter at the Simon Silverman Phenomenology Symposium at Duquesne University in March 1999, and to Tina Chanter for her rich comments on this chapter at SPEP. A shorter version of this chapter was published in *Confluences: Phenomenology and Postmodernity, Environment, Race, Gender* (Pittsburgh: Simon Silverman Phenomenology Center at Duquesne University, 2000).

neocolonialism, and stunt the imaginative life of those very individuals they seem to profit most. Among Frankfurt School theorists, Marcuse was most determined in his pursuit of a vision for a free society. He used psychoanalytic theory in order to propose a type of person who would not obsess over the need to perform for Capital, but who would exercise expressive drives instead. However, while Marcuse was in some ways unique among critical theorists, he shared their failure to grasp the social drives that allow for more enticing conceptions of human freedom. Marcuse, along with other first- and second-wave critical theorists, grounded his philosophical anthropology in the myth that man's most primitive urges are narcissistic. The grounding of the human psyche in childhood narcissism made it difficult to theorize how we might learn to care for the particular other except through an education based on fear and trauma or guilt and internalized aggression.

Irigaray augments the tradition of critical theory with a more powerful phenomenology of psychic drives. She locates the origin of desire in quasi-ethical exchanges between children and their mothers, and from this origin she enlists sociality as a basic libidinal drive. With this reconception of human psychology in pro-social erotic drives, Irigaray carries forward Marcuse's emancipatory project. Capitalist growth and aggressive drives are to be restrained by social goals for erotic exchange. Not since Aristotle has a major philosopher so strongly placed sociality at the center of human life. But while Aristotle identifies male friendship as the *telos* of the *polis*, and dismisses relations of marriage and family from the public scene, Irigaray argues that the romantic couple is the anchor of the state and the basis for a new type man to be joined with a new type of woman. With this transformation of classical philosophy, Irigaray is able to do what no other European philosopher has yet done. She has developed a vision of man as the social animal that includes women too.

There are, however, problems with Irigaray's challenge to critical theory. Irigaray's vision for a more just society is propped up by an invisible stratum of society that is left behind. This stratum consists of those who labor so that others might enjoy more beautiful lives. Whether marked by class and religion or other signs of lesser types of people, this stratum of workers tells us more about social justice than can be seen from what Tina Chanter aptly and excellently describes as Irigaray's "Ethics of Eros."[1] It is Irigaray's significant contribution toward a global ethic of freedom as well as some of her project's limits that I explore in this chapter.

---

[1] For the most complete philosophical account of Irigaray's ethics, see Tina Chanter, *Ethics of Eros: Irigaray's Rewriting of the Philosophers* (New York: Routledge, 1995).

Toward a Critical Poetics

The modern fiction of the autonomous individual diverts attention away from the critical infrastructure of human society. One dimension of this infrastructure is cultural. Another is economic. Images from the entertainment industry and metaphors from high, middle, or low culture forge fundamental links in human capacities for cognition and empathy. These imagistic and discursive links set the stage for our ability to judge ourselves and others on moral grounds. Post-Kantian normative philosophies (including Habermas, Derrida, and Levinas, as well as deontological philosophers in the Anglo tradition) do not help us to see these critical links when they focus our attention on an ontological gap between moral and worldly force. These philosophers may be partly right about disjunctions between realms of force. There are gaps between social expectations and what we may desire to do. However, the gigantic proportions of the gaps that these thinkers espouse encourage us to see the moral subject without his or her social, economic, and corporeal element. The fact is that the human primate (like other primates) does not attain to intellectual or moral heights outside of his or her element. On the contrary, outside of the social field, the human primate diminishes into a broken and dispirited creature.

Our fundamental weaves of thought, emotion, and image grow by way of the nurturing education and institutional practices through which we were raised. This weave, however, is not entirely (perhaps only minimally, as the tip of the iceberg) accessible to our full discursive awareness. Hegel was wrong to think that he could totalize our consciousness in his system of concepts. Much of the weave of life is visible only at the periphery of consciousness. Music and art may allude to it but cannot bring this weave into the sharp focus that exists for objects and persons at the center of our visual field. As a consequence of the partial invisibility of this web, even the most exemplary moral subjects, if these include the great philosophers, inevitably speak from the power and privileges of their social positions. This moral error is only readily seen from the point of view of those moral persons who stand outside of the positions occupied by these subjects.

An important contribution of post-Hegelian philosophers, including Marcuse and, as we shall see, Irigaray, is that these thinkers take seriously the charge that the individual grows or diminishes through the nourishment of the social web. For Irigaray, who has been influenced by Lacan as well as Freud, this means that the individual emerges in the realm of the "Symbolic" (language and other signifying structures that bind social practices), and that linguistic meaning rests on the "Imaginary" (or culturally based fantasy). Unlike Lacan, Irigaray gives much attention to how these structures should be transformed on behalf of the oppressed.

Patricia Huntington defines Irigaray's transformational project in terms of a "critical poetics."[2] As Huntington explains, this critical poetics aims to foster a society that is not "hom(m)osocial," which means one that would not be based one-sidedly on the social desires of men (or *des hommes*) (*ES*, 132). As Huntington argues, Irigaray will be useful to critical theory only if we bring her conceptions of gender and identity into a larger theoretical frame. Drucilla Cornell's idea of a "reiterative universal" is one important component of this larger task.[3] Cornell's claim is that Irigaray's corrections to Lacan can be only one of many possible ways for women to explore a female imaginary in order "to symbolize their own desires as universal." Huntington adds that while critical poetics is necessary for normative philosophy, this project cannot usurp the central role of communication in moral philosophy or critical theory. She elaborates upon the larger tasks of a communicative ethics by drawing upon Iris Young's conception of ethical exchange in terms of asymmetrical reciprocity (*ES*, 277–301).[4]

To a large extent, I shall expand upon these claims. My contribution will focus on some of Irigaray's more recent attempts to make dialectical mediation and communicative exchange central to social practices. I take as central to Irigaray's work the "asymmetrical reciprocity" that Young explores as the basis of social ethics. In the context of Irigaray's work, I will emphasize the less discursive dimensions in communication as well as quasi-biological capacities for bodily attunement (including blood pressure, hormonal changes, and sleep and energy cycles). These more poetic and bodily dimensions of "communication" have been studied extensively in recent child development research. This research focuses on the social capacities of infants to respond to adults through rhythmic movement, nondiscursive sounds, and facial display. Theorists compare this communicative capacity to leaps of imagination that Baudelaire invoked in his poetry under the term "correspondences."[5] Correspondences bring together

---

[2] Patricia J. Huntington, *Ecstatic Subjects, Utopia, and Recognition: Kristeva, Heidegger, Irigaray* (Albany: State University of New York Press, 1998), 132; henceforth *ES*.

[3] Drucilla Cornell, *Beyond Accommodation: Ethical Feminism, Deconstruction, and the Law* (New York: Routledge, 1991); *The Philosophy of the Limit* (New York: Routledge, 1992).

[4] Iris Young, "Asymmetrical Reciprocity: On Moral Respect, Wonder, and Enlarged Thought," *Constellations: An International Journal of Critical and Democratic Theory* 3, no. 3 (1997): 340–363.

[5] See "A Correspondence Theory of Ethical Exchange" in Cynthia Willett, *Maternal Ethics and Other Slave Moralities* (New York: Routledge, 1995), 92–94; henceforth cited as *ME*.

incommensurate dimensions of sensation in productive relationships. Just as the blast of a horn may evoke the color red, without the sound and the image sharing any common properties, so too may a child respond to an adult's movement with sound that the adult might or might not feel to be appropriate. The sense of the appropriate may never lend itself to total discursive explanation or argumentative defense. Waves of rhythm and tonality, texture and color, propogate expressions of human affect with potentially cosmic proportions. Irigaray gives us the basis for understanding these nondiscursive correspondences, tone and rhythm, for example, as central to the ethics of human relationships.

This expanded notion of embodied sociality also has political significance. Through correspondences, we may join together incommensurate experiences of diverse social groups in order to produce large-scale forces for social change. Feminists and critical race theorists, post-slavery and post-Holocaust philosophers, may come from different social locations and use different languages to join hands through corresponding senses of right and wrong. Without practical and theoretical efforts to establish these correspondences, groups occupying different social positions and speaking different languages will work at cross-purposes, when they might instead energize one another. A more expansive conception of the encumbered dimensions of human sociality brings Irigaray's overall project closer to Huntington's own concerns for a communicative ethic. A concept of embodied and embedded sociality and its relation to political engagement is crucial for third-wave critical theory.

I want as well to point out ways in which we might critique the kind of pluralism that could be implied by such claims as (1) all critical race theorists and feminist projects yield a corresponding sense of justice without dissonance or underlying conflict; or (2) even Cornell's otherwise important point that Irigaray's poetics reflects only one perspective of many possible and equally valid female perspectives.[6] It is always useful, I think, to bring ethical claims into relation with what Fraser and Nicholson term a large, empirical narrative of the economic and political structures that condition social and communicative practices (Chapter 4). This large, even global, narrative critiques and negotiates sharply conflicting views of social justice, including differences between francophone and anglophone feminisms, on the basis of a humanistic vision of freedom. In this chapter, I will argue that

---

[6] Drucilla Cornell is in fact fully aware of the concerns that I am elaborating upon here. See her remarks on Irigaray's heterosexism in her interview with P. Cheah and E. Grosz, "The Future of Sexual Difference: An Interview with Judith Butler and Drucilla Cornell," *Diacritics* 1, no. 28 (Spring 1998): 19–42.

Irigaray's own poetic imagery is implicated in invisible conventions that reinforce the high status of a specific class. The privileging comes at the cost of taking into account the political and domestic concerns of less privileged social groups. Irigaray's blindness to the relevance of class and status in her analysis of gender traces back to her incomplete analysis of aggressive drives in the human psyche. We will need to acknowledge the inevitable impact of these drives on human behavior before we can build a society evolving from and sustained by free libidinal relationships. Ethical attunement does not happen in a vacuum, but in a space that is warped by asymmetries of power and social recognition. A central task of ethics is to attune ourselves to social dissonance, establishing limits on games of power for the sake of everyday freedom.

Irigaray's Ethics of Eros

In some respects, Irigaray's "ethics of eros" represents a francophone counterpart to what in America is called "care ethics." While Irigaray's ethics emphasize sexual and artistic dimensions of nurturing, her ethics also cast the moral person in something of the same depoliticized and sentimentalized space in which those of us from the white middle class talk about love in America. Both Irigaray and Anglo-American philosophers influenced by Gilligan critique the one-sidedness of traditional male-oriented ethics. These ethics are anchored in a form of reason that is stripped bare of affective sociality. As we have seen in Part 1, the ways in which Gilligan's psychological study of care ethics is brought into play with rationalistic Anglo-American normative theory and Habermasian discourse ethics vary. However, some of the most engaging uses of Gilligan's work pose a kind of marriage between traditional masculine and maternal moral functions in a single unified and gender-neutral moral subject.[7] The moral subject is redefined as a union of impartial reason and empathy (Myers, Benhabib) or care (Tronto). This picture of the unified subject would salvage the Enlightenment notion of autonomy as the universal human goal.

Like her Anglo-oriented colleagues, Irigaray also critiques the male bias of conventional views of moral reason and seeks to complement this one-sidedness through an ethics of love. Unlike many of her Anglo-oriented

---

[7] See, for example, Diana Tietjens Meyers, *Subjection and Subjectivity: Psychoanalytic Feminism and Moral Philosophy* (New York: Routledge, 1994), and Joan C. Tronto, *Moral Boundaries: A Political Argument for an Ethic of Care* (New York: Routledge, 1993), esp. 162–163; cf. Seyla Benhabib, *Situating the Self: Gender, Community and Postmodernism in Contemporary Ethics* (New York: Routledge, 1992), esp. 1–17.

counterparts, Irigaray does not aim to integrate traditionally male and female components of the moral person into a single gender-neutral subject. She aims instead to demonstrate that conventional claims about motherhood and manhood are based on a repression of the eroticism of the flesh, and to demonstrate how this eroticism is gendered. The cultural and individual elaboration of tactile eroticism yields a conception of the moral person that is influenced by Romanticism. This moral person is not the self-defined rational individual of classical liberalism plus or minus degrees of sympathy. This person's autonomy is developed through erotic capacities for sympathetical communication, and is akin to what Kelly Oliver calls "communion."[8]

Irigaray argues that mainstream European cultures overemphasize male imaginary and symbolic structures. She argues also that widespread resentment of feminine and maternal power has shaped mainstream male self-representations. As a result of the deep-rooted cultural hegemony of men (in fact, of an anti-female bias in many constructions of masculinity), women are confronted by warped representations of femininity and motherhood. Moreover, they are under the temptation to constitute their sexual identity in servitude to male desire. "Even today, [Irigaray writes], we become the slaves of those phantasies, of that ambivalence, that madness, which is not ours."[9]

But then what is the ambivalence, or madness, of men? Phallic images of manhood in our culture (e.g., images of male "hardness" in connection with power) impede emotional intimacy. The experience of romantic love drums up phallic sexual desire but also awakens more erotic drives of the flesh. It is the latter, more diffuse, erotic drives that render men ambivalent about love, and that are fully lost in the psychoanalytic tradition. The conventional assumption is that male ambivalence about love reflects the classic Western focus on phallic penetration. According to this picture, heterosexual desire elicits images of castration and loss of self in an abyss or other boundaryless womb-like experience. Variations of this picture of heterosexuality include images of regression to childhood dependency and threats to autonomy and freedom.

But things are not what they seem. Irigaray's investigations lead one to suppose that the more subversive threat to male identity does not stem from those

---

[8] Kelly Oliver develops this conception throughout her numerous works; a good place to begin is *Family Values* (New York: Routledge, 1997), in which Oliver critiques the concept of autonomy and calls for a ethic of communion (see, e.g., 228). See my introduction for a fuller discussion of Oliver's work.

[9] Luce Irigaray, *Sexes and Genealogies*, trans. Gillian C. Gill (New York: Columbia University Press, 1993), 18; henceforth cited as *SG*. References to the original French text are from *Sexes et Parentes* (Paris: Minuit, 1987).

sexual drives represented by penetration. The more subversive threat is rooted in fleshly drives to be with another person. It is these more diffuse erotic drives that signify danger for mainstream male heterosexual identity and that can constitute a revolution for conventional norms of autonomy and reason.

The numbing of the flesh and the hardening of the body in phallic self-representations block human capacities for communication and sympathy. Moreover, male barriers against the eroticism of the flesh transfer to encounters with the natural world. The social systems of Western man are not based on cultivating the fertility of the planet. Our social systems are based on artificial economic processes. These processes take wasteful accumulation and destructive warfare as the norm of modern human history. As she explains, "How often our nerves are set on edge. We are driven to compete in the rat race of modern life—so maddened and overwhelmed by the pace of existence.... Wars break out when peoples move too far from their natural possibilities.... This was often true in the past. It will continue to be so if we fail to set up an ethics of the couple as an intermediary place between individuals, peoples, States" (*SG*, 5).

It is a mistake to place the modern autonomous individual, the traditional bonds of the extended family, or classical hom(m)osociality at the heart of the community. Irigaray insists that we take the heterosexual couple as the elementary sociopolitical unit. Mainstream conventions of manhood, motherhood, or the abstract moral person jeopardize loving relationships between men and women, and thereby warp the social web. Conventional individuals strive for status (or "objective merit" and individual accomplishment) first, and expressive interpersonal relationships only second. Our social structures reinforce these priorities in our measures of personal identity and accomplishment, or in what Marcuse termed the "performance principle." In order to show that modern society does not require the repression of libidinal drives, that on the contrary, political society should have as its highest aim the cultivation of these same drives, Irigaray asks that we rethink the fantasies that we share about our libidinal origins and the consequences for our personal and political goals. That is why, Irigaray argues, "social justice cannot be achieved without a cultural transformation, the nature of which we can barely conceive. Social injustice is due not only to economic inequalities in the strict sense. Our needs are not restricted to housing, clothing, and feeding ourselves.... Our need first and foremost is for a right to human dignity for everyone."[10] And if the sexualized body impacts core

[10] Luce Irigaray, *je, tu, nous: Toward a Culture of Difference*, trans. Alison Martin (New York: Routledge, 1993), 21–22; henceforth cited as *TD*.

experiences of self-identity, then "we need laws that valorize difference" (*TD*, 22).

Irigaray aims to subvert mainstream representations of male and female differences through genealogical critique (i.e., by interpreting the mythic elements embedded within discursive accounts of human origins). She examines how our sense of identity takes root in imaginative representations of our beginnings in a maternal womb. She critiques the Oedipal theory because she sees this theory as a major variant of a conventional narrative in Western culture. According to the usual story, early infancy (and, by analogy, primitive human experience) takes place in a realm of immediacy. Our earliest consciousness is assumed to occur in an asocial, narcissistic bubble or an even more primitive (and chaotic) state of biological drive. The child is said to break out of immediacy by entering into a world that is structured by a series of oppositions, including divisions of subject and object, and right and wrong. Irigaray challenges the Oedipal theory and other conventional variants of this common narrative. While Anglo-oriented theorists may introduce the insights of care ethics (and object-relations psychology) to balance such conventional poles of selfhood as dependency and autonomy, feeling and reason, and connection and separation, some of the more intriguing dimensions of Irigaray's revisions of psychoanalytic theory point beyond these poles altogether.

My reading of Irigaray takes its cue from the preamble of *Sexes and Genealogies*. There Irigaray indicates her intention to move beyond conventional poles of mainstream Western culture, beginning with the separation of culture (or, in the United States, what we understand in terms of "social construction") from nature (or what we sometimes term "biology"): "In our day and age it seems less important to analyze where the split between nature and culture occurs than to mark the places where growth has been sterilized, misunderstood, repressed" (*SG*, vi). In fact, for Irigaray, it is in this gigantic gap between nature and culture that the proliferation of dualisms in Western culture take root. Conventional manhood is staged as a separation from the maternal sphere, and acquisition of power over the natural realm that this sphere represents. It is as an artifact of this split that quasi-ethical forces of nature are reduced to more exclusively biological ones. This reductive thinking hinders not only our understanding of nature but also our understanding of ourselves. Central to Irigaray's project is her attempt to address how our failure to understand the quasi-ethical forces of nature leads us to sever our human identity from the eroticism of the flesh. In the United States, this concern translates into issues around sexuality and gender. Anglo-America feminist theory exacerbates the effects of the artificial split between nature and culture when it overemphasizes the distinction between sexuality and gender. While analytic distinctions between sexuality and gender are useful for understanding distinct forces for social change, Irigaray would have us enlarge our perspective on human identity by focusing on ways in which sexuality and gender are dialectically related.

One also wonders if the analytic split between nature and culture does not hinder the role of imaginative seeing and thinking in philosophy. This is especially true if imagination is reason operating in the flesh of sensory awareness. A symptom of this larger problem occurs in the schizophrenic misreading of Irigaray's poetic discourse.[11] There is a tendency to read her work on the body in terms of essentializing, scientistic categories of biology, and her work on the symbolic and imaginary as a form of social constructivism. In fact, her nuanced dialectic aims to wrap around the conventional poles and prepare for a more relational, even lyrical discourse of the moral person. Irigaray helps us to learn how we might cultivate poetic dimensions of human identity. These dimensions take us back to the earliest stages of human development, to the parts of ourselves that are most "natural." Central to Irigaray's task is a reconsideration of the meaning of childhood.

The Umbilical Cord

Every major philosophical vision rests upon some more or less vague notion of individual development from childhood, or, as some philosophers prefer, of human origins. A pervasive image in our culture is the association of presubjective existence with what we poetically represent as the "womb." The image of infancy in a womb may appear to be so fundamental as to lie beyond question, but it is not. Of course, there is no question that the human fetus develops in a uterus. The images that are used in order to describe early human experience, however, are laden with value, indeed, with the basic elements of our mythologies. Modern writers and theorists associate primitive human existence with repetitive cycles of biological drives or presubjective experiences of fusion in the fluids of the mother's body. Developmental psychologists measure the development of subjectivity in terms of acquiring a sense of limits, or rules and principles of restraint and responsibility. In modern political systems, these limits come to mark the conventional moral rights and legal boundaries of the autonomous individual. Psychoanalytic theorists argue that the mature moral subject must repress autoerotic drives that bind the child to his mother and accept symbolic castration. More

---

[11] Tina Chanter addresses this concern thoroughly in *The Ethics of Eros* (see note 1).

generally, modern Western theories and social practices assume (problematically, as I will argue in Part 3) that separation from the maternal sphere (which can expand to include the domestic and natural spheres and even the entire nexus of social relations that is included in the term "convention") is necessary in order to acquire the boundaries of personhood.

Irigaray does not question (never as fully as I think she might) the mythology of separation as a crucial component in stories of identity. She does aim to change the meaning of separation so that it is no longer based on repression, and not on any obvious version of castration trauma.[12] In order to show that socialization does not require repression of presubjective drives, she must also transform the basic images and fantasies that we have of our presubjective existence. She does this by challenging directly the image of womb as the basis for presubjective life. As we shall see, the implications for adult life will be startlingly original. She will be able to depict the passions of love not as a regressive threat to—or, as we see in the work of some care ethicists, a secondary support for—autonomy. Instead, Irigaray argues that in romantic love the male and female self attain the most advanced stage of moral and political development. It is erotic passion, not cognition or character, that defines our center as human beings.

Oddly, Irigaray gives little attention in her theory of embodied identity to the female pathology of anorexia. She does describe a parallel "male" pathology. Male subjectivity, Irigaray argues, revolves around a "repressive, moralizing, conception of sexuality" for the citizen-worker and the cathartic release of pent-up male libido in what I call quasi-hubristic violence (SG, 3). These alternating cycles of work and aggression stem from what Irigaray argues to be the "original sin" of Western culture. This sin is not the biblical crime against the Father in Heaven; it is against the mother here on earth. Our culture from classic to modern times represents the mother / child relation in terms of natural or biological functions. We then construct the moral subject in terms of control over a range of natural drives or biological appetites expressed in early childhood. Among these natural drives is a poorly understood but very strong libidinal drive to be with the mother. Male-oriented cultures may come closest to glimpsing the

---

[12] Cf. Margaret Whitford, *Luce Irigaray: Philosophy in the Feminine* (New York: Routledge, 1991), 84. Alison Weir focuses on Irigaray's earlier writings on the "two lips" of female autoeroticism, and argues that Irigaray disavows separation, eliminates the basis for social mediation, and deconstructs the basis for personal identity. See *Sacrificial Logics: Feminist Theory and the Critique of Identity* (New York: Routledge, 1996), 90–111. Irigaray's more recent location of the flow of fluids through the umbilical cord in early human life gives her a basis for reaffirming separation, mediation, and identity.

power of this erotic drive when it is viewed through the template of sexuality. The Oedipal theory is an example of this kind of distortion. This theory views all erotic energy in terms of stages toward the development of so-called normal male heterosexual identity. The Oedipal theory also traces our most productive social practices to the sublimation or repression of heterosexual erotic energy. But as Irigaray's work suggests, the Oedipal theory is just one more example of the way in which we have failed to see the original erotic energy between children and their mothers, and how this energy might be cultivated (or as Freudians write, "sublimated") in the most refined tasks of society.

Of course, male-biased cultures perpetuate a wide range of distorted views on the erotic drives between the mother and child. Perhaps most typically, this relationship is viewed through the image of the womb as a safe refuge, a kind of original image of home, or a prelapsarian paradise. Early childhood experience is pictured as innocent of conflicts based on moral dissonance or economic and social distinctions. As I will argue, this is not adequate to the complexity of early experience.

Irigaray aims to alter traditional associations of the mother with the womb or womb-like functions by focusing on images of the placenta and umbilical cord.[13] This shift parallels Irigaray's earlier attempt to transfer the primary focus of female sexuality from the vagina to the tactile sensitivity of the two lips. Like the imagery of the two lips, the imagery of the placenta and umbilical cord transposes the path of our libidinal drives from cycles of fusion and repressive separation toward a dynamic of mediation and connection. Still, as we shall see, this dynamic is predicated on the experience of loss that she wrongly believes to be a necessary element for both mother and child in the process of birth.

Irigaray describes the exchange of fluids between the mother and the fetus that occurs through the placenta and umbilical cord as "almost ethical" (*TD*, 41). The exchange could not be fully ethical because it does not involve a relationship between two subjects. Nonetheless, the mediation of fluids that occurs through the fleshy contact of these organs prepares Irigaray to transform the basic parameters of moral philosophy. The central focus of ethics is not the development of moral autonomy through rational self-choice. Irigaray invites us to place at the heart of ethics that she calls the "amorous exchange."

[13] For a discussion of the placenta as mediator, see Gail M. Schwab's "Mother's Body, Father's Tongue," in *Engaging with Irigaray*, ed. Carolyn Burke, Naomi Schor, and Margaret Whitford (New York: Columbia University Press, 1994), 249–262.

If Irigaray's ethics is going to transform moral identity from a dynamic of fusion and separation to the "amorous exchange," then it will be important to understand the libidinal connection between the mother and child in terms that do not reduce to the autoerotic pleasures of oral, anal, and phallic drives. The traditional representation of the maternal function through the fluids of the womb, and the elaboration of this original experience of immersion through oral, anal, and phallic identity, displace friendly exchanges between mother and child in a boundaryless experience of fused oneness.

The functions of the placenta and umbilical cord pose the fetus and the mother as two distinct beings. We might imagine the placenta as fingerlike weaves of tissues reaching out between the mother and the fetus; these tissues are not fluid; they meld, I would say, but do not merge. In dialogue with Irigaray, biologist Helene Rouch reports that "it's the mediating space between mother and fetus, which means that there's never a fusion of maternal and embryonic tissues" (*TD*, 39). The umbilical cord, "that primal link to the mother," connects the "whole" child with the "whole" mother through the "mediation of her blood" (*SG*, 14). The fetus produces hormones for the mother while the mother gives to the child nourishment and air.

This is a relationship based on exchange that Irigaray describes as more than biological, and hence as almost ethical. Although it is not clear what Irigaray means by the expression "almost ethical," I would argue that this experience is for the fetus an original expression of social drive. While Irigaray does not claim that the fetus has any awareness of the exchange, we might suppose that fleshy contact and vital fluids form an original source of pro-social pleasure. When the fetus fails to get the nutrition that it needs from the mother, when the mother herself is overworked and exhausted by the demands of her society, then the exchange may be felt for both mother and fetus as painful. The pleasure and pain experienced in this exchange would predate and redefine the pleasures and pain of swallowing, sucking, and chewing (or oral drive). The tactile and fluid stimulation of the fetus in the uterus may also explain the newborn's compelling need for touch and for the milky smells that are associated with the mother. My supposition is that the presubjective pleasure in fluid and tactile exchange lays the ground for human sociality.

Certainly, for Irigaray, a presubjective experience of fluid and tactile exchange is the basis for ethics. And yet it is not an experience that in any way is "symmetrical" or even "mutual" between the mother and child (*SG*, 14). The experiences between the mother and child are not only different; they are also in many ways unequal. Unlike the mother, the fetal consciousness lacks intentionality, and perhaps also the ability to imagine or desire what is absent. These capacities make a central dimension of subjectivity. The fetal consciousness also lacks communicative capacities and intersubjective experiences (assuming, of course, that these capacities correlate with the development of subjectivity). If the development of intersubjectivity were to be defined in terms of recognition of the face of other persons, and this were to be measured through the development of social smiling, then we might conclude that the child lacks a social sense of the self until several weeks after birth (*ME*, 63–67). On the other hand, the mother is more than embodied experience; her ability to sustain the pregnancy depends upon, to borrow from Foucault, a disciplined routine for the care of the self. Her ability to care for her self and her attitude toward her pregnancy reflect political and social forces that define dimensions of her personal space. If the mother is routinely or traumatically subjected to violation, then she may not have the desire to care for herself or the child.

Irigaray's discussion of the asymmetrical reciprocity between the fetus and mother, however, is not directed toward social practices and political force (or what she associates with the French term "*le pouvoir*") but to what she understands in terms of procreative power (and associates with the term "*la puissance*"). She identifies as the "most elemental identity tag [of the person]: the scar where the umbilical cord was cut" (*SG*, 14). This scar marks the site of an original ethical debt that the child owes to the mother. It is a debt that our Western social systems have barely acknowledged. Aristotle argued that children owe a debt to their fathers that they can never reciprocate. This debt was to be paid back in terms of the greater love and respect that a child gives to the father than the father need return. Nietzsche and Freud expand upon Aristotle's conception of original debt. They explain how the son's sense of debt to his own father multiplies into a sense of guilt before an invisible god. For Marcuse, this sense of debt transforms into the obsessive drive to work. In the postmodern world, the sense of debt translates into the drive to perform for the simulacre of Capital.

Irigaray demonstrates that the roots of the troubled soul run deeper than these men were willing to see. Our cultures' focus on infinite debts that are owed to personal, political, or religious fathers obscures what for Irigaray is an even more original source obligation, and that is the debt we owe to our mothers. Moreover, Irigaray argues, the power of the mother is not of the same kind as the power that has been attributed to fathers. She distinguishes the maternal power (*la puissance*) to conceive and nourish from male power (*le pouvoir*) aimed at control over desire and mastery over things (*SG*, 12). This distinction between two sources of power plays a major role in Irigaray's moral psychology. It is also a distinction that I think we might call into question.

Autonomy and Power:
Fort/Da and the Circle Dance

Irigaray traces the differences between the two kinds of power back to the ways in which children acquire autonomy. She uses traditional psychoanalytic theory (Freud and Lacan) in order to link selfhood with autonomy and to locate the emergence of the subject with the moment when the child begins to speak. In contrast with the tradition, however, she views this threshold through her altered picture of presubjective experience and a greater sensitivity to female identity. Freud developed his theoretical speculations on self-formation by reflecting upon a game that was played by a little boy (Freud's grandson). According to the story, the boy throws a toy, or, at this threshold stage, an "almost-thing," while babbling a syllable that approximates the word "*fort*" (German for "gone"). A variation of the game involves attaching the toy to a reel and uttering "*fort*" as the toy disappears, as it happens, over the edge of a curtained cot, and then babbling "*da*" ("here") as he reels the toy back in. Hence, the game is called "*fort/da*." The game enables the child to realize that objects may continue to exist despite the fact that they are not seen. The disappearance of the object, however, does not have only cognitive implications. As children learn to think about object permanence, they also express a desire to be with their absent mother and develop phobias of being left with strangers.

Irigaray elaborates upon some of the implications of Freud's story. She suggests that the game that Freud observed demonstrates the style in which boys acquire a sense of identity in Western culture. Boys develop a sense of independence from the mother through the pleasure they experience in skills of mastery over objects. They develop the rudiments of speech in order to indicate their control over objects. What the Freudians miss, Irigaray argues, is the significance of the fact that the game is played when the mother (who is also Freud's daughter) is absent. Irigaray argues that the boy comes to terms with the mother's absence by turning his desire away from his mother to toys. Neither Freud nor Irigaray mention the employment of a nanny. Nor do they mention the presence of other children and adults (e.g., the grandfather, who claims only to observe). Irigaray instead focuses on the fact that the boy, who is defined as "alone" at those times when his mother is absent (regardless of whether others are present), uses toys as a substitute for his mother's presence. Irigaray argues that this path to autonomy is misguided. The boy who acquires autonomy by establishing a sense of control over objects has failed to come to terms with his feelings of loss for his mother. A more sound path to autonomy would begin by acknowledging the attachment to the mother and then dealing with, not denying, the pain of what Irigaray terms the "original separation."

One might address the more complex intersubjective dimensions of early childhood (relations, for example, between infants and their fathers, siblings, and a vast array of potential caregivers), beginning with contemporary research on face-to-face encounters in infancy. Irigaray underemphasizes intersubjective dimensions of child rearing, and, as we shall see, this failure raises some questions about her project. The intersubjective dimensions of child rearing point toward economic and social sources of power as well as quasi-biological drives for power that should not be left unchecked by moral philosophy. I will return to these concerns later. At this point it is important to note Irigaray's significant contribution toward a phenomenology of presubjective drives.

Irigaray observes the presubjective drives between children and adults in "gestures" that accompany the child's first efforts at language. Elaborating upon psychoanalytic theory, Irigaray argues that the gesture involved in the little boy's game of *fort/da* tells much about how boys acquire a sense of self. The arm that raises and lowers the reel prefigures the phallic identity that Freudian theory locates at the symbolic core of the modern, performance-oriented subject (*SG*, 96).

Clearly, one can see that this account of identity thought the game of "*fort/da*" is not gender neutral. The boy learns to deal with the mother's absence and acquires the first syllables of language in a gendered style. We would want to raise questions about how girls might differ. However, for Irigaray, the problem is more complicated. Her work does not lend itself to any uncritical acceptance of gender difference. Her point is not just that boys and girls enter into the symbolic stage in different ways. She also argues that the conventional identity of boys in patriarchal Europe (she focuses on German and French cultures) is based on repressing the feminine from the beginning, and therefore needs to be altered (*SG*, 96). Boys have developed a sense of autonomy through playful games that alternate in cycles of aggression (throwing toys) and possession. Presymbolic styles of play prepare the boy to enter into a social world based on related cycles of overproduction and wasteful expenditure—the very same cycles that Marcuse understood in terms of the performance principle and its tie to drives toward death and destruction. Irigaray's claim is that these cycles trace back to a mistaken way in which boys learn to deal with their mother's independence. Assuming that toys are substitutes for interaction with the mother, the boy learns to deal with his frustration over his mother's absence (Irigaray understands this frustration as a kind of mourning for a significant loss) by taking it out on his toys. He throws his toys as though to say, "I don't need you" and then reels the toys back in as though to say, "I will have you on my own terms." He denies his sorrow and constructs his self in stoic terms. Then he substitutes for the independent mother (whose power he cannot control) objects that he can control (*SG*, 31).

The boy's sense of self is based on refusing to recognize the mother's significant power in relation to his own identity. He deals with his mother's power by denying her importance and then substituting toys over which he has control. Male selfhood is defined by a problematic response to the contingency and complexity of human interactions, beginning with the boy's stoic response to the mother's power. From this stoic denial of emotional investment in a relationship with the mother, the boy turns his attention to games of mastery (*le pouvoir*) and episodes of violent destruction. But then the boy's sense of identity is not just a valid choice that one might accept as part of a more pluralist society. Male identity is problematic, and needs to be regenerated in ways that recognize female power. This change would begin with the recognition of the mother's power. Irigaray insists that maternal power, unlike conventional male power, is based on *la puissance* and not *le pouvoir*.

Irigaray does not discuss how little boys might take a different path to the development of autonomy. She does discuss different ways in which little girls deal with their growing awareness of their mother's power and their own sense of self. Irigaray believes that a girl would not be likely to represent the mother as an object: "She does not play with a string and a reel that symbolize her mother, because her mother is of the same sex as she is and cannot have the object status of a reel" (*SG*, 97).

Irigaray lists three ways in which she believes that girls deal with her mother's independent power: "*(1)When she misses her mother, she throws herself down on the ground in distress, ... she loses the power and the will to live, [and] she neither speaks nor eats, totally anorexic.*" I take it that self-destructive cycles of binging and bulimia would mirror male cycles of overproduction and destructive waste of resources. More recently, these cycles also appear in male and female obsessions with exercising to build the hard body. Irigaray's brief remarks suggest that these various male and female pathologies trace back to failed ways of dealing with the mother's enormous power to frame central desires of our lives. While the boy denies the mother's power, the girl denies her own. Of course, this route is pathological.

"*(2) She plays with a doll, lavishing maternal affection on a quasi subject.*" If girls focus their attention on dolls rather than on balls and related objects, then they may develop the fantasies that form the basis for individual identity differently than boys, at least in our culture. Girls may focus their attention more on developing relationships than on cognitive or physical skill. Certainly Irigaray's own emphasis on the presubjective bonds of intersubjective relationships contrasts with male philosophers' tendencies to place self-reflection or self-control at the center of their moral philosophy. For Aristotle, the highest form of friendship excludes erotic passion. For Marcuse, the highest man prefers a more solitary life based on the sublimation of narcissistic drives in self-reflection.

"*(3) She dances and thus forms a vital subjective space open to the cosmic maternal world*" (*SG*, 97). It is to this third possibility that Irigaray gives the most emphasis.

Irigaray describes "this dance as a way for the girl to create a territory of her own in relation to the mother" (*SG*, 98). The sense of ownness, or autonomy, that would develop out of the dance differs significantly from the sense of autonomy that develops through motor activities like throwing balls and taking control over objects. Irigaray claims that the language that grows out of the dance is playful and expressive, apparently more lyrical and erotic, and less defined by the crisp oppositions of *fort/da*. She argues that the erotic movement "characteristic of the female is whirling around rather than throwing" and retrieving objects. "The girl tries to reproduce around and within her an energetic circular movement that protects her from abandonment, attack, depression, loss of self" (98). "The girl-subject does not have objects as the boy does. It splits into two [mother/daughter] in a different way and the ... goal is to reunite the two by a gesture, to touch both perhaps so that birth is repeated. ... Women do not try to master the other but to give birth to themselves. They only stoop to master the other (the child, for example, insofar as they have the power) when they are unable to engender their own axis" (*SG*, 99). And if the male axis is confined to reeling in objects, woman's axis "moves ... from the ... earth to the ... sky" (*SG*, 100). It is as infinite as it is sublime.

While boys learn to be conventional men by playing games of control, women—insofar as they do not lose their axis—give birth to themselves and to others in a process that is divine. In effect, Marcuse's search for the "new type of man" finds its answer in Irigaray's provocative juxtaposition (if not sharp opposition) between possessive, guilt ridden man (who is, as for Marcuse, once again defined as pathologically disconnected from the maternal sphere) and artistic woman. Of these women, she writes: "Their absolute need is not for a penis or phallus but for the chance to be born to themselves, to find autonomy, to be free to *walk*; walk away and back, however it pleases them" (*SG*, 100).

Marcuse dismissed women as "neurotic housewives" who were exiled from the sources of power that confined them in their sterile homes in 1950s suburbia (see Chapter 5). According to Marcuse, these women exhibit the symptoms of a pathological society, but could give us no glimpse into a better one. On the other hand, Marcuse suggests, images of female beauty in classic and modern art would serve to provoke men to think of a more beautiful world. In such a world, men would not be reduced to perform for the up-and-down cycles of Capital. Instead men would develop intellectual and imaginative capacities for self-reflection, while advanced technology would minimalize the psychic drain of human labor.

Irigaray teaches us to see through Marcuse's dream. The self-reflective man that Marcuse celebrates never breaks out of the narcissistic bubble from which he imagines that he comes. Therefore when Irigaray turns to the wives of these reflective men and proposes for these women a more sublime life, that life will not be anchored in childhood narcissism, but in the social eroticism that binds children and their mothers. The girl's need to evoke the mother's presence through her play with dolls is surpassed only by the cosmic force that summons the girl to dance. Dance bridges inner and outer spaces through a power. That power is sensual and spiritual. It is the maternal expression of the human soul.

Maternal spirituality does not purge the body of the flesh; it does not function as a catharsis of embodied subjectivity. Irigaray envisions a spiritual force that nourishes the soul in ecstatic connection and physical exaltation. Aristotle and a parade of modern moral philosophers who march after him fail to include among the virtues that they celebrate what must be central to an ethics of the flesh. This is the virtue of grace. As dance scholar Ann Wagner explains, in our culture "the absence of grace in its theological and esthetic dimensions, coupled with the presence of law, is striking. The fruits of the law are fear and retribution. The law can produce justice but not joy." [14]

The little girl's attunement with cosmic forces grows out of her original bond with the mother. Irigaray invites her readers to reinterpret Catholic iconography and Western mythology through the figure of this original connection. She compares the tissues of the placenta to "a more or less white, more or less transparent veil" (*SG*, 30). She writes that the original

[14] Ann Wagner, *Adversaries of Dance: From Puritans to the Present* (Urbana: University of Illinois Press, 1997), 396.

veil—the placenta—should evoke for us the gift of life. This transparency of the veil should symbolize the "mystery of a first crypt, a first and longed-for dwelling place, the happy time when he [the son but also the daughter] ... owed his whole life to [the mother].... He lives off her, feeds on her, is wrapped up in her, drinks her, consumes her, consummates her" in a spiritual moment that precedes any distant religious "call" or limited ethical "claim" (*SG*, 32). "This is a gift that permits no mastery during its term, an infinite debt, [from a] ... diffuse ... presence" (*SG*, 32). Irigaray sees the exchange of fluids and flesh through the placenta as invoking the work of mediation that gives access to the spiritual world. This work of mediation takes shape through the rituals and poetic images of her religion. "The messages from the beyond" come from angels, Irigaray explains. These angels share their "whiteness" with the tissues of the placenta (*SG*, 33). She calls upon the angels to return with "this veil, through which there once took place ... the sympathy between two bodies capable of mutually decoding one another" (*SG*, 36). Our task as modern subjects in need of spiritual sustenance is to "wait for this to happen ... —this sympathetic deciphering of bodies, skins, membranes, mucuses." The spirituality brings us back home to the bliss we "knew" once upon a time in the placenta (*SG*, 36).

Religious traditions may offer a challenge to Judeo-Christian monotheism by turning our attention to genealogies that celebrate a particular history of ancestors to which the individual might owe thanks. Irigaray appropriates monotheism's focus on a more abstract cosmic force. She challenges in this monotheism "the fact that men have taken sole possession of the divine." Her aim is to displace "God the father" for the sake of the angels who would aid in our communication with a cosmic force that may be feminine (v). "Hasn't the angel taken off from her, flown away from her? Skin and membrane that can hardly be perceived, almost transparent whiteness, almost undecipherable mediation, which is always at work in every operation of language" (38–40). The social eroticism of the mother gives way to spiritual forces that trace back, beyond any specific history of ancestors or their ghosts, to a spiritual force that is, apparently, more pure and more divine.

I have concerns with Irigaray's vision of a more beautiful society and more sublime world. Perhaps girls define their autonomy more often than not in some of our modern cultures through dolls and dance while boys traverse space through games of sport. Perhaps boys play these games in order to acquire a sense of themselves in their power over objects and in exercises of self-control. Perhaps. But it is also true that for the most part boys enjoy close contact with others, and often prefer to play with other children. And the value of these other children does not amount to their function as substitutes for mothers. The pleasure in children's games increases dramatically with the social display and recognition of physical or cognitive skills. Even more, their pleasure increases with friendship. Girls may enjoy dolls and dance, but they enjoy dolls and dance much more when they are at the center and not the periphery of the social stage. And girls no less than boys are possessive of their toys and their space. The social stage for acquiring autonomy is more complex than Irigaray allows. Just as drives for control constitute dimensions of the most intimate play, so too interpersonal demands for attention and friendship relay drives for power. Children are driven by the needs for power as well as needs to connect, and these two kinds of needs mix at the core of the moral person.

And what about the mother whom Irigaray represents in terms of a feminine power (*la puissance*)? Again, Irigaray uses gender difference in order to set up a false distinction. Irigaray interprets maternal power as though it were a cosmic force. Surely, normal mothers, no less than their children, are driven by power. Irigaray divests the female subjectivity of any impurity of *pouvoir* in order to align that subjectivity with a divine cosmic force. The problem is that this cosmic force washes away the subjectivity of the mother along with her drive for power. Similarly, Irigaray's celebration of the gifts of the maternal body conceals the mother's laborious interactions with the social and political world, including individual routines and social rituals for the care of the pregnant self.

There is no subject who does not possess some element of power in the complex field of relationships that define social life. The mother's exercise of power extends well beyond the boundaries of the immediate family into the political economy. If that mother enjoys something of a life of leisure and privilege in the class-structured societies of Europe, she may be supported by low-paid servants and immigrant workers. In order to sustain her power, she must play games of "*fort/da*," certainly with the servants, if not also with her peers for the distinctions of status and power that define class-based societies. Have these women "lost their axis" as Irigaray's theory of identity and cosmic force seem to imply? Or are such divisions of power and status built into human animal society and moral psychology in ways that Irigaray fails to see? Irigaray reduces the mother's role in caring for her pregnancy to the bodily exchange through the umbilical cord. She white-washes the difficulties in the exchange when she pictures it as an original source of sympathy. Anything that blocks that original sympathy is associated with "the devils, ... [whose] job is to disrupt and to confuse" (*SG*, 39).

Evil is placed over there (*fort*) and original sympathy over here (*da*). But this is an old rhetorical game, known no less to girls than to boys. Irigaray's contribution to the politics of gender plays its own secret game of *fort/da*.

Clearly, any dream of human society that does not acknowledge games of power as core to our existence is naively romantic, just as any attempt to reduce society to those games is hopelessly cynical. Either option fails to come to terms with how democratic transformations of society are possible through a greater awareness of visible and invisible sources of power. From Irigaray, we would need a more dialectical concept of social force in human society, one that acknowledges both *le pouvoir* and *la puissance* in the complex and overlapping ways in which men and women develop their identities.

A Lover's Discourse and Its Critical Limits

In many ways, the strengths and weaknesses of Irigaray's vision of human society show up most strongly in her relationship to Aristotle. Aristotle located the household as a part of the productive and reproductive economy.[15] The friendship between marriage partners was for the sake of economic needs, and therefore was inferior to the friendship between the highest type of men.[16] Aristotle believed that these higher types of men would love each other for their excellence of character alone. Due to their excellence they were hardly moved by the economic pressures and emotional wounds that prevail among the lower types who seek "utility" in friendship. The relative immunity to material pressures and personal vices made it possible to avoid lack or need as a basis for friendship. These ideal men would base their friendships on generous pleasure and extraordinary excellence alone. The aim of the polis is the cultivation through education of the desires and virtues of these higher men.

Irigaray discerns in the subordination of women and heterosocial relationships to biological and economic functions not just the failure to recognize women, but "the beginning of a failure of respect for nature." She argues that this underlying alienation from nature and from our own embodied subjectivity characterizes the dominant tendency of Western culture. With the establishment of the hom(m)osocial polis, we lose a sense of the ethical dimensions of nature. Instead of cultivating heterosexual friendships, men and women use their own "bodies to release neuropsychic

---

[15] Aristotle, *Politics*, trans. Ernest Barker (Oxford: Oxford University Press, 1995), Bk. 1, Chap. 3 1253b1–14.

[16] Aristotle, *Nicomachean Ethics*, trans. Terence Irwin (Indianapolis: Hackett, 1985) Bk. viii, Chap. 12 9.74.

tensions and produce babies." "What we need is to work out an art of the sexual, a sexual culture" (*SG*, 3). Therefore, in sharp opposition to Aristotle, who anchors the polis in the cultivation of the highest pleasures of male friendship, Irigaray argues for "an ethics of the couple." For Irigaray "the couple" dislodges male friendship as the privileged relationship, or "intermediary," "between individuals, peoples, States" (5). If for Aristotle the polis serves first and foremost to secure the social virtues of male friendship, for Irigaray the telos of the community rests on the eudaimonia of the heterosexual couple in romantic love.

Visual and poetic images have focused the male fantasy of sexuality on penetration, viewed penetration as a return to the womb, and reveled in sexual passion as a challenge to the strong boundaries that define normal identity. Irigaray invites men to view their sexuality quite differently. She assumes that men will continue to take the phallus as central to their experience of sexuality. She does wonder, however, if men might not transform the prevailing cultural associations of the phallus. Why not, Irigaray suggests, view the phallus less as an instrument for control, a tool for penetration, or weapon in sexual conquest, and more as a fleshy organ of connection between sexual partners? The asymmetrical exchange of fluids through the contact of flesh might be experienced as nourishing both to the self and to the other. Indeed, one could imagine a society where sexual relationships are cultivated beyond the cathartic release of neuropsychic tensions and sexual performance, and develop into central sources of spiritual rejuvenation.

But then, Irigaray suggests, might not the phallus bear a strong kinship to the umbilical cord that once tied the man to his mother? If sexuality reinvokes something of the intimacy of the first libidinal relationship, it might be experienced as a source of nourishment rather than as a type of conquest. The view of the phallus as a cord of connection would bring sublime love back from a threat of confused boundaries, co-dependency, and lost subjectivity. Male sexual satisfaction would be forged differently from the violent imagery of explosive release of pent-up force and the sadistic scenarios (including rape and other forms of violation) that this release too often invokes in fantasy if not in reality. If the phallus is viewed as akin to the umbilical cord, then men might give up stoic games for control for the sake of pleasures that nourish the self alongside the other.

Irigaray explains this alternative projectory for male identity in terms that significantly alter traditional drive psychology: "At the very place where there once had been the cord, then the breast, would in due time appear, for the man, the penis which reconnects, gives life, feeds and recenters ... bodies" (*SG*, 17). The implication is that the umbilical cord, breast, and phallus would displace oral, anal, and phallic drives as the embodied sites of self-articulation. If modern narratives for moral development turn on scenarios of fear and guilt in the acquisition of social rules and moral law, Irigaray views development through cultivating the pleasures of mediation and creative reconnection. While the imagery of cord, breast, and phallus are once again a bit too close to reducing motherhood, early childhood, and heterosexual encounters to biological functions focused on some body part, Irigaray intends to use the imagery in order to alter our preconscious fantasies and anchor intersubjective encounters in drive psychology. These preconscious fantasies must change if we are to develop an ethics of eros as an alternative to the guilt-ridden imperatives of a disembodied or hardened will and the cynical realities of power.

Irigaray does not aim to eliminate moral law and political society. She does aim to alter their meaning by replacing the disciplined or self-interested citizen with the erotic lover as the center of society and the basis of individual rights. Because Irigaray's efforts to transform the meaning of male as well as female identity threaten conventional lines of the ego, her work can invoke rage. But Irigaray's intention is to subvert the conventional defenses in order to make way for an expansive sense of male and female power. This power would admittedly begin with the humbling recognition of loss and limits of male identity, but it would also cultivate more fertile sources of subjectivity. Irigaray expresses the loss and the gain, again by eliciting new meaning for the male organ: the penis "evokes something of life within the womb as it stiffens, touches, and spills out, passing beyond the skin and the will. As it softens and falls, it evokes the end, mourning, the ever open wound. Men would ... return to the world that allows them to become sexual adults capable of eroticism and reciprocity in the flesh" (*SG*, 17). Traditional images of male heterosexual desire associate sex with loss and re-submergence in the maternal womb. This same tradition defines manhood in sharp opposition to behaving like a child or being like a woman. If sex threatens the borders between manhood and its opposite, it does so only as a thrill from which man reemerges with the conventional boundaries of the self intact. Irigaray dares men to cultivate their more diffuse sources of erotic pleasure and rejuvenate their moral identity through the transformational avatar of becoming like the child and the mother.

Irigaray does not envision love, and certainly not romantic love, as the social bond that ties together the entire community. On the contrary, the locus of love is narrowly defined as the couple. But Irigaray does suggest that the poetic speech that heightens romantic love supports the more fully expressive styles of communication and sympathy (the ethical culture) that allow social systems to flourish. The discourse that would hold together social systems is not a disembodied Symbolic. The abstract language that is valorized in modern social systems diminishes the expressive capacities of the person, and appropriates erotic energy for sterile games of power. Irigaray wants "a language that is not a substitute for the experience of *corps-a-corps* [or being with the mother] as the paternal language seeks to be, but which accompanies that bodily experience, clothing it in words that do not erase but speak the body" (*SG*, 19).

Such a language would recall in our imaginations the intimate pleasures once experienced through the interwoven fingers of the placenta. Irigaray describes this erotic experience as at once carnal and spiritual, as a sacred bond. The sympathy that gives pleasure in sexual love would invoke the "inconceivable nearness" of a maternal presence that, Irigaray writes, is "without form or face" and who "flows in and out of" fetal and infant life (*SG*, 33). This maternal spirit may lack form and face but it is not silent. The flesh that is not hardened by the polemics of the moral will (one pole of conventional manhood) does not return us to "the blurred shapes, blocked movements, duels for dominance" (the pole of mythic animality). Beyond the nature/culture divide, carnal love speaks the music of the earth, a music that is unheard of by "the Father if his will is that flesh be abolished" (*SG*, 47). Safe from the flesh-devouring Father of patriarchal lore, the maternal spirit speaks as a "sympathetic deciphering of bodies, skins, membranes, mucuses" (*SG*, 36). This spirit does not command the will; it touches the soul.

Nor does this maternal spirit set itself against the earth; instead it makes itself felt through the "rhythms of nature," through, for example, the opening and closing of flowers. The flower is, unlike the animal, the "pure apparition of natural generation" preferred by Irigaray (*SG*, 47). Thus for Irigaray the warrior eroticism and animal imagery valorized by Nietzsche's Dionysian *Übermensch* and resisted by the rigid god of moral law would yield to an eroticism of more tender desires, troped in the language of fertility, flowers, and flesh. And beyond the sovereign man celebrated by both Dionysian and Apollonian models of ethics would grow the power, not of the Nietzschean superman, but what we might call in good humor the *Über*-couple.

For this world beyond convention is created by a very ideal sexual love. Men in love who would dare "an exile from any will belonging to any existing community," who would seek as their "only guide ... the call to the other," these men would find themselves outside of the zones of conquest and in the poetry of the flesh. In that poetry are kept "Love, pain, life and death, ... secret, enigmatic, barely breathing out their melody beyond or through all speakable words" (*SG*, 49).

Such a love is not completely alien to the traditional poetics of male identity. Irigaray accepts the view that erotic drives of love constitute a threat to what men have called autonomy. However, according to the traditional view, men are to emerge from their sexual liaisons with the will intact, and so return to a community of men, a community, Irigaray might have written, of "men without skin."[17] Irigaray proposes the elements for a counter-mythology. According to this counter-myth, manhood would no longer be sustained through tests of will but in expressions of love. Masculinity would be expressed not in the hand that grasps but in the impassioned play that opens to the other. Still, love flourishes, for Irigaray as for the romantic tradition, only in exile from community. For it is in love that men strip away the abstract and artificial conventions that bind all existing communities. In love, men would become "strangers to exchange, business, marketplace." No longer having words, "abandoning all control, all language, and all sense already produced," these men would find their spiritual dwelling in the flesh of another (*SG*, 51, 53). From this spiritual dwelling would arise a new type of ethical community, one that tames savage capital and instrumental force with the music of love.

In Irigaray's view, this love must threaten the boundaries of any existing self. Certainly it breaks through the illusion of abstract autonomy and the reality of instrumental calculation that makes up the modern subject. Love that stems from the tactile drives between mother and child rather than from fantasies of fusion promises to give spiritual sustenance to a more elevated self. The amorous exchange that defines the romantic couple can lay the foundation for a universal ethical cultural based on a difference that is sublime.

The Work of the Caregiver and the Power of the Mother

Irigaray's story of human origins prepares us to understand how human sociality is as old as our skin. Her mythology does not suffice for understanding how the primordial encounter is embodied in webs of power. These webs of power act as a second skin, bending lines of erotic exchange in fields of force. There is no dimension of human life that would escape the impact of these fields of force. Even in the most abstract kinds of legal and moral communication, discursive space is curved by lines of power. Certainly these lines of force operate in the intimate space of lovers. Therefore, the individual cannot rely on a sanctuary of sublime love or a court of impartial legal judgment to place him or her outside of these lines of force. Needed instead are counter-forces (in law, culture, education, or material re-

---

[17] Toni Morrison, *Beloved* (New York: Penguin, 1987), 210.

sources) that might check hubristic sources of power and nourish exuberant forms of human sociality. Without restraints on the social, cultural, and/or economic registers of friendly exchange, these forces will continue to play at the periphery of our vision in secret games of power.

Irigaray's emphasis on the corporeal dimension of erotic exchange supplements Platonic and Hegelian philosophies of human desire. She shares the failure of these two traditions to develop democratic conceptions of work and power. In particular, her dialectic of love recalls Plato's myth of Eros in the *Symposium*. Irigaray's belief in a cosmic force for sympathy recalls the communal rituals of love and reconciliation in the young Hegel. She shares dialectical philosophy's critique of the abstract universal (i.e., a concept that generalizes) and prefers the concrete universal (or a narrative that relates distinct sources of meaning). Hegel uses the struggle between male and female power in the tragedy of Antigone and Creon in order to explain the origin of ethical and spiritual culture, or what he calls *Geist*. Diotima's speech in Plato's *Symposium* explains the ambiguities of human desire through a tale about a resourceful father and a needy mother who have produced a son named Eros. Like Plato and Hegel, Irigaray places sexual difference at the origin of dialectic. Of course, for Plato and Hegel male and female sources of meaning are not equal, and for Irigaray this is the problem with traditional dialectic. Hegel argues that Antigone must learn to bend family and religious concerns to the economic and military needs of the state. Plato portrays maternal and paternal forces as unequal resources in the philosopher's erotic assent to divine wisdom. Plato and Hegel may grant a greater place for female sources of power and wisdom than does Aristotle's hom(m)osocial celebration of male virtues, but these philosophers are hardly egalitarian. Irigaray is right in aiming to rectify dialectic with a somewhat more balanced view of male and female origins of desire. She errs when she attempts to strip human subjectivity of its will to power and substitute for real power and human connection a cosmic extension of the lonely self.

Irigaray's distinction between male and female sources give us insight into ways in which misguided ideas of fertility and reproduction perpetuate a defective series of analogies. Philosophers as diverse as Plato, Aristotle, and even Hegel view procreation through the myth that men implant a seed in the woman's womb. The womb is viewed as empty space or earthly soil, providing little more than nourishment for the seed. This passive view of the womb reflects the view that maternal care for the child is more or less biological and possesses no ultimate source of political (*le pouvoir*) or spiritual power (*la puissance*).

This view of maternal passivity proliferates in stories of creation in traditional and modern cultures. Monotheistic religions and monological philosophies search for a single origin or unifying principle for human experience. In monotheistic religions, this is the male sky-god who visits the abyss below in order to generate life. In Hegel's cosmology, *Science of Logic*, this single origin is Being, which penetrates into the Nothing in order to generate Becoming. For Aristotle, metaphysics focuses on the forms that impregnate matter.

Our notions of artistic creativity are based on similar analogies. The artist views him (or her) self as creating a figure out of background or imposing form on matter.

This same metaphysics of form over matter generates notions of a moral agent who might restrain material desire with an ethical imperative.

Therefore, when Irigaray writes that there are two sources of order, and not one, when she argues that women have sources of creative power equal to men, she alters the fundamental weaves of our thought. From this recognition she asks for a spirituality that would place female gods alongside male gods. She roots cultural forms in a nature that is already almost ethical. She asks for a dialectical cosmology based on not one but two principles of being; an ethics based on two universals; and a basic law that includes rights for women alongside rights for men. And, as Irigaray writes of the man who is a poet and a lover, the beauty of words, indeed the power of artistic creation, would emerge at the edge of meaning, yes, but also in response to the call of the other. From this more ethical source of creation, the cultural landscape would change. Our stone-chiseled monuments to stoic power would yield public space to lyrical expressions of human accord.

Irigaray's moral individual does not develop from the childhood narcissism to abstract thought. The person develops from presubjective social drives and childhood dance to adult love. In some ways, Irigaray's path to moral development differs so radically from the conventional theories that it can provoke wonder or ridicule. In other, more troubling ways, it mirrors those conventions sufficiently so as to reinforce them. Kohlberg supports modern moral psychology by positing a stage of moral development that severs cognition from life. Irigaray reorients developmental psychology toward the experiences of pregnant women and their children and lovers. However, her account of these experiences borrows too heavily from the sentimental discourse that belongs to our romantic conventions. She would have us believe that maternal attachment and childhood play could be severed from games of status and power. She asks us to celebrate mothers "without form or face" and lovers who dwell "in exile from the marketplace." I wonder if these mothers without form and face have not been stripped of both their power and their subjectivity in order to be taken up into rhythms of the cosmos. I also wonder how lovers can live without a source of labor. Where does this labor come from? Irigaray imagines that lovers might cleanse their skin of the sedimentations of power and create a paradise from out of nothing. But then I cannot imagine how an ethics of the flesh operates in a world defined through the politics of skin.

The fantasy of the noumenal couple, no less than that of the fantasy of the noumenal man, is fabricated from the conventions that it claims to leave behind. It is from the prevailing conventions that Irigaray takes the heterosexual couple as a norm. She neglects homosexual couples, communal relationships, and friendships based on nonsexual sources of pleasure. The claim that the couple is the minimal social unit reflects the diminished social life of postindustrial society. The isolation of the couple from communal ties may be less a romantic dream than a consequence of the modern marketplace. It is this same marketplace, and not nature, that divides society into two spheres, the domestic sphere based on love and the productive sphere based on paid labor. Irigaray envisions lovers leaving behind social conventions and entering into a virginal space that is an idyllic refuge from the outer world. However, it is this image of the refuge, an image that has often in our modern tradition been associated with the womb and domesticity, that points to the limits in Irigaray's critical poetics.

The romantic couple that she celebrates is less a counter-myth than a conventional fiction that allows us to forget for a moment the inevitability of relationships based on work and power. No less than Aristotle's model of perfect hom(m)osocial friendship, Irigaray's heterosexist vision of marital bliss places key relationships in society beyond the sphere of those lower types who are chained to the marketplace. Yet no one is more dependent on the marketplace than those who claim to inhabit some more noumenal realm. Aristotle makes clear that his society requires wives and noncitizen workers in order that the beautiful people could enjoy lives of excellence. Irigaray places wives alongside husbands at a center of society that is based on love and joy. However, like Aristotle, she leaves behind the servants and other noncitizen workers who must work so that her lovers can play. It is not an ideal that could be universalized, and the attempt to do so would only exacerbate class divisions, about which it is in denial.

The Angels of Eros and the Ghosts of Beloved

Irigaray gives us the white body and the pure spirit of the mother, but not the material subject. She consigns the mother to a quasi-natural domain that is almost but not fully ethical. Her role is to nourish the fetus through a biological organ. Irigaray misses the ways in which the pregnant subject must take care of her self, sometimes through difficult times. She imagines an unscarred (*blanc*) skin of the placenta as the basis for the perfect exchange between the mother and fetus. She compares the virginal skin of the placenta to the translucent flesh of the angels. Angels are said to be pure emblems of eros sent by the gods to remind us of our origins and allow for sympathy among ourselves. Yet Irigaray's genealogical method has taught us how to unearth political motives for more pure claims. She presents her angels as through they were untouched by the struggles of the material world. One wonders whether human relationships can ever escape wounds from conflicts past and present. One wonders, where are the ghosts of those who were lost?

Irigaray advances critical theory beyond Marcuse by expanding our understanding of embodiment beyond the release of tensions in oral, anal, and phallic drives. She introduces proto-social drives to be with the other. We are compelled to seek in the other the warmth of their flesh, the rhythms of their body, and the music of their voice. We are driven by the presence of the body of the other. We respond to their embodied presence through rhythms of our own movement, the sounds of our own voice, and the generation of fluids. The embodied response crosses paths of sensory stimulation, melding image and sound, touch and gaze, in a synesthesia of correspondences. These correspondences do not stop with the boundaries of the sensual other but reach out to forces that are natural, lunar, and even cosmic. Love is not only about relating to the other through care or communication; love celebrates the everyday mystery of human creation. It is not a discourse. It is a poem.

Irigaray's philosophical psychology falls short by two steps. First, while Irigaray expands drive theory in order to develop broader conceptions of male and female eroticism, she fails to connect her phenomenology of drive with a theory of intersubjectivity. The lack of such a theory blinds her to the ways in which drives are elaborated by social interactions between subjects. Rape does not just release neuropsychic tensions on the body of the other. It constitutes an act of arrogance. It is energy directed against another subject. Its aim is humiliation. From classical Greek culture, we understand hubris as a significant crime. The crime is defined as the violation of another person so as to cause shame or dishonor for one's own pleasure. The origin of this pleasure is in intersubjective relationships and not merely in quasi-biological needs. A theory of hubris needs to be introduced into modern culture by way of what Hegelians have understood in terms of a dialectic of recognition and Frederick Douglass redefines in terms of social death and slavery.

Second, Irigaray fails to grasp that women no less than men, that indeed all animals, are driven by games of power. Irigaray simplifies children's games by assuming that toys and gestures signify the mother's absence. In fact, these games develop physical and cognitive skills that are original sources of control and pleasure for the maturing child. Irigaray imagines male identity through totems of animality and juxtaposes the purity of the female self. Women, she remarks, are like flowers; we open and close in response to nature's rhythms. We sing its song. But women, like flowers? Flowers do not walk. And what happened to our ties with the female members of other animal species? Do not female animals contend no less than male animals for signs of rank and privileges of power? But then eros is no angel.

Irigaray fails to elaborate upon ways in which we are all engaged in social battles for power and status. She does not see how scars from battles past and present warp the space that we call home. She certainly does not acknowledge the ways in which class and cultural inheritances inflect her universalist conception of gender difference.

Still, Irigaray's contribution to critical theory of freedom is significant. Marcuse had seen how the performance principle cramps human expressive capabilities. He had urged us to check Capital for the sake of a new type of man. But this new type of man, the man of leisure, was all too familiar to the housewife whose own leisure was defined as raising his children and caring for his needs. This man was the absent father, and his life was defined far away from the social intimacies of the family. Irigaray carries forward Marcuse's task when she insists on gender as an essential part of our political and moral identity. She is right to transform the meaning of our gendered identities rather than assume that we might transcend them. She is also right to argue that we must include a more expansive concept of erotic bonds as central to any better world.

Marcuse traced the evolution of liberalism from the possessive individual to the performance principle. He aimed to find in human psychology a drive that was stronger than the performance principle, a drive to express individual creative force in art and thought. Irigaray's vision makes us question the underlying narcissism of Marcuse's new man. She invites us to reimagine the Marcuse dream by joining a new type of man with a new type of woman. She leads us to wonder how much better we might live as human beings—no, as social animals—if we would better understand the individual from his or her origin in the family. From this origin we might alter our vision of the telos of modern society. The rights-bearing citizen would not be the possessive individual of classical liberalism; nor would it be the narcissistic man celebrated by Marcuse. No, Irigaray's vision leads us to wonder if the rights-bearing individual of modern social systems is not first of all the lover, the worker, and the friend. But this would alter the meaning of the law.

III

A Discourse of Love, a Practice of Freedom

7

The Mother Wit of Justice

Eros and Hubris in the African-American Context

"Who better to know what freedom means than the slave."[1] So speculates the contemporary writer John Edgar Wideman. Wideman explains that freedom was the fire that kept the plantation worker in America alive. The vision of freedom ran deep and wide through plantation communities. Its truth was spiritual. If the slave were to lose sight of that vision, Wideman remarks, that slave was doomed. The Civil War held out the

Beverly Guy-Sheftal, Opal Moore, Mechthild Nagel, Deborah Achtenberg, and Thomas Tuozzo have contributed enormously to my understanding of the issues in this chapter. I am also grateful for the perceptive comments of William Wilkerson on an earlier version of this chapter. A version of the chapter appears in William Wilkerson and Jeffry Paris, eds., *New Critical Theory: Essays on Liberation* (Lanham, Md.: Rowman and Littlefield, forthcoming).

[1] John Edgar Wideman, interviewed on the documentary "Judgment Day," episode 4 of "Africans in America," PBS, April 8, 1999.

promise of a Second American Revolution, one to complete the work of the first. But if the Civil War brought an end to chattel slavery, it did not bring the freedom that it had promised. Observing the long-standing racial hierarchy in America, critical theorist Patricia Hill Collins concludes, "The more things change, the more they stay the same."[2] What is the promise of freedom against the changing same of race in America? What did the plantation worker mean by the term "freedom"?

One might think, as did Walt Whitman, that the cure for democracy is more democracy. A majoritarian system, however, does not guarantee protection to minority groups. The civil rights movement extended formal rights of citizenship to African Americans. These rights eased but did not erase long-standing racial hierarchies. If we are to overcome racial hierarchies, we will need to search for the deeper meaning of freedom in the context of a modern democracy.

Patricia Hill Collins develops some of the basic concepts for the project in her social theory,[3] using an Afrocentric perspective to reground European critical theory. This perspective turns our focus from the center to the periphery of modern social systems. From the periphery of modern power, Collins replaces romantic themes of the alienated man torn by a double consciousness or the exoticized Other who does not speak with her more politically savvy concept of the "outsider within" (*FW*, 5). The concept of the "outsider within" draws attention to the fact that modern alienated subjects do not inhabit—in fact do not aspire to—some space beyond the reach of modern social and economic structures, including capitalism. In the modern world, individuals are situated at the intersections of diverse sources of power. The outsider struggles for social and economic survival under oppressive conditions with no way out of these modern systems of markets and mass culture. Collins's example of the outsider within is the black domestic worker in the white household. Collins does not allow the theorist to position the domestic worker as the subdued object of our own ethics of generosity, compassionate concern, or charitable interest. We are led instead to focalize our theoretical perspective from the domestic worker's point of view. The change of focus supports what Collins, among others, including critical race theorist Kimberle Crenshaw, describes as an intersectional analysis of social identity.

[2] Patricia Hill Collins, *Fighting Words: Black Women and the Search for Justice* (Minneapolis: University of Minnesota Press, 1998), 13; henceforth cited as *FW*.

[3] For Collins's account of her relation to Frankfurt School Critical Theory, see *FW*, 254 n. 4.

As Collins observes, in "a system of interlocking race, gender, class, and sexual oppression, there are few pure oppressors or victims."[4] The African-American woman is not locked in a traditional, Hegelian-style dialectic between the objectifying gaze of the white racist and inner resources of the self. Du Bois's romantic concept of the double consciousness of the black man does not address the domestic worker's need to deal with incommensurate demands made by black men, white employees, and her own children, among others in interlocking systems of power. An analysis of these interlocking systems scrutinizes the ways in which individuals both have and do not have power (FW, 59). While what Collins terms the "both/and" perspective reengages dialectical language, she avoids the binary categories and polarizing tactics of the romantic, European model. Old styles of dialectical subversion and class (or race or gender) warfare fail to capture the heterogeneous sources of identity in the modern service economy.

Modern communitarian and individualistic theories of democracy lack tools for addressing the ways in which hybrid social forces define the parameters for individual identity. These theories, however, offer some partial concepts for new critical theory. African-American writers know well the central impact of communal and historical forces on individual identity. As Collins observes, African Americans have taken back the term race from reactive white supremacists. While white racists have used science in order to claim significant genetic differences, African Americans use race to establish, if not invent, a common heritage within America and "'perceived kinship relations between blacks ... throughout the diaspora'" (FW, 24). Social categories such as race are necessary in order to discern group-based injustices and construct group-based remedies. This does not mean, however, that critical theorists do not need as well a concept of individual right. As Patricia Williams points out, both positive rights that emphasize community responsibility and negative rights that are centered on individual freedoms serve as indispensable weapons in legal struggles against racism.[5] The trick is understanding what concepts of community and right would offer serious justice to the outsider within the racial system of modern America.

[4] Patricia Hill Collins, *Black Feminist Thought: Knowledge, Consciousness, and the Politics of Empowerment* (New York: Routledge, 1990), 194; henceforth cited as *BF*. See also Kimberle Williams Crenshaw, "Mapping the Margins," in *Critical Race Theory*, ed. Kimberle Crenshaw et al. (New York: New Press, 1995), 357–383.

[5] Patricia J. Williams, *The Alchemy of Race and Rights* (Cambridge: Harvard University Press, 1996), 154.

In a classic analysis of black alienation, Howard McGary explains why the liberal concept of right is ineffective against the social ills of racism.[6] Liberalism, McGary observes, rests upon a relatively sharp distinction between internal and external constraints on individual freedom. Among internal constraints are biological or psychic ills that might hinder one's free action. Among external constraints are such violations as theft of property or lack of opportunity for employment or housing. Liberal rights may guarantee some protection against external constraints to freedom. However, as McGary argues, one of the significant harms of racism lies outside the liberal paradigm altogether. McGary terms this harm "self-alienation." McGary's use of the term "alienation" seems at variance with Collins's preference for the term "outsider within." However, his analysis of alienation dovetails very well with Collins's remarks on mixed forms of power. McGary explains that the expression of race-based attitudes is part of the norm of white-controlled societies. These attitudes constitute what we can identify as a source of social force. Social forces affect the individual's psychic and even biological sense of well-being (recall the high incidence of stress-related illnesses such as high blood pressure or even, as now is being argued, the high level of child mortality among disempowered groups). In a hostile racial climate, the African American can experience alienation from the social world, and this alienation can assault the self. Race-based alienation is not the same thing as alienation from work but, like work-based alienation, race-based alienation can cut deep into the sense of who one is and what one desires. As McGary points out, however, hostile social forces do not necessarily damage personal identity. On this point, McGary, like Collins, recognizes that the individual stands at the intersection of many sources of power. McGary explains that African Americans may lack recognition from white-controlled societies, and yet sustain a strong and unalienated sense of self from family and community.

Multiple and conflicting social forces traverse the multiple centers and peripheries of modern capitalist systems. While these forces make up the air we live and breathe, no single force defines the individual. Social forces are not strictly speaking either "internal" or "external" to the individual, or so I would argue. The sources of social force include discursive forms of power (such as commercialized art and the media, and cultural wars over the language and the symbols that we use). These sources also include events from

---

[6] "Alienation and the African-American Experience," in Howard McGary, *Race and Social Justice* (Malden, Mass.: Blackwell, 1999), 7–26; henceforth cited as *AA*. The essay also appears in numerous anthologies, including Cynthia Willett, *Theorizing Multiculturalism: A Guide to the Current Debate* (Malden, Mass.: Blackwell, 1998).

past history that affect our wealth and our spirit. We might say that these sources are both external to the individual, who is not necessarily defined by any of them, and yet also internal to what contemporary liberalism too narrowly conceives in terms of rational autonomy, self-esteem, and bodily integrity. As McGary observes, the act of resisting social forces that are alienating or harmful costs psychic and bodily energy (*AA*, 16). And because racism exerts quasi-internal and quasi-external kinds of constraints, liberal theories of justice leave this force partially obscured from vision. But then what basis for right would protect the individual from constraints based on racism? What notion of harm describes the impact of a hostile social force?

McGary points out that this question cannot be answered by the simple turn to a liberal notion of group rights. Even if African Americans have such group rights as equal employment opportunities, they may still suffer from estrangement in a way that whites do not (*AA*, 16). McGary's conclusion is that the only solution available in liberalism is for the individual to attain a strong sense of autonomy (or self-choice) with the support of ethnic communities.

McGary's tentative remarks recall recent efforts on the part of various philosophers to marry an ethics of care with a moral concept of individual autonomy. I have argued that these approaches go some way but perhaps not far enough toward challenging the social minimalism of the modern liberal tradition of individual freedom (Chapter 1). Our liberal tradition much needs a thicker account of human sociality. We moral philosophers have also not given nearly enough attention to the social and economic impact of those whose carework sustains the so-called self-directed, autonomous individual. The question is whether or not there is a richer basis for social freedom than the autonomous self propped up by the anonymous service of unseen others.

Racism has been and continues to constitute an assault upon the social being of the individual. Slave owners broke up families and communities and suppressed Afrocentric social practices both for economic motives and for social control. As Frederick Douglass observed, the plantation economy functioned through tactics aimed to render a people "morally, politically, and socially dead."[7] Moreover, as Douglass foresaw, the end of the plantation system would not mean the end of slavery or its tactics. To free the slave from individual masters only to make him a slave to the economy, "to emancipate the bondsman from the laws that make him a chattel, and yet subject him to laws and deprivations which will inevitably break down his

[7] From "The Present and Future of the Colored Race in America," in *The Life and Writings of Frederick Douglass*, ed. Philip Foner (New York: International Publishers, 1975), 3: 352; henceforth cited as *LW* followed by volume number.

spirit," hardly constitutes significant change (*LW*, 3:,350-351). Economic slavery no less than chattel slavery casts the black worker in the role of the "social pest"—the enemy of a system that is at war with itself. The process is of "little gain" to the emancipated slave. And, he adds, it is of even "less gain to the country" (*LW*, 3:351). With this warning, Douglass establishes himself as a major prophet of the "changing same" of racial arrogance, the race tragedy of America.

In the final part of this book, I take up what Collins, among others, argues to be the spiritual core of freedom in the love and justice tradition of black America. Collins discerns the meaning of this freedom by returning to the words of an ex-slave in Toni Morrison's *Beloved*. The slave, as Morrison writes, searches for "a place where you could love anything you chose." As I understand this vision of freedom, it exceeds narrow parameters that locate the self in discourses of ownership or self-choice. Female and male narratives of love and freedom—my primary examples include Morrison's *Beloved* (Chapter 9) and Frederick Douglass's *My Bondage and My Freedom* (Chapter 8)—may differ in focus. As Claudia Tate observes, "In the work of many Black male writers, the significant relationships are those that involve confrontation with individuals outside the family and community. But among Black women writers, relationships within family and community, between men and women, and among women are treated as complex and significant" (cited in *BF*, 98).[8] Male narratives staging confrontations outside the community may accommodate the more traditional, romantic language of alienation and double consciousness than do the women's narratives. However, both styles of narrative subordinate metaphysical (and economic) claims to self-ownership to more basic rights of the individual as a social being.

The invocation of a freedom that is at once spiritual and economic resonates with a theme of social justice that lies buried in ancient European, African, and Asian texts. I will examine only one of these many sources, one from the ancient Greek world. Disconnected passages in Aristotle's works reflect (if only dimly) the popular Greek understanding of injustice as the violation of sacred social bonds. The conception of violation as a social crime constitutes what in popular Greek culture is called hubris. Tragic hubris occurs through partly seen, partly unseen acts of arrogance. Arrogance is a social crime, and it goes unchecked in race-torn America today.

Modern writers in the African-American context have reflected upon the crimes of arrogance in a land plagued by racial violence. They challenge

[8] Patricia Hill Collins draws this conclusion from Claudia Tate's edited collection, *Black Women Writers at Work* (New York: Continuum Publishing, 1983), esp. 92.

the constricted ideologies of liberal freedom. They demonstrate how constricted ideologies sustain unacknowledged forms of social and economic control. Many of these writers would not doubt the central claim of the liberal theorist John Rawls, that "each person possesses an inviolability founded on justice, that even the welfare of society as a whole cannot override."[9] But black critical theory exposes the social vacuum of the modern tradition of liberal right. The basic rights of the person cannot rest on metaphysical, psychological, or economic conceptions of self-ownership. On the contrary, black critical theory teaches that just as surely as the origin of the person is not merged but with-the-other, so the goal of freedom must be in the inviolability of the individual-in-relationship-to-others. The primary bearer of rights and opportunities is not the self-interested and rational person per se; the primary bearer of rights is the social person. It is this person that rights must protect. As the Greeks partly understood, the violation of the social person constitutes an act of hubris. The function of the law is to protect the social individual from violation, and to cultivate the erotic power of the individual-in-relationship-to-others.

Toward the Erotic Core of the Modern Subject

Kelly Oliver argues persuasively that modern European conceptions of the subject render relationships of love impossible. Neo-Hegelian theories of recognition (e.g., that of J. Benjamin) assume that "master/slave" style conflicts are normative for the formation of the subject.[10] Neo-Lacanian theories of subjectivity (e.g., those of J. Butler and J. Kristeva) take as a norm the abjection of the mother. In a fascinating analysis, Oliver demonstrates that both psychoanalytic and Hegelian theories reflect the failure of mainstream Western culture to develop adequate models of subjectivity.[11] Our intimate relationships with our mothers provide the prototype for all subsequent social relationships, and yet this original relationship is portrayed as asocial. The scenario of asocial intimacy defines what Oliver terms the "paradox of love."

Oliver draws from the work of Kristeva in order to elaborate upon the lack of love in modern culture. Quoting from Kristeva's *Tales of Love*, Oliver

---

[9] The quotation from John Rawls serves as the epigraph for Drucilla Cornell's *At the Heart of Freedom* (Princeton, N.J.: Princeton University Press, 1998), 3. I will return to Drucilla Cornell's revision of Rawlsian liberalism later. Further references to Cornell's text cited as *HF*.

[10] Kelly Oliver, *Beyond Recognition: Toward a Theory of Othered Subjectivity* (Minneapolis: University of Minnesota Press, 2000).

[11] Kelly Oliver, *Family Values: Subjects between Nature and Culture* (New York: Routledge, 1997), 3; henceforth cited as *FV*.

writes: "Modern man dwells 'in exile, deprived of his psychic space, an extraterrestrial... wanting for love.'"[12] "Kristeva describes a threatening body that has completely colonized the soul.... 'In the wake of psychiatric medicines, aerobic, and media zapping, [Kristeva asks,] does the soul still exist?'" (*SS*, 143–144). Kristeva's remedy to the modern crisis is to replace the stern father of traditional psychoanalytic theory with the loving father: "For Kristeva, only the loving father can feed and fill the psyche." While the stern father uses disciplinary tactics in order to educate the child into the abstract norms of modern social systems, the loving father allows the child to invent a psychic space of its own.

Although Kristeva teaches us much about the crisis of the soul in modern culture, her critique of the norms of psychoanalytic theory does not venture far from modernity's centers. As Oliver argues, the desire to cultivate one's own psychic space does not sufficiently challenge modern narcissism. Oliver asks: "If Narcissus suffers when he realizes that he sees only his own image reflected back to him, that he is alone, then doesn't he need companionship and communion, communication and a shared discourse instead of his own individual discourse? Are modern men ... looking for [new forms of] ownership or the gift of love?" (*SS*, 145).

Oliver points out the need to nudge Kristeva's critique of psychoanalytic theory two steps further. First, if we were to view the mother as a social person (and not as an asocial zone of eros), then we might assume that the mother could provide the source of love necessary for the maturation of the child. Second, if the mother is a loving subject, then abjection would not be necessary in the process of maturation (*SS*, 137). Irigaray invites us to view both the mother and the child (if not a host of other unacknowledged caregivers) as "whole creatures" in "communion" with one another.

One more step might be necessary as well, as I have suggested in the discussion of Irigaray (Chapter 6). We might also think of the mother as a political and economic power in relationship with various others (including fathers, domestic workers, or employers), all of whom mediate her relationship with her child. From this perspective, I would question the contemporary American representation of maturation in terms of the separation of the child from the mother altogether. If the mother and child already enjoy a multifaceted social relationship, then symbolic rituals of separation would seem to function more to devalue the mother's domestic work and disconnect the mother from her adult children than to perform a necessary function for subject formation. Actual violations of the connection between

[12] Kelly Oliver, *Subjectivity without Subjects* (Lanham, Md.: Rowman and Littlefield, 1998), 144; henceforth cited as *SS*.

the mother and her child can induce trauma, and theories of separation do not shy away from this fact. On the contrary, major theories from Hegel through Lacan and Levinas glorify trauma-inducing separations as though they test manhood or moral conscience. As I will argue further in later chapters, the experience of the Middle Passage and slavery in America argue for the reverse in African-American culture. Separation from the mother, family, or community does not make the man; it may break him.

These three steps beyond the work of Kristeva need to be brought back into a post–Frankfurt School philosophical anthropology. Some theorists who are critical of narcissistic conceptions of subjectivity draw upon a neo-Hegelian notion of recognition in order to focus on the subject's "desire for the desire of the other." But, as Oliver argues, the desire for recognition is also narcissistic: "Theories dependent on notions of recognition reinscribe a type of master-slave relationship within the very act of recognition of the other.... Recognition presupposes a recognizer who has the authority and power to determine who is in and who is out" (SS, 173).

For this reason, Oliver is right, I think, to reject neo-Hegelian theories of the subject. She turns instead to African-American and post-Holocaust texts, and proposes a notion of subjectivity based on "witnessing an other" who is "beyond recognition." "Unlike recognition, ... witnessing admits that the other comes first" (SS, 175). Oliver argues persuasively that the notion of witnessing has much to contribute to moral philosophy. It is an especially significant moral charge for those of us who enjoy asymmetrical positions of power over others. We might, however, take one more step here as well, and incorporate an awareness of the asymmetry of subject positions into our third claim made vis-à-vis francophone philosophy: no encounter with the "other" can escape the heterogeneous sources of power that structure modern societies.

In particular, Collins's analysis of the "outsider within" at the "intersections of power" alters the focus for normative philosophy in two significant ways. First, Collins's analysis asks us to focus our theories or narratives from the point of view of those at the peripheries of power. A witness theory of ethics (depending upon how it is understood) may continue to focalize ethical encounters from the view of those who occupy the centers of power, and who seek to help. Second, Collins's analysis places not the bare Other but embedded and embodied human relationships at the center of analysis. It is both the complicity and the intimacy between differently empowered subjects, not the bare need of the Other, that would orient new critical theory. This analysis of relationships allows us to work out underlying political and social conflicts behind charitable acts of moral goodness (my main concern here is with the type of view represented by Levinas) as well as blatant acts of domination and cruelty.

No individual can remove herself from complicity in interlocking systems of power. Neither the human animal nor liberal society is free from the aggressive drives that sustain struggles for status. However, these drives might be restrained through a dialectic of subversion and mutual recognition. As Oliver warns, however, we would have to theorize dialectic outside of the Hegelian (or Marxian) quest for mastery over a material world. Collins provides some of the key concepts for this task. In the modern world, we emerge as subjects by struggling *both* within *and* against specific histories of power. Oliver's critique of Hegel needs to be brought into the core of dialectical critical theory. A dialectic from the position of the outsider within would not take as its telos the self-defined, self-originating, and arguably self-involved subject of mainstream liberal culture. As Oliver explains, "ethics cannot be based on the rights or reason of an autonomous subject if all subjects are inherently social in the constitution of their very subjectivity" (*FV*, 231). Liberal theories (including J. Rawls's) are designed to protect the rights of the rational individual, and not the affective needs of the social individual. Hence, liberals are not prepared to make the interventions into the market and commercialized culture that would be required to overcome what romantic theorists analyze in terms of alienation from capitalism or from antiblack racism, and what might better be described in terms of the need to check hubristic sources of power for the sake of the social individual. But then the question is, how does one define the rights or reason of the subject who is of eros born?

Drucilla Cornell responds to the problems of difference and misrecognition by reenvisioning a liberal concept of individual rights. Her significant innovation is to bring to the heart of liberal theory a sexual dimension of the individual, and, in particular, "to introduce the issues of sex and sexuality into the analytic framework of John Rawls' *A Theory of Justice*."[13] In order to develop a liberal theory of equality that is rich enough to address issues of sexual difference, she foregrounds what Rawls argues to be one among many primary goods, self-respect. Special attention to the primary good of self-respect prepares her to redefine equality in terms of the "equal protection of certain minimal conditions of individuation" (*ID*, 4).

Cornell lays out these minimal conditions via francophone and, in particular, Lacanian theory. These conditions are the right to bodily integrity,

---

[13] Drucilla Cornell, *The Imaginary Domain: Abortion, Pornography, and Sexual Harassment* (New York: Routledge, 1995), x; henceforth cited as *ID*.

the right to symbolic forms, and the right to the imaginary domain. She points out that sex and sexuality play central roles in the formation of personhood. Therefore, basic law should protect the "imaginary domain" against the kinds of degradation or shame that would "limit psychic space for free play with one's sexuality" (*ID*, 9). Cornell acknowledges that her minimum conditions of individuation require an appeal to some empirical notions of human psychology. She believes that her three conditions are "tailored broadly enough so that almost all psychological and psychoanalytic schools would agree that these conditions are necessary for the achievement of any sense of self" (*ID*, 18).[14]

There are a few questions that I have with Cornell's powerful revision of Rawlsian theory. I will articulate these concerns in such a way as to sharpen contrasts between the Enlightenment liberal subject (defended by Rawls and reinterpreted by Cornell) and the social humanism to which I turn. My aim is to generate a gestalt switch from the self-owned, self-chosen, or self-respectful individual of liberalism to the social person who expresses his or her individuality through the capacity to form libidinous relationships with others. While the liberal concept of rights and liberties prioritizes the need to protect the individual's capacity for choice in the private sphere, the social humanist concept of right begins with an understanding of how market and cultural forces traverse our private space, including the space of the imaginary domain. This latter concept of right prioritizes the need to protect the individual from hubristic market and cultural forces, and to cultivate the social basis of personal identity.

Following Rawls, Cornell argues for the need to establish a theory of justice on the basis of a noncontroversial philosophical anthropology. Cornell's own remarks, however, borrow from an original and somewhat controversial weave of neo-Kantian and psychoanalytic sources. She locates the basis for rights in the disembodied "noumenal" (or "contentless" and "autonomous") person as theorized originally by Kant. At the same time she claims that the embodied experience of sexuality is core to the formation of the moral and legal person. This is an intriguing but, I think, somewhat

---

[14] Cornell elaborates upon the "right of the imaginary domain" in *At the Heart of Freedom*. She begins by establishing her claim through a revision of the Rawls doctrine that "each person possesses an inviolability founded on justice" (3). She argues that the "freedom to create ourselves as sexed beings ... lies at the heart of the ideal of the imaginary domain" (ix). "Some formal-equality feminists have ignored the reality that hearts continue to starve, no matter the new opportunities available to women" (ix). "What has been missing is the protection of each person's imaginary domain, that psychic and moral space in which we, as sexed creatures who care deeply about matters of the heart, are allowed to evaluate and represent who we are" (xi). The imaginary domain is "an essential right of personality" (ix).

paradoxical position to defend. If quasi-biological sexual drives (which have been interpreted through media images) invade the noumenal core of the person, then in what sense is the core noumenal, or otherwise without content? Cornell argues that her empirical claim regarding the centrality of sexuality in personal identity is based on broad agreements across psychological and psychoanalytic theories of the subject. She elaborates upon these agreements by drawing upon a traditional, or noncontroversial, Lacanian framework. One problem with this traditional framework is that it excludes race from playing the crucial role in the formation of the modern subject. According to Frantz Fanon, the modern subject forms his identity precisely through ideas about race, and these ideas are not always secondary to, or otherwise dependent upon, more basic ideas about sexual identity (as I believe the traditional Lacanian paradigm implies).[15]

Our modern ideas about what it is to be a person are rooted in specific ethnic, racial, and cultural styles, and in histories of domination and freedom. Justice theory needs to recognize the ways in which our most abstract ideas about the self (not to mention the very tendency to abstract) may be embedded in specific cultural histories, and then establish legal means to redress specific forms of domination rather than simply secure minimal rights of personality formation that abstract from these forms of domination—or at least this is what I would claim. Laws need to recognize vulnerable group status in the United States, and design specific and asymmetrical laws protecting these vulnerable social groups in appropriate ways. For example, Native Americans should be granted rights to land, Spanish should be recognized as an official language of the United States, and African Americans should receive reparation for slavery, discrimination, and wrongful incarceration, at least to the degree necessary to achieve economic and social equality. The need for these specific laws and rights grow out of understanding historical narratives of identity formation, more so than appealing to minimal rights of personality formation.

Moreover, as Oliver argues, the bare-bone premises of psychoanalytic theory exemplify perhaps noncontroversial but nonetheless highly problematic views with regard to human sociality and mothering. Cornell bases the right to bodily integrity on the Freudian thesis that the child's first developmental task is to organize its fragmentary experiences of embodiment into an experience of its body as its "own." She quotes Oliver Sacks: "What is more important for us, at an elemental level, than the control, the owning and operation, of our own physical selves?" (*ID*, 34). Cornell originally formulates

---

[15] Shannon Winnubst, "Is the Mirror Racist," work in progress.

her position by borrowing from Lacan the thesis that the child develops a sense of autonomy through the mirroring of the self that occurs in relationship to the caregiver (*ID*, 35).[16] The claim that the definitive aim of maturation is the development of autonomy, and that autonomy is primarily focused on developing a sense of one's own wholeness, obscures the primordial import of human interaction. The Lacanian use of the mirror-metaphor fails to do justice to the complexity of the mother's subjectivity in her relation with her child. The Lacanian framework sets her up as a passive prop for the child's developing ego. An awareness of these social forces calls for regrounding the liberal concept of right, so that the moral development of autonomy retreats to a secondary issue in the drama of the social person.

Moreover, specific historical forces (including racial politics) affect the relationship between the mother or other caregivers and the child in ways that are central, and cannot easily accommodate the Lacanian framework that Cornell employs. What does it mean if an underpaid, black day-care worker disciplines a white child from the middle class? How does this woman deal with the racist valorization of white skin in beauty magazines when it comes time to return home to her own children? The Lacanian framework does not readily articulate the distinct economic, quasi-biological, and cultural forces that compose psychic and physiological space. These traversive social forces loom large for those whose economic, cultural, and political projects are routinely violated or otherwise challenged by unfriendly employers, racist mass media, and a biased judicial system. Cornell describes the right to the imaginary domain as guaranteeing a "sanctuary" for the individual to create infinitely varied sexual identities (*ID*, 23, 8). She argues for the need to get the state out of the business of giving form to intimate life (*ID*, 26). The right to the imaginary domain also entails that "states no longer force women to play the role of the primary caretaker in families.... Some women who continue to do so would be freely expressing themselves in an intimate life that is their own" (*ID*, xi).

---

[16] In an exciting footnote to Drucilla Cornell's recent book, *Just Cause* (Lanham, Md.: Rowman and Littlefield, 2000), she states that she would no longer support the Hegelian (and Lacanian) concept of reciprocal symmetry (156 n. 14). In another footnote, she explains her interest in psychoanalytic theory in terms of the "elaboration of psychic laws that are ethically justified in the name of achieving adequate separation and individuation" (156 n. 3). She might view my own project as a bit too close to the movement for the "remoralization" of representations of women and men (15). I see my efforts here more along the lines of reimagining the collective ideals of society, to which she also appeals. So here, too, I think there is only a difference of emphasis, and yet one that I hope adds momentum to the project of a gestalt-switch from bourgeois to social liberalism. Cornell's book is henceforth cited as *JC*.

It is important to support the right of the private individual to create for him or herself an imaginary realm, but this right is not nearly sufficient in an era when the imaginary is inevitably bombarded, indeed, constructed by larger social images and narratives. It is arguably impossible for the individual to create his or her own imaginary domain without the active engagement of others. Many of us are overwhelmed by social forces that restrict our ability to feel what we want to feel, to express our deepest desires, and to hold on to our most precious relationships. Moreover, it is not clear that the legal protection of a private "sanctuary" could provide a realistic barrier against hyper-modern forms of social power, including the impact of television images in the bedroom. For these reasons, Enlightenment liberalism's double focus on two sources of power, the private individual versus the state, is one more modernist binary that needs to be thrown into question (although not by any means eliminated). Clearly, corporate culture respects neither side of the line, situating both individual and state as pawns in more global games of power. The modern liberal state is less in the business of giving form to intimate life than is business. Sexual, racial, and ethnic fantasies of personal life are inhibited or promoted more effectively through economic and electronic resources (including mass culture) than through government regulation in the liberal state. A more effective state needs to check hubristic powers in the marketplace, and lend its support to those of us who are struggling for the resources to define ourselves.

The intractable individualism of the liberal model of the state downplays the ways in which we draw (and need to draw) our sense of who we are from our experiences with each other within a history, and a natural and social environment. We cannot step outside of modern systems of racial and sexual politics into a private sanctuary any more than we can step outside of our skin. Nor do we always want to. Our social practices can drain but they can also sustain our psychic and physical health. They can weaken or strengthen our sense of who we are. It is, as Cornell also so well teaches us, a mistake to postulate some privileged dimension of the self that is immune from the impact of these forces. In order to develop a theory of law that can address head on these nebulous and often conflicting social forces, we need to alter our focus from the individual-in-opposition-to-the-state to the individual-in-relationship within local and transnational systems of economic and cultural power. This altered focus takes us beyond the classic liberal concern for protecting a realm of self-ownership and self-choice, and toward the right of individuals to develop their erotic capacity to relate to others against overwhelming economic, racial, and other dehumanizing social forces.

Michael Lerner has argued that "fetishizing the freedom to choose as our highest goal in life" conspires against humanizing relationships.[17] Sylvia Ann Hewlett and Cornel West expand upon Lerner's admonitions against classic liberalism in *The War Against Parents*.[18] Indeed, they pose a direct challenge to the individual-vs.-state type of liberalism found in Rawls. For Hewlett and West, a liberalism centered on self-fulfillment reflects the narcissism of a consumer-oriented society. They argue that liberalism misses the web of care that sustains social systems. Their first concern is not with the fulfillment of the individual but with the well-being of the family. They argue that "untrammeled choice and uncluttered freedom get in the way of the altruistic, other-directed energy that is the stuff of parenting. The recent liberalization of our divorce laws is a case in point" (*WP*, 94).

According to Hewlett and West, the problem Americans face today is not that there are women who are compelled by the state to serve as mothers for the nation; the problem is that parents fail to receive the support from the state that they need for their families. They cite studies claiming that 85 percent of working women with school-age children feel that "they cannot fulfill their responsibility to their children and work a forty-hour week" (*WP*, 107). The absence of public policy supporting families means that these women need to work in order to help pay the rent and put food on the table. The issue of women's independence from the parenting role may be less significant than the fact that, as Hewlett and West so well argue, "big business, government, and the wider culture have waged a silent war against parents, undermining the work they do" (xiii). "In late-twentieth-century America, parenting has become a countercultural activity" (xii). The failure to support parents pushes up child poverty rates and school drop-out rates. "More and more babies are being born without a skin—with none of that protective armor that in the past was provided by loving parents and supportive communities" (29). "The parent-child bond is the most powerful of all human attachments" (xiv). It is also the basis for establishing the bonds of friendship and compassion that build the infrastructure of society (41). The destruction of this bond means that "entire web of care is breaking down." While Drucilla Cornell argues for the rights of the sexed individual, Hewlett and West propose what they call the parents' bill of rights. It is the social individual and not the classic liberal individual who is the subject of these rights.

---

[17] Michael Lerner, *The Politics of Meaning: Restoring Hope and Possibility in an Age of Cynicism* (Reading, Mass.: Addison-Wesley, 1996), 95.

[18] Sylvia Ann Hewlett and Cornel West, *The War Against Parents* (Boston: Houghton Mifflin, 1998), 96; henceforth cited as *WP*.

The claim is that there is no way that governmental policy does not play a constitutive role in defining the family. Hewlett and West argue that the effect of public policy on the family has been especially visible to African Americans since the Middle Passage. The forced separations and break-up of community that began with slavery were replaced by well-intentioned liberal programs such as the Aid to Families with Dependent Children (AFDC) and the child protective services of foster care. AFDC supported only those families without fathers, leaving many fathers with no option but to leave their families. The foster care system removes children from poor parents instead of supporting the families (*WP*, 123). This is not a small problem. One-third of the men between the ages of twenty-five and thirty-four earn less than the amount necessary to keep a family of four out of poverty (*WP*, 174). This rate is much higher for African-American men. "We rarely recognized how 'welfare,' a set of programs that render men redundant . . . recalls and renews the deep wounds of slavery" (*WP*, 182).

The Parents' Bill of Rights takes the G.I. Bill of Rights as its model. Benefits such as tax breaks, wage increases, day care, and parental leave programs are designed to apply universally to all parents regardless of race, gender, income, and so forth. These programs are to be financed by establishing firm limits on corporate greed. And the Parents' Bill of Rights, like the G.I. Bill, is based on the ethical principle of service to the country (*WP*, 230). Finally, while Cornell argues for maximizing child-care alternatives for the nuclear family, Hewlett and West praise the parenting virtues of "honor and sacrifice" and of biological parents raising their own children (249).

No doubt Hewlett and West are right to urge strong government policies to support families. They are also right to recall biological and libidinal bases for parent-child bonding. These bonds have been assaulted by government policies from slavery to workfare. Perhaps there is no greater pathos than the destruction of the individual through the weakening of family and community relationships. However, Hewlett and West's proposals are not sufficiently critical of the ways in which what they champion as an "ethic of service" might perpetuate the social category of a servant class. The problem with the ethic of service is that not all are guaranteed to serve an equal amount. Just as men of color and working-class white men have performed more than their fair share of military service, so women of color and working-class whites continue to perform a disproportionate share of the so-called honorable but disempowered and unremunerated work of caregiving. Collins astutely draws our attention to ways in which the "paradigm of individual sacrifice" "can border on exploitation" for women. She cites a psychological study of battered black women: "One significant factor in [the] study distinguished Black women from those who were not—almost all of the battered women held privileged positions in their families of origin. As young girls, the African-American women who were battered had seen themselves as important family members, and other family members depended upon them. But although they held high self-esteem and felt powerful, their identities were also wrapped up in pleasing and accommodating the needs of others … [which] left them vulnerable to abuse" (FW, 29–30). Hewlett and West propose to make it more difficult for women to attain a divorce. Women do not need an ethic of sacrifice or a liberal ethics of self-esteem as much as they need a fair share of social power and protections (including full childcare remuneration) for their chosen family roles.

Moreover, Cornell is right to emphasize our need to protect the parenting rights of gays, lesbians, and transsexuals among other rights for the "sexuate being." The heterosexual nuclear family was never more than one model, and not necessarily the best, for raising children. Indeed, the nuclear model of the family evolved alongside the myth that the child is passive, and that rearing the child is not work. Because much creative and exhausting labor is involved in child rearing, one can imagine that children may be better raised through extended sources of care. This extended model of care continues to be a viable model of child rearing in both modern and nonmodern societies. Hewlett and West acknowledge that these extended sources of care in the community are critical for individual well-being. However, they overlook the ways in which various forms of community and extended family relationships can be critical for child rearing. They also overlook the vital right of gay, lesbian, and transsexual individuals to raise children. But then how do we negotiate between a liberal justification of rights for the sexed individual and a communitarian conception of parents' rights? How do we break out of self-oriented individualism without slipping into an ethic of service to family and country?

Irigaray's efforts toward revising the liberal conception of autonomy provides some partial clues for resolving the differences between Cornell's liberalism and Hewlett and West's communitarianism. Irigaray invites us to reroot human subjectivity in our erotic attachment to our mothers. She asks us to practice autonomy as a ritual of reconnection rather than as a game of mastery. But Irigaray is able to make only a partial break from the class-and-race-based systems that she critiques. One doubts that as social animals we will ever find ourselves in a sanctuary outside of interlocking systems of economic and cultural power. Certainly, Irigaray's own racist appeal to the *blanc* flesh in a dream of perfect sympathy leaves white-skin privilege and the wounds of racial arrogance unacknowledged and unchecked. Her exclusive celebration of the mother obscures the debts we owe to the many who labor for the sake of our well-being. How might we go about recognizing the labor that sustains the fabric of our relationships? If African-American women have had a disproportionate share in the sex, care, and other service work in our society, then it is to the theoretical writings from these women that we should turn.

The Visionary Pragmatism of African-American Women: Jazz Freedom

The modern liberal subject is dependent upon a host of caregivers, low-wage and often disenfranchised workers, and social institutions to prop up the private domain of his or her self-determination. Exploited service workers seem to be well within the view of the wealthy middle-class subject, and yet the subject who prizes his or her autonomy acts as though s/he does not see them. No doubt, the liberal ideology of autonomy trains those who dwell at the centers of power not to register certain facts. It trains us not to register the peculiar property of white-skin privilege. It trains us as well to minimize the fact that the modern, liberal subject cannot thrive outside the womb of a disproportionately nonwhite service economy. The knowledge practices of the modern subject are part of a long history of the dissociation of thought, feeling, and action. They are practices that separate reason and care, love and work, and black and white. They are practices that mask the hubris that lies at the center of white capital. In order to understand the nature of this peculiar power, we need to distance ourselves from white norms of knowledge and learn practices of knowledge that are historically nonwhite. From alternative modern cultures emerges a vision of justice that acknowledges the social individual at its core. From these alternative modernisms, I would argue that that focus of rights should not be the self-interested or rational individual, but the individual-in-relationship-with-others. This model of the individual takes us beyond classical liberalism, but short of the classical Marxist emphasis on the economic interests of groups, to the social needs of individuals.

Collins explores differences between black and white practices of knowledge. She explains how Afrocentric and Eurocentric practices emphasize differently the value of oral and visual-print media for constructing knowledge-based communities. For African Americans, "the sound of what is being said is just as important as the words themselves in what is, in a sense, a dialogue of reason and emotion" (*BF*, 216). She explains that "written documents are limited in what they can teach about life and survival in the world. Blacks are quick to ridicule 'educated fools' ... [as those who] have 'book learning' but no 'mother wit'—knowledge, but not wisdom" (*BF*, 208).[19] It is not wisdom to separate poetry, politics, and knowledge. On the contrary, the reassociation of what has been artificially severed is at the heart of wisdom for an oppressed people. Otherwise, that power to oppress goes unseen and unchecked.

For the black women whom Collins has known, wisdom teaches survival through a relentless focus on a future that is free. Collins describes the mother wit of black women as a "visionary pragmatism";[20] she traces the roots of this wisdom to a black tradition of love and justice; she claims both that the roots of this wisdom are black and that its aims are "universalist"; she argues that black women bring a philosophy of both struggle and connection to critical theory; and she argues that the "love and justice" tradition offers an overarching moral framework for modern life that is both individualistic and communal (*FW*, 29, 188). Finally, she compares the love and justice tradition to the musical tradition of jazz: "One effect of this oral mode of discourse is that individuality, rather than being stifled by group activity ... actually flourishes in a group context (*BF*, 99).

The relationship between the love-and-justice tradition and the music of jazz is complex. The oral discourse of freedom in America has been amplified by the expressivity of jazz. Jazz communicates a pattern of sound and a rhythm that can revitalize the individual, tapping into dimensions of the soul that liberal culture does not see or even hear. In her novel *Jazz*, Toni Morrison addresses the connection between music and freedom. The novel contrasts the improvisational style, erotic energy, and group spirit of jazz with two troubling and equally polarized styles of music. Both styles constitute in part black responses to white violence. One style is heard in the sad and stoic and sometimes preachy militancy of drums beating out a rhythm of "fellowship, discipline and transcendence." The other style is heard in the "Hit me but don't quit me" tunes of blues.[21] Morrison's novel fuses feelings of self, ideas of freedom, and musical styles. Her novel warns of the temptation to take on the excessively proud rhythms of self-righteousness just as it warns of the temptation to surrender to bluesy cycles of libidinal explosion and violent rejection, where undercurrents of anger are "disguised ... as ... roaring seduction" (59). The novel also warns against the

---

[19] Collins is quoting from Geneva Smitherman, *Talkin and Testifyin: The Language of Black America* (Boston: Houghton Mifflin, 1977), 76.

[20] But see also Leonard Harris's extensive work in pragmatism, including his edited collection, *The Critical Pragmatism of Alain Locke* (Lanham, Md.: Rowman and Littlefield, 1999).

[21] Toni Morrison, *Jazz* (New York: Knopf, 1992), 59, 60.

uneasy dialectic between these two sensibilities: "Alice [the guardian of the young woman, Dorcas] thought the lowdown music ... had something to do with the silent Black women and men marching down Fifth Avenue to advertise their anger over two hundred dead in east St. Louis" (57). The polemical but interwoven styles turn up throughout Morrison's novels, including, for example, in the differences between the proud and self-righteous Sethe and the blues man, Paul D, and Sethe's failed attempt (like Alice's) at stoic disavowal of this dizzying cycle of passions in *Beloved*. At the end of *Jazz*, the narrator, who is in many ways a jazz spirit, reflects back on the *metamorphosous of desire* in the characters in the novel: "I was so sure ... that the past was an abused record with no choice but to repeat itself. ... I was so sure, [but the characters] danced. ... Busy, they were, busy being original, complicated, changeable—human" (220). The point of jazz improvisation is the erotic freedom of the individual through the reconnection of what the hip, head, and heart know. Earlier Alice had tried "to keep the heart ignorant of the hips and the head in charge of both" (57). In Drucilla Cornell's own fascinating discussion of the novel, she explains that "what Morrison is attempting to represent is not that jazz itself is a threat to Alice Manfred's person. Rather, Morrison's aim in this novel is to articulate the conditions under which jazz is audible" (*JC*, 42). Suppose we continue Cornell's thought by understanding the meaning of jazz in the novel as synonymous with desire. The question is then, under what conditions are one's own desires audible? From here I want to ask, what is meant by the freedom to desire? How does the meaning of freedom tap down into the hip, heart, and head so as to revitalize the social being of the human soul?

In a subtle analysis of the many faces of evil, Roy Martinez exposes the inner recesses of Europe's "rational individual" and calls for philosophers to rethink their definition of the human.[22] While his conclusions teach us much about the alternative modernism that Collins seeks, his beginning point is not slavery but Auschwitz. Martinez recalls that "Auschwitz was clearly and distinctly conceived, meticulously calculated and planned, systematically executed and mellifluously justified by its agents. It does not suffice to dismiss Auschwitz as the product of a reason gone haywire." Repeating the words of Lyotard, Martinez challenges us to think how we modernists might strengthen—not our abstract powers of cognition—but our social bonds: "The question of the social bond, when it is put in political terms has always been raised in the form of a possible interruption of the social bond, which is simply called 'death' in all of its forms:

[22] Roy Martinez, "An Ethic of Compassion in a World of Technique," *Laval Theologique et Philosophique* 54, no. 1 (February 1998): 83–90.

imprisonment, unemployment, repression, hunger, anything you want. Those are all deaths" (90).

Martinez argues that chief among the "countermeasures" to social, moral, and political deaths is the virtue of compassion: "Contrary to the received view, to be human is not determined by the sheer rational distinction of the species, but rather by its ability to share the suffering of others, and its willingness to relieve them of it" (89). Collins takes up the call for compassion in the context of an intersectional analysis of oppression. The multidimensional analysis of power prepares us to incorporate an ethics of the social bond into a concrete and universalist framework for justice.

This framework is designed to challenge forms of oppression that cannot be articulated or addressed in a liberal theory. At the center of this framework lies the moral and legal concern with the kinds of assaults on the soul that McGary analyzes in terms of alienation and that Collins revisits with her intersectional analysis of power.

Collins takes as her starting point what Audre Lorde terms "the power of the erotic." With this term, Lorde offers a materialist analysis of eros that both parallels and differs from the classic Marxist analysis of alienated labor.[23] Marxist analysis has well demonstrated how capitalist modes of production strip the individual of meaningful modes of work in order to increase profits for an elite middle class. In these analyses, work is taken to be a central source of identity in ways in which it may not be for black persons in antiblack societies. As Collins explains, "Work is a contested category" for African Americans. She quotes an urban worker in order to underscore what she sees as "the difference between work as an instrumental activity and work as something for self: 'One very important difference between white people and black people is that white people think you are your work'" (*BF*, 46). African Americans who are alienated from work in white-managed economies and do not see realistic opportunities for non-alienating work may define themselves through social and cultural achievements instead. This is in contrast with many whites, who may identify themselves through their work despite its alienating affects. Perhaps the persistent marginalization of blacks at all levels of the white-dominated market system has enabled blacks to challenge more thoroughly the basis for power and meaning.

Certainly, something like this scenario seems to be implied in Collins and Lorde's various remarks on the "power of the erotic." Rather than focus on the need of the worker to possess or control the conditions or fruits of

---

[23] See also Ann Ferguson's interesting analysis of erotic work in *Blood at the Root* (London: Pandora, 1989).

one's labor, Collins and Lorde focus on the need to reclaim the erotic power that has been "annexed" or "appropriated" by white systems of domination. Lorde develops the thesis in her essay "Uses of the Erotic."[24] She argues that eros is one of many kinds of power, noting that psychic and emotional meanings of power are missed by classic Marxist or liberal analyses of alienation. She also argues that "the principal horror of any system which defines the good in terms of profit rather than in terms of human need, or which defines human need to the exclusion of the psychic and emotional components of that need—the principal horror of such a system is that it robs our work of its erotic value ... and fulfillment" (55). The labor theory of value is based on a recognition of the self in the product of one's labor. Under capitalist (or Marxist) formulations, the individual is defined in large part through his or her labor. At least in theory, labor bequeaths the prize of individual (or collective) ownership. The capitalist (and Marxist) does not really ask for anything more. The aim of Lorde's alternative materialism is to shift the focus of social critique from meaningful productive work (note that here I would include the artistic and intellectual works of the cultivated but lone individual; see Chapter 5) toward meaningful erotic work. Or as Lorde explains, the aim is to "make our lives and the lives of our children richer and more possible" (55).

The power of the erotic is suppressed in white culture. Lorde explains that white cultures reduce eros to sexuality, and channel sexuality into restricted forms of heterosexuality. The dynamic of the erotic, she argues, is naturally expansive; its power is perverted when it is restricted to a single object. Collins adds that this more expansive erotic power emanates from those black women she knew as a child. "There was not the individualized, sexualized, private romantic love currently commodified and marketed by American media, but rather a proclaimed, actively struggled-for, passionate love ethic" (FW, 200). Collins calls this the power of "mother love," and she distinguishes this love from any kind of "natural, instinctual female condition." She explains that the ability to survive oppression has been rooted in these women's love for their (biological or nonbiological) children and their community. She also observes how "the power of intense connectedness and ... caring deeply for someone can foster a revolutionary politics" (FW, 200). Eros is a healing art. It rekindles the ethical bonds of a people in struggle. It is also a political art. It serves as a major catalyst for social change. Eros is a threat to a culture that is based on oppression.

[24] Audre Lorde, *Sister Outsider* (Freedom, Calif.: Crossing Press, 1996), 53–59.

This is because the power of the erotic is a significant source of energy for a social system. At issue is who controls this energy. Lorde observes that "every oppression must corrupt or distort those various sources of power within the culture of the oppressed that can provide energy for change" (53). In "Sexual Politics and Black Women's Relationships," Collins elaborates upon Lorde's thesis by locating it at the core of Toni Morrison's novel *Beloved*. "Freedom from slavery meant not only the absence of capricious masters and endless work but regaining the power to 'love anything you chose,'" Collins writes, citing phrases from Morrison's novel. The characters in the novel "saw that system of oppression function by controlling the 'permission for desire'—in other words, by harnessing the energy of fully human relationships to the exigencies of domination" (BF, 182).

Because erotic power can be a catalyst for social change, it is the direct if unexpressed target of oppressive social systems. "Political economies of domination ... aim to thwart the power as energy available to subordinate groups" (*BF*, 182). "By distorting Sethe's ability to love her children 'proper,' slavery annexed Sethe's power as energy for its own ends" (*BF*, 181).

The racial caste system produces conflicting perceptions of what structures American society. Collins's remarks on these conflicting perceptions help us to see why the power of the erotic is less a biological and more a spiritual and political force for black culture than it is for white culture. She argues that Afrocentric worldviews and the economic conditions of poverty challenge the "radical split equating private with home and public with work" (*BF*, 47). The color line between white capitalist society and the black community marks a more relevant distinction for African Americans, many but not all of whom have been poor. Women-centered networks of "fictive kin" or "othermothers" (i.e., networks missed by Hewlett and West's analysis of parenting) generate shared responsibilities for raising children (*BF*, 119). And as Collins argues, this shared sense of responsibility implies that children have not been viewed primarily in terms of property or ownership in the African-American community (*BF*, 123).[25]

Drawing upon a black literary tradition, Collins makes further connections between the meaning of freedom and relationships based on a black tradition of care (*BF*, 137). She cites Marita Golden, who writes that it was from her son's love that she found more "freedom than any love I had known."[26] Golden describes this experience of freedom as having "expanded" her self. Alice Walker focuses on the significance of the face in re-

---

[25] Collins's source is bell hooks, *From Margin to Center* (Boston: Beacon Press, 1984), 144.
[26] Marita Golden, *Migrations of the Heart* (New York: Ballantine, 1983), 240–241.

lationships of love, and sees the friendly exchange between her self and her child as more sisterly than maternal: "My child loves my face ... as I have loved my own parents' faces.... We are together, my child and I, Mother and child, yes, but sisters really, against whatever denies us all that we are."[27] The asymmetrical power between a mother or othermother and child may foster less a relationship of dependency than a ground for mutual strength and spiritual renewal.

If children and caring adults know each other through the face and its expressions, then it is human expression and not the oral, anal, or phallic organ, not even (as Irigaray supposes) the umbilical cord and placenta, that is the primary vehicle of intimacy. As a consequence of this altered site of human connection, the dynamic of love in the black tradition does not take the same pattern as the dynamic of love in white culture. While Freudian and post-Freudian writers portray love as a threat of immersion, black writers like Lorde and Walker present love as a force for the expansion of the human personality in relationship to others. Eros is most decidedly a primary source for, and not a primitive threat to, subjectivity. Again, Collins explains: "Self is not defined as the increased autonomy gained by separating oneself from others.... Rather than defining the self in opposition to others, the connectedness among individuals provides Black women deeper, more meaningful self-definitions" (*BF*, 105–106).

The implication for political theory is striking. Freedom is not to be defined through the classic individual-versus-state liberal model. This model poses freedom in opposition to constraints on autonomy, and fails to grasp the role of the market and mass culture in our private lives. Certainly, if freedom means to "get to a place where you could love anything you chose," self-determination is important. But more fundamental to social justice than the ability to choose is the ability to sustain human relationships. Freedom's most sublime meaning is eros. As we shall see in the next section, the connection between eros and social justice may elude the categories of liberal and Marxist theories, but this connection has a place in older conceptions of democracy and social justice. For the ancient Greeks, the violation of the bonds of human sociality constitutes what they called hubris. One of crucial ethical functions of law and literature was to establish limits on hubris in order to protect the citizen's significant social and personal relationships. As I will argue, there are strong parallels between what the Greeks called hubris and what black theorists write about racial injustice in modern societies. In order to gain a better understanding of these parallels, we need to

[27] Alice Walker, "One Child of One's Own," *Ms* 8, no. 2 (August 1979): 75.

examine briefly some ancient sources. Among the most informative of these sources is tragic drama.

Hubris and Human Rights

Greek audiences, made up primarily of common laborers and farmers, would have viewed the politics of hubris as central to the meaning of tragic drama. In the *Poetics*, Aristotle gives us some hints about the function of drama in Athenian democracy. However, this elite "outsider-within" Athenian culture (recall that Aristotle was from Macedonia, and was a foreigner in Athens) fails to address what for the ancient Greek *demos* (or people) was central to popular drama, the social crime of hubris.

Aristotle argues that the *pathos*, or terrible suffering, that tragedy unleashes results from *hamartia*, or an error of judgment or character (*Poetics*, 53a10).[28] As Aristotle observes, the tragic hero is described as "one of those people with a great reputation and good fortune, e.g. Oedipus, Thyestes and distinguished men from similar families," which accurately locates the tragic actor among the elite (*Poetics*, 53a10). He argues further that the tragic actor commits an act of violation as the result of "error" rather than "vice and wickedness" (*Poetics*, 53a10). Aristotle turns to the topics of vice and wickedness in the *Nicomachean Ethics*. In the *Ethics*, he locates hubris as the consequence of either vice (as in the arrogance of the rich and powerful, 1124a289; or as in the crimes of one's enemies, 1125a8) or of moral weakness (as found in sexual abusers, 1148b27). Hubris is distinct from, and worse than, mere error. Terence Irwin connects various passages in the *Ethics* with a discussion of hubris in the *Rhetoric* and gleans that "an act of hubris involves attacking or insulting another, but in a special way: so as to cause dishonor and shame to the victim for the agent's pleasure" (*Ethics*, glossary, 432).[29] In the *Politics*, Aristotle observes that if envy is the characteristic vice of the poor, arrogance is the characteristic vice of the rich and powerful (1295a34).

This Macedonian's interpretation of tragedy as an innocent error reflects a skewed elite view of tragic drama. For the common Athenian people (*demos*) of the ancient democracy, *hubris*, and not *hamartia*, would have more likely been

---

[28] Aristotle, *Poetics*, trans. Richard Janko (Indianapolis: Hackett, 1987), 53a10.

[29] Aristotle, *Nicomachean Ethics*, trans. Terence Irwin (Indianapolis: Hackett, 1985); see esp. Irwin's glossary entry for "wanton aggression," which is how he translates hubris (432). Cf. *The Basic Works of Aristotle*, ed. Richard McKeon (New York: Random House, 1941), *Rhetoric*, 1739a1.

recognized as the cause of tragic suffering.[30] The legal system in democratic Athens recognized hubris as a crime of arrogance, punishable by law. And as the famous case of Alcibiades reminds us, hubris is a type of crime that is "characteristic of the young, and/or of the rich and/or of the upper classes."[31] Hubris is a crime of power. The elite protagonists of tragic drama would have been among the paradigmatic instigators of this crime. Under ordinary conditions, hubris was not a crime that could be committed by the subaltern.

Aristotle remarks that tragic error leads to a dialectical reversal of fortune from happiness to unhappiness. The protagonist's error must be revealed in a context in which ignorance leads to knowledge. This knowledge occurs in the climax of the drama, and is defined in terms of a scene of recognition. Aristotle lists the essential elements of this scene of recognition in his discussion of Oedipus and yet he does not lay out in full what for the communal Greek citizens must have been this scene's central importance. He notes that Oedipus comes to realize who he is at the same time that he comes to realize that those he took to be enemies were in fact friends. He observes that tragic violence in general targets "friendly relationships, e.g., brother against brother, son against father, mother against son or son against mother" (*Poetics*, 53b20). These friendly relationships typically center around a household: "the finest tragedies are constructed around a few households" (*Poetics*, 53a19). His location of the cause of tragedy in a simple error does not fully explain the escalating violence that leads to the downfall of the agent. Nor do his brief remarks make clear how such a simple error would bring down in one fell swoop not only the tragic actor and his household, but also a city.

Richard Janko's remarks on the Greek language in his translation of the *Poetics* provide us with some more clues to understanding what is obscured by Aristotle's notion of tragic "error" and abbreviated discussion of "friendly relationships." Janko notes that in the Greek context, friendship, or *philia*, is "much stronger than in English, denoting someone connected by blood, marriage, or the sacred ties of hospitality" (see *Poetics*, glossary entry, 208). For the racist and patriarchal Greek citizen, these ethical ties were certainly neither universalist nor egalitarian. However, both elite and non-elite Greek citizens assumed that the individual does not stand alone but in a web of relationships. Aristotle (writing during the demise of democracy, and near the rise of the Empire) begins to back away from this classic, democratic Greek

---

[30] See Ruby Blondell, Mary-Kay Gamel, Nancy Sorkin Rabinowitz, and Bella Zweig, eds. *Women on the Edge: Four Plays by Euripides* (New York: Routledge, 1999), 19; cf. Josiah Ober, *Mass and Elite in Democratic Athens* (Princeton, N.J.: Princeton University Press, 1989), 162.

[31] N. R. E. Fisher, *Hubris: A Study in the Values of Honour and Shame in Ancient Greece* (Warminster, Eng.: Aris and Philips, 1992), 1.

idea of friendship when he subordinates all other friendships to intimate relationships based on mutual admiration of shared virtues, and an extension of proper self-love (*Ethics*, 1168b, 1171a14). In the *Ethics*, Aristotle discusses the role of political friendship, which probably refers to the broader social friendships of the earlier era (Book 9, Chapter 6). However, he restricts these forms of friendships to those who are "respectable" and excludes the "inferior" class of people (or again, the *demos*).

For the ordinary honor-loving Greek, the individual and his few intimate friends is not the significant unit of political society. The citizen is defined as the head of a household, and the household is defined through its links in the *polis*. It is because the individual is part of the household and a *polis* that an assualt on friendly relationships unravels the social infrastructure of the *polis*, and then returns to destroy the agent. This escalating pattern of violence that brings down one or more cities linked by oaths of friendship, and boomerangs back to destroy the agent, defines the horror of Greek tragedy.

Aristotle's focus on individual error in his discussion of the cathartic poetics of tragedy does not give full due to the ecstatic sociality of the ancient Greek citizen. For the Greek citizen, the knowledge that comes about through tragic suffering is not the reflection of the exiled protagonist on his error. In drama, one learns who one is as one learns of the significance of "friendly relationships." At the center of the tragedy is the assault on these relationships. For this reason, hubris cannot be understood primarily as an excess of judgment or a character flaw. The crime of hubris is not first of all an individual vice or innocent mistake, but an assault on social bonds. It does not only bring down an individual; it destroys a city.

Crimes of hubris violated codes of honor and hospitality among friends and strangers (*xenos*). The horror of these crimes (in large part, the nature of evil) is the abusive pleasure that the powerful enjoy in asserting their superior status over those of lesser status. It is true that the Greeks lacked the modern liberal concept of a negative right, if we understand this kind of right as a restraint against government interference on the private individual (*DA*, 10). The Athenians, however, had available a political tool that liberal democracies lack. The recognition of hubris as a moral and legal crime allowed the working poor and subsistence farmers who made up the masses to establish restraints on the power of elite social groups.

Man is by nature the social animal.[32] Based on this Greek insight, Aristotle argues that the purpose of the city is to promote the good life through various kinds of friendship (*Politics*, 1280b29). Aristotle also argued

---

[32] Aristotle, *Politics*, trans. Ernest Barker (Oxford: Oxford University Press, 1995), 1252b27.

that the law was to prohibit such social vices as hubris (*Ethics*, 1129b25; *Politics*, 1295a34). Aristotle's reflections on Greek democracy teach us much about what is missing in modern systems. But if Aristotle undertakes his *Politics* with a classical Greek vision of the *polis*, he occludes this wisdom from his discussion of tragedy in the *Poetics*. The ironical reversal that defines Greek tragedy is not a mere change in fortune for drama's haphazard protagonist. What for the Greeks must be the major irony (the dialectical reversal) of tragedy is that the crime against the other is a crime against the self. The mythic god or beast might exist alone. Sociality is the element of man. This is tragic wisdom.

Inasmuch as Aristotle occludes from his discussion of tragedy the political and social implications of the Greek theater, and focuses instead on individual character or judgment, he obscures what must have been for the Greek people the essence of social ethics. The dialectic of reversal and recognition in tragic drama is not primarily about excess of character or error of judgment. The virtue of moderation was not primarily about controlling the excessive appetites of the excellent man as portrayed in Arisotle's *Ethics*; in his work on ethics, Aristotle stops short. The ethics of self-control (among other virtues) was practiced for the sake of sustaining "friendly relationships." Tragic drama warns of the ways in which we destroy each other as we destroy ourselves.[33] If tragic art depicts the pathos of hubris, it is so that we may learn how crimes of arrogance tear at the social fabric of our existence.

Eros and Hubris in the African-American Context

The ancient view of justice reemerges in modern African-American contexts. However, modern writers develop the classical themes of eros and hubris from a different origin and toward a different end. Aristotle's practical philosophy reflects the standpoint of the elite outsider within the leisure class of Athenian democracy; it is not clear to what degree the Greek democrats questioned the natural status of the slave. Contemporary critical theory reflects the visionary pragmatism of the outsider within America's racialized service economy. The highest aim of Aristotle's ideal polis was to cultivate the social virtues of the leisure class. Modern writers in America develop ideas of social existence in ways that bear a kinship to ancient Greek

[33] For a discussion of a tragic dialectic of reversal and recognition driven by ecstatic desire, see Cynthia Willett, "Hegel, Antigone, and the Possibility of Ecstatic Dialectic," *Philosophy and Literature* 14, no. 2: 268–283.

themes, holding social bonds to be sacred for justice. However, these writers contest the race-and-class divisions of democracies old and new.

The ideas of social existence developed by these writers carry forward the discussion of eros and hubris through a three-dimensional vision of human identity and social freedom.

First, these conceptions of identity and freedom reach down deep into the power of the erotic at the core of personality. The Western tradition misses the power of the erotic in its speculation on our presubjective origins in "animal-like" appetite. This tradition posits basic drives that are narcissistic or biological but not social. For this tradition, these basic human drives may engulf or consume but they do not respond discretely to the warmth and the touch, the syncopated rhythms and the abrasive tone, the embodied presence of the other. As we shall see in Chapter 9, Morrison evokes the power of the erotic in the sermons of Baby Suggs. "We Flesh," Baby Suggs calls out as she tells of a body that is born not of sin but of an intimacy that may be given or denied. For writers like Lorde and Morrison, the most primordial impulse of eros is not turned inward but outward in an epic quest for human relationship—or wider universality, as the dialectical thinker might say. The draining of erotic energy under conditions of oppression challenges our expressive capacities and blocks the energy for libidinal relationships and social change.

The liberal state protects the religious freedom of the individual, but this liberal right does not suffice for protecting what after Nietzsche we might call free spirit. Religious rituals based on confessing sin or individual responsibility need to give way to state-funded celebrations in the public sphere that rekindle our social energy. At the same time, we must challenge those social practices that appropriate or distort the flow of this energy for the sake of material profit or arrogant power. Firm limits need to be set on corporate greed. Taxes on corporate wealth need to be appropriated in order to support childbearing in households, low-wage labor across national boundaries, and social activities in communities.

Second, these modern writers pose the person as a social event. Hegel misrepresented this event when he stages the inaugural encounter with the other as a threat to the narcissism of the self. Given the premise of originary narcissism, Hegel's dialectic can find no other path for checking the hubristic impulse to dominate except by way of the stoic turn in Hellenistic culture. African-American writers conceive the struggle for recognition differently. Texts emphasize the significance of human expressive and social capacities, focusing on the face-to-face encounter between mother and child. In Morrison's novel, the ghost from the middle passage (also in some sense Sethe's daughter, Beloved) is portrayed as having lost her sense of self as she is separated by the white slave traders from her mother. Beloved expresses the pathos of loss through her yearning for her mother's "face," and she exhibits the symptoms of traumatic separation through her refusal to distinguish her mother's face from her own. In his depiction of slavery, Frederick Douglass focuses on the cruelty of practices that severed families and denied mothers the "intelligent smiles" of their children.[34]

From both these writers, we learn that the distorted representation of the face (e.g., the caricature of the black face in white art) and the displacement of the face (e.g., in the representation of the person as a biological organ) are issues of social justice. Legal or ethical codes need to restrain the arrogant misrepresentation of one group of people by another group of people in sites of public consumption or at work. Mothers, in fact all caregivers, need to be recognized and fully remunerated for their cultural and economic work, and all work must be evaluated in relation to its contribution to our social needs. Rituals of friendship need to join with family rituals as central parts of our political and economic culture.

Third, we learn from these writers how the child might mature through erotic rites of reconnection rather than stoic rituals of separation. For both Douglass and Morrison, cathartic rites of reconnection heal the social and psychic wounds that threaten to tear us apart. Douglass orchestrates the agonistic contest for social recognition as a spirited reply to the hubris of white domination. The violence of the contest is checked by Douglass's desire to re-create the basis for social bonds. Morrison tells a kindred story in *Beloved*. The tormented daughter Denver does not leave behind her family in order to stake out an identity alone or submerged in a larger community. Denver decides who she is as she brings the community back to her family, and together they work against the terrible forces from the past that haunt the present.

In these narratives, Morrison and Douglass give us significant lessons for social justice. If the struggle for freedom collapses into a sacrificial ritual or a politics of retribution and revenge, then justice falters. We must work instead for the spiritual renewal of social bonds. The renewal of these bonds requires confronting economic and cultural debts that hegemonic powers, including modern liberal states, owe for crimes committed in the past that contribute to present wealth and cultural power. In America, one of the worst of these crimes is slavery. Core to white arrogance is the refusal to acknowledge the role of slavery in perpetuating cycles of racial violence in

---

[34] Frederick Douglass, *My Bondage and My Freedom*, ed. William L. Andrews (Urbana: University of Illinois Press, 1987), 39.

contemporary America. This means understanding the high rates of incarceration of blacks in America as just one more chapter in the changing same that begins with the Middle Passage. We cannot begin to overcome racism and other crimes of arrogance in contemporary institutions until we make reparations for social crimes past and present. Basic constitutional laws must protect us against large-scale social practices or persistent acts of arrogance. These laws must secure rights for individuals to claim as the first priority the existential, social, and material resources that they need in order to develop their capacities to form friendships in the family and across social groups and state borders.

For the ancient Greeks, hubris names the violation of the bonds that make up a fully human existence. The crime of hubris can lead to horror. This horror is not easily contained. The veiled consciousness of the perpetrator means that he both knows and does not know the humanity of the one that he assails. Secret pleasure comes from knowing what one is not supposed to know. Power comes from denying what one knows. The Greeks believed that those who have been assaulted would not rest until things were set right. This is what makes for the angst of the privileged classes. The elite create for themselves the terms of their own undoing. The symptoms of this undoing will not disappear until we come together to recognize who we are and where we have been, and make amends.

8
The Genealogy
of Freedom in Slave America
Frederick Douglass

Classic works of social and political philosophy in the Marxian and liberal traditions anchor conceptions of freedom in theories of property and rights of ownership. In classical liberalism, the interest in the individual resides in the right to own property. From this core value came a model and a metaphor for understanding the other rights of citizenship. Modern philosophy even went so far as to borrow from the interest in private ownership a means for conceptualizing moral freedom. Just as the economic agent had free

This chapter was originally written for a volume of essays on African-American thinkers, edited by Lewis Gordon (Blackwell Press, forthcoming). I am grateful to Lewis Gordon for comments on the earlier version. For more recent philosophical essays on Frederick Douglass, see Bill E. Lawson and Frank M. Kirkland, *Frederick Douglass: A Critical Reader* (Oxford: Blackwell Press, 1999).

access to a private realm of property, so too the moral agent had free access to a private domain of mind. In both the political philosophy of the liberal state and the modern metaphysics of morals, the core of individuality would reside in a private sphere of ownership, and freedom would mean autonomy.

Marxian philosophy emerged out of the struggles of the working classes in Europe. This perspective did not see in private ownership the model and metaphor for freedom. Instead Marxists saw that property relations created class-based inequalities. The core value of liberalism divided society into those who owned property and those who did not, compelled those who did not own property into relations of economic dependency upon those who did own property, and made a mockery of freedom. For Marx, freedom from the social and economic alienation of liberalism would require common ownership over all forms of property.

Frederick Douglass (1817–95) wrote in the midst of these modern debates on the meaning of freedom. His numerous writings include three versions of an autobiography (published in 1845, 1855, and 1881), a fictive narrative (1853), and numerous articles for the antislavery newspapers that he edited, *The North Star* (1847), *Frederick Douglass' Paper* (1851), and *Douglass' Monthly* (1859–63). He was a successful orator both in the United States and abroad. His best-known speeches include "What To the Slave Is the Fourth of July?" (1852) and the oft-requested "Self-Made Men" (1866). Later in life, Douglass served as minister to Haiti (1889–91). While Douglass's political philosophy changed over the course of his life, he expropriated the popular theme of the self-made man from liberal philosophies of self-ownership.[1] So, too, Douglass from time to time joined his voice with socialist calls for worker unity against economic dependency.[2] However, his formulations of freedom arose in response to specific experiences of oppression.

Douglass did not occupy the position of the white worker or white property owner in America. His primary interest was not in extending rights of ownership based on the moral attribution of rational self-control. Douglass began his career as writer and public speaker after having escaped from a youth spent in various forms of chattel slavery. By his own account, this youth culminated in an encounter with a slave breaker whose purpose was to break the spirit of rebellious slaves, to whom Douglass had been hired out

[1] Eric J. Sundquist, *To Wake the Nations* (Cambridge: Harvard University Press, 1993), 83–92.
[2] Philip S. Foner, ed., *The Life and Writings of Frederick Douglass*, vols. 1–5 (New York: International Publishers, 1975). See editor's introduction, 3: 14–15, 53–54; henceforth cited as *LW*, followed by volume number. See also Angela Davis, "Unfinished Lecture on Liberation—II," *Philosophy Born of Struggle*, ed. Leonard Harris (Dubuque, Ia.: Kendall/Hunt Publishing Co., 1983), 130–138.

in 1834. Douglass emerged from the encounter victorious, his sense of self well intact. However, this particular encounter served to dramatize what for Douglass must be the central preoccupation of the slave and ex-slave in America. As suggested in an epigraph from Coleridge placed at the front of his second autobiography, *My Bondage and My Freedom* (1855), this central preoccupation evolves around how it might be that "a person is eternally differenced from a thing."[3] It is from thoughts regarding this ontological difference that Douglass probes into the deeper meanings of freedom and bondage.

The significations of freedom and bondage in Douglass's corpus are not singular but multiple, and his political philosophy is not subject to any single or abstract analysis. Douglass believed himself to be the bastard son of a white master and a black slave, Harriet Bailey. He came from Maryland, a southern state bordering the North. He lived during a time when a neo-classical mythos of democratic freedom was intermixed with a quasi-logical defense of modern race-based slavery. It was a time when wealth as measured in terms of number of colored persons could be increased through the sexual-economic productivity of rape. Douglass believed himself to be the offspring of this strange mix. His response to American modernism was likewise mixed, both radical and conciliatory. He did not attempt to extricate himself from the American system and seek a homeland in Africa or in an exclusively black community. Instead, Douglass devoted most of his life to challenging some of the more ghastly contradictions in the American conception of liberty and selfhood. From these challenges to the American system came not only an exposure of the hypocrisies that restrict the range of freedom; Douglass's personal and intellectual struggles against racism and slavery reveal the derivative nature of major European and Euro-American conceptions of freedom. His narrative accounts of these struggles suggest that for Douglass freedom appears only superficially in the mastery that the person exerts over his mental and physical possessions. That is, freedom does not reside primarily in individual or collective forms of ownership or control, and therefore should not be theorized in terms of autonomy. Freedom lives or dies in the relations forged between persons. Throughout his writings Douglass portrays freedom in terms of a social and ethical force that he calls spirit.

That a deeper moral and social vision would come from those who stood further from the sources of power was a principle that Douglass brought

---

[3] Frederick Douglass, *My Bondage and My Freedom* (Urbana: University of Illinois Press, 1987); henceforth cited as *MB*.

with him in modified form from his early alliance with the Garrisonians. These Christian abolitionists believed, as Douglass writes, that "Of all men beneath the sky, the slaves, because most neglected and despised, were nearest and dearest to his [god's] great heart" (*MB*, 216). Sadly, these same abolitionists did not question, in fact perpetuated, one of the underlying dichotomies of oppressive Western cultures, namely, the difference between pathos and logos, or tragic suffering and philosophical representation. For the Garrisonians this meant that the pathos of the slave did not entitle him to represent the moral truth that he embodied. "'Give us the facts,' said the Garrisonian to the slave; 'we will take care of the philosophy'" (*MB*, 220). While Douglass is thought to have been under the powerful sway of the Garrisonians at the time he wrote his first autobiography (1845), ten years later he was poised to challenge the Garrisonians directly. His second autobiography, *My Bondage*, makes clear that for Douglass these white abolitionists lacked the source of moral insight necessary for understanding the deeper layers of freedom. The stigmata of moral education appear, Douglass explains, as a "diploma written on my back" (*MB*, 219). Whatever was operating behind the backs of the Garrisonians, they had not experienced slavery and they lacked the moral authority to represent those who stood "nearest and dearest to [god's] great heart."

Douglass's own spirited break with the Garrisonian abolitionists carries with it a more complicated understanding of moral authority than that which can be found in any simple reading of his philosophical commitment to racial justice or of his personal acquaintance with slave suffering. Douglass not only questions the separation of logos from pathos in abolitionist ethics; throughout his writings, he also casts doubt on any simple opposition between moral authority and power. For Douglass, the moral authority of the slave resides not only in his pathos but simultaneously in the power that the slave musters under extreme conditions of moral challenge. It is this more dialectical notion of moral authority that accounts for Douglass's break with the Garrisonians, and that in fact is exhibited in the spirited challenge to these white men. For the dissociation of logos and pathos in Garrisonian ethics turns upon yet another problematic dichotomy of Christian and modern liberal cultures, namely, the separation of moral and political spheres. The Garrisonians adhered to this separation with the fervor of the extremist. As Douglass explains of Garrison, "The bible was his text book—held sacred, as the word of the Eternal Father—sinless perfection—complete submission to insults and injuries—literal obedience to the injunction, if smitten on one side to turn the other also" (*MB*, 216). For Douglass, the separation of morality from politics bars the abolitionist from using all political means necessary in order to counter the insults and injuries of slavery. This separation also blocks the abolitionist from understanding the ways in which moral force is at its core intermixed with the dynamics of power.

In order to grasp this more fundamental challenge to modern morality in Douglass's writings, we need to examine one of Douglass's more radical claims: "Slave holders," Douglass writes, "have made it almost impossible for the slave to commit any crime, known either to the laws of God or to the laws of man. If he steals, he takes his own; if he kills his master, he imitates only the heroes of the revolution. Slave holders I hold to be individually and collectively responsible for all the evils which grow out of the horrid relation.... Make a man a slave, and you rob him of moral responsibility" (*MB*, 119).

If slave ethics exceeds the normal bounds of "moral responsibility," if the slave cannot be held "accountable" before the laws of man and God for the mediating violence of ethical practice, this moral madness is not criminal but "heroic" (cf. *MB*, 119). The none-too-clear distinction between the criminal and the heroic is critical for a transformative political ethics. This distinction also reverberates through old-world sources of wisdom. Crimes of power were called *hubris* in ancient Greece.[4] These crimes were "many-formed" (*polymeres*). But they were also thought to include the most horrifying forms of injustice, and to lead to revolts and revolutions (*stasis*). Those who carried out acts of revenge against the hubris of their oppressors were not thought themselves to have committed an act of hubris. On the contrary, "the *hybris* of the responding party is ... justified, and not 'really' *hybris* at all" (*H*, 250). Of course, the masters will argue differently, but the people (*demos*) will know that they are wrong.

After having laid the foundation for a slave ethics in violence, Douglass discusses the moral character of that type of slave holder represented by one of his masters, Captain Thomas Auld. "I thought him incapable of a noble action," Douglass writes. "The leading trait in his character was intense selfishness.... Capt. Auld was not a *born* slave holder—not a birthright member of the slave holding oligarchy. He was only a slave holder by *marriage-right*," an "accidental slave holder" (*MB*, 119, 120). "There was in him all the love of domination.... He could be cruel; but his methods of showing it were cowardly, and evinced his meanness rather than his spirit" (119).

So, too, in the ancient world the people were said to be wary of those who claimed to be their just rulers. The ruling classes were known to

---

[4] N. R. E. Fisher, *Hybris: A Study in the Values of Honour and Shame in Ancient Greece* (Warminster, Eng.: Aris and Phillips, 1992), 26–28, 250; henceforth cited as *H*.

develop peculiar habits at the expense of the ruled. Among these habits was the tendency to indulge in acts of humiliation and cruelty for the sake of pleasure as well as profit (*H*, 26). As one scholar writes, "Hybris is revealed above all in the selfish, shaming enjoyment of pleasures, in the exercise of one's own power and the enjoyment of one's superiority" (*H*, 31). The crimes of the master were often directed toward sensual enjoyment, but in any case mixed oblique forms of erotic enjoyment with the display of power (*H*, 29–31). It is this peculiar mix that defines their cruelty.

The slave who rebelled against "all law known to man and god" (to all law known to the white owner and to his god) could also be cruel. Aristotle warns of those who avenge acts of hubris against either themselves or against those for whom they happen to care. "Those attacking because of their anger (*thymos*) do not spare themselves in their behaviour, as Heracleitos observed, saying that it was difficult to fight with *thymos*, since it bought its wish with its life."[5]

The cruelty of the rebel slave, however, had a limit and a just purpose. The terms that Douglass uses to describe the outraged slave are strikingly similar to those used to describe the "natural slave holder." The rebel slave, as Douglass writes about himself, was one possessed by a "daring spirit," that is, one who would do battle to the end, "heedless of consequences" (*MB*, 149). Only a few pages earlier in the book, Douglass had described with some admiration that "generous, dashing slave holder [his white father?], who is fearless of consequences" (*MB*, 120). The implication is that the moral madness of the rebel slave may make him cruel, but it does not, apparently, make him mean. That is, the slave who rebels against his unnatural condition bears a kinship with that white man who is a "whole-souled" enslaver. His methods evince the requisite spirit for revolutionary fervor.

Naturally, the slave despises the "assumed attitudes of the accidental slave holder." Indeed, Douglass is quick to add, the slave cannot respect any kind of slaveholder. Still, Douglass does portray the heroic slave in terms that recall a political mythology that was familiar to white slaveholders. According to the myth, the warrior establishes a claim to moral authority over the slave through victorious battle. Southern culture had long perpetuated this classical mythology of conquest over an inferior race in order to establish its right to slavery. When Douglass portrays the rebel slave as more authentic, that is, more authentically daring or spirited than the cowardly slave holder, he is stealing the grounds to authority right out from under the feet of his master. But if he steals, he takes his own. If there is to be domination, it is the

[5] This fragment of Heraclitus (fr. 85DK) is quoted from Aristotle's *Politics* (1315a14–31) in *H*, 30.

rebel slave and not the accidental slaveholder who merits the privileged place. In any case, the glorification of the angry spirit of the warrior appeared to be the only realistic option in a political system that would not recognize black manhood except through the mask of criminality. The slave lives, as Douglass writes, "in an enemy's land" (*MB*, 206). This is not a situation that is conducive to white Christian principles of good neighborliness.

The African-American experience of living in the enemy's land did on occasion approximate and draw from the Jewish experience of exile. However, the black history of bondage and freedom is different. While the Jewish diaspora would give rise to what Levinas in mid-twentieth century conceptualizes as an ethics of "hospitality towards the stranger," Douglass's experience of segregation and moral distance as an ex-slave in the North led him to challenge directly the position of the social outcast within American society. Douglass did not cope with alienation by separating himself from white society; he countered alienation by usurping parts of white culture almost as though by right of conquest. His comparison of the rebel slave with the natural-born slaveholder is a case in point. But something deeper was at stake in Douglass's war against an unnatural domination. The object of this war was not conquest in a foreign land. In his telling and retelling of his own life story to a largely white audience, Douglass was demanding the kind of "practical recognition" (*LW*, 2:361) that one might expect to enjoy in a place that one called "home" (*MB*, 206).

Indeed, as William Andrews suggests, Douglass's experience of racial exclusion and isolation in the North leads him away from nineteenth-century themes of the self-reliant individual and toward a reconceptualization of freedom through the metaphor of the home (see editor's introduction in *MB*, xi–xxviii). The warm, communal virtues of home and the values of cultivating the personal, ethical, and spiritual dimensions of the self were also part of the nineteenth century's romantic movement and therefore a part of European and Euro-American culture. In fact, these values associated with the home were used against the economic and social nightmares of what the industrializing eighteenth century had valorized as the public sphere. But while the intimate social and psychological values of home would provide a comfortable metaphor for nineteenth-century revisions of moral truth, the experience and significance of the home for blacks born in slavery contrasts sharply with the nostalgia for a pre-industrial home in white culture.

For whites, the home signified a place of private retreat or moral virtue protected from the sublimated warfare of the workplace. This image of home culminated in the nineteenth-century cult of white womanhood, which made for "idols," not "wives," Douglass observes, as he tells how the white master prefers the company of the slave (*MB*, 42). So while Douglass's experience of isolation in the North led him to see that to be "free from home" is not freedom, the meaning of this metaphor of the home is not taken, so to speak, from the house of the white master. Douglass does not understand what he calls home in terms of the sentimental care of the idealized white mother. The home that Douglass has deepest in mind stems from his early memories with his black grandmother, associations that he developed in the second autobiography. From these early associations, Douglass projects a vision of home and a philosophy of freedom that cross humanist with antihumanist themes in a mixture that does not fit into the normal categories of the nineteenth-century Euro-American imagination.

Douglass's autobiographical rendering of the significance of home and his political philosophy of freedom come together quite forcefully in the aptly titled second autobiography. Douglass draws from his personal story, not an allegory for the first principles of freedom, but a lived knowledge for what he argues had become in white America overly theoretical and abstract (cf. *LW*, 2:361). In fact, for Douglass, freedom is not to be represented in the form of an abstract principle or theory at all. If Douglass's first autobiography had emphasized the role of literacy in liberating Douglass from the mentality of the slave, *My Bondage* makes it clear that it is not from books, principles, or dialogues on the nature of liberty taken from the house of the master that Douglass understands what he calls the "veriest freedom" (*MB*, 85, 32). The more originary experience of freedom Douglass knows already as a young child in the home of his grandmother.

The home that Douglass knew as a young child did not, as did the white home in nineteenth-century white imaginary, provide a partial refuge from the horrors of the capitalist workplace. The black home provided a partial refuge from white society. For white America, the private domain of domesticity was born of the antinomies of European modernism. This modernism opposed a female sphere of moral sentiment to the active sphere of male contest. As a major European philosopher of nineteenth-century Romanticism, Hegel aimed to bridge these divisions. He used his dialectical conception of philosophical method to bring together the moral claims of the female sphere and the public sphere of men, and to rename freedom spirit. The Hegelian philosophy of freedom did not question the traditional assumption that spiritual progress would require as a necessary stage the dialectical negation of the female domain of feeling and intimate connection. According to that assumption, boys must leave home and everything that home represents in order to become men. For Hegel, the agonistic individualism that was valorized in the marketplace, in manhood, and in modernist philosophies would give way to a sense of belonging to something larger than oneself. And for Hegel, this homeland larger than the self was the bourgeois German state. Freedom signified belonging to a homeland that was held together through the consensus politics of a universal and rational will.

For Douglass, the claim to black manhood invokes a different dialectic with a different origin and a different goal. Like many slaves, Douglass was separated very early from his biological mother. He was, however, more fortunate than many slave orphans. While many slave children were raised by strangers, Douglass was raised by a grandmother and an extended family. Douglass characterizes this difference in terms of a family ethics: "Being [among] the children of my grandmother's daughters, the notions of family, and the reciprocal duties and benefits of the relation, had a better chance of being understood than where children are placed—as they often are—in the hands of strangers, who have no care for them, apart for the wishes of their masters" (*MB*, 3). *My Bondage* uses this family ethics in order to lay the groundwork for a revolutionary politics.

The extended discussion of his childhood sets up sharp contrasts between the ethics of the white family and the black. While the idealized white mother was to exemplify the soft and protective virtues of care, Douglass's equally idealized black grandmother mixed these more tender traits with virtues that were associated with manliness. "She was a good nurse," Douglass writes, "and a capital hand at making nets for catching shad and herring"; she was also "somewhat famous for her good fortune in taking the fishes" (*MB*, 28). The transformed virtues of the woman as huntress did not produce children who were either soft and sentimental or restrained and rational. It also did not produce children who were unrestrained and mean. The white boy, Douglass observes, is pampered by nurses who give "lectures on propriety of behavior"; they are made to "recite pretty little verses ... from the nursery" and "swallow pretty little sugar-coated pills, to cleanse his blood" (*MB*, 32). The suggestion is that white family practices strip both women and boys of their strength and courage. In contrast, Grandma Betsey Baily is described as "a woman of power and spirit." She is as her stature, "marvelously straight in figure, elastic, and muscular" (35). And it is these same traits that she cultivates in her little boy. Douglass testifies to the results: "Freed from all restraint, the slave-boy can be ... a genuine boy, doing whatever his boyish nature suggests; enacting, by turns, all the strange antics and freaks of horses, dogs, pigs, and barn-door fowls, without in any manner compromising his dignity" (31). A boy so raised, Douglass comments, "cries but little, for nobody cares for his crying; learns to esteem his bruises but slight, because others so esteem them. In a word, he is, for the most part of the first eight years of his life, a spirited, joyous, uproarious and happy boy" (32).

In many conceptions of male identity formation, little boys become men through rituals of separation from the mother and her spiritless domain of domesticity. The biological mother, like the womb from which the boy supposes that he comes, signifies in the modernist fantasy both the comforts of belonging to something larger than the self and the dangers of submerged identity. Manhood and moral maturity entail disciplining the pleasure-loving desires of the child according to the abstract and individualistic principles of the rational will. In the gender-divided world of the nineteenth century, boys have been expected to master these principles of restraint and discipline from fathers who lay down the law.

Black children born into slavery were not only separated from their mothers very early on; they often did not even know their mothers. Their caregivers would not have been so readily associated with the omnipresent comforts of the womb. It was even less likely that they knew a law-giving father. "Genealogical trees," Douglass observed, "do not flourish among slaves. A person of some consequence here in the north, sometimes designated *father*, is literally abolished in slave law and slave practice" (*MB*, 28). Douglass did not live his childhood under the sentimental care of a biological mother or the rational will of the distant father. His autobiography does not relate a story about a boy who becomes a man through a dialectic of separation from the mother and initiation into the law-bound society of the father. The consequence for Douglass's conception of self is striking. For even as a young child of seven or eight years of age and still under the care of his grandmother, Douglass reports that he felt himself to be a "man" (35). Indeed, it was not until he left his black family that he became what the white master would call a boy.

In slave society separation from the mother signifies something very different than it does in patriarchal European and non-European societies. Douglass points toward this difference when he wrote that "the practice of separating children from their mothers ... is a marked feature of the cruelty and barbarity of the slave system. But it is in harmony with the grand aim of slavery, which, always, and everywhere, is to reduce man to a level with the brute" (29). In sharp contrast with the ethical practices and psychological symbols of identity formation in many patriarchal cultures, the Douglass autobiography demonstrates that the separation of the child from the "joyous circle" of the maternal family, and the subsequent relocation of the boy to the realm of the distant white father, does not make the man; it threatens to break him.

Slavery destroys freedom not only through the physical, economic, and legal mechanisms that would force men and women to serve as domesticated animals, as chattel slaves; slave holders who were outnumbered by their slaves would also rely upon psychological mechanisms to ensure their domination. The aim of these mechanisms was to undermine the psyche of the slave in a process that Douglass describes as spirit-breaking. A primary strategy for breaking the slave was to sunder him from family and friends. It is this strategy that Douglass came to articulate more fully in his second autobiography. A second strategy, and one that was already central in the first autobiography, involved subjecting the slave to hard labor. When the two strategies are woven together as part of a single narrative, as they are in the second autobiography, they serve not only as an extensive commentary on the spirit-breaking tactics inflicted by whites on blacks in slave society; this larger narrative also exposes the pathologies of character formation in many patriarchal cultures.

In modern culture, separation from the sentient bonds of the family gives way to the formation of the rational will and the necessary discipline for entry into the working world. The dialectic of separation and discipline constructs the conventional poles of white manhood. The goal of manhood is autonomy. Significantly, a variation of the dialectic for identity formation in white America reappears with a vengeance in the (de)formation of the slave. In the slave world, separation from the ethos of the family prepares for the disciplinary practices of slave labor. It is as though the white man makes the black man perform white manhood but in an extreme form.

What Douglass knew well by the time of his second autobiography is that the remedy for oppression does not lie in white conceptions of manhood or freedom. If the black man is to overcome the insults and injuries inflicted by white racism, he must turn away from the abstract norms of identity formation in white society and summon from the black family an ethics of spirit.

The narrative indicates the significance of this alternative ethics by subordinating (but not excluding) Douglass's achievement of literacy in the European alphabet and related exercises in abstraction to alternative processes of spiritual growth. While early and final chapters of the narrative emphasize the values of home for Douglass's conception of freedom, the plot attains its climax and the dialectic its moments of reversal and recognition in Douglass's confrontation with the slave breaker. And, not surprising, this "manly" encounter does not reinforce themes of separation from the maternal sphere. On the contrary, the encounter reinvokes the spirit that Douglass knew already as a young child in the home of his grandmother.

The event with the slave breaker occurred when Douglass was an adolescent, well after his separation from his grandmother and what he described as his "gradual initiation into the mysteries" of the slave masters, beginning with the "almost fatherly" Captain Anthony (*MB*, 54). This separation from attachments and initiation into mysteries took the form of what for Douglass was a "law which I can clearly comprehend, but cannot evade nor resist" (128). The dialectic of separation from family and friends and subjection to labor repeats with ever greater fury. After leaving Captain Anthony's house, Douglass was passed to a family in Baltimore, where he learned to read and write. Finally, he ended up in the hands of Captain Auld. His inclination to defend himself against false accusations as well as his endeavor to impart instruction to his fellow slaves provoked the fear that he was another Nat Turner. Douglass did not deny the charge. In response to such "impudence," Auld declared that Douglass needed to be taught a lesson, to render a "visible improvement" in his "character" (125–126). Thus Douglass was to be "put ... out—as he said—'to be broken'" (126).

The man to undertake this special education was Mr. Edward Covey, a known slave breaker. As Douglass observed, the techniques of education used to break the slave do not differ from those used to tame a wild horse or ox. The combination of intense labor and harsh discipline reach their intended effect for the man as for the ox when the animal is rendered "tame and docile" (*MB*, 132). Danger stems from the animal that knows the cruelty of the master but has not been subjected to sufficient discipline for full submission: "The ox is the most sullen and intractable of animals when but half broken to the yoke" (132). "I was somewhat unmanageable when I first went there," Douglass continues, "but a few months of this discipline tamed me. Mr. Covey succeeded in breaking me. I was broken in body, soul and spirit.... Behold a man transformed into a brute!" (136).

Covey's methods for breaking the will are one variation among a classic repertoire. The particular variation used by Covey does not rely on humiliation, psychosexual acts of violation, or even, as Douglass noted, the sadism of the lash: "Frequent as the lash was used, Mr. Covey thought less of it, as a means of breaking down my spirit, than that of hard and long continued labor" (133). The technique is basic, lacking the sociopsychological dimensions of more sophisticated forms of cruelty. The critical element is power. As the tormenter, Covey must make known his total power over his victim. For Douglass this means that he was "but the sport of a power which takes no account, either of my welfare or my happiness" (128). The tormenter assigns tasks that are nearly impossible and then punishes failure with the "savage fierceness of a wolf" (133). The tormenter's rough manner of address, together with a cold and distant demeanor, forbids any expression of reasonable complaint or moral plea. "When [the tormenter] spoke, it was from the corner of his mouth, and in a sort of light growl, like a dog, when an attempt is made to take a bone from him" (131). The slave breaker's methods of surveillance subject the victim to total fear: "He would creep and crawl, in ditches and gullies; hide behind stumps and bushes, and practice so much of the cunning of the serpent, that [his slaves called him] *'the snake'*" (134). The relation between tormentor and victim is like that between predator and prey. There is no intersubjective space in which one could anchor an ethical appeal. The aim is to drain the psyche of the slave and render him like the thing devoid of self.

The particular circumstances of Douglass's own situation, however, enabled him to regenerate the forces that he needed in order to regain his soul. It was not that Covey's tactics failed to achieve their intended aim. Douglass reports that after half a year with Covey, he was essentially dead inside, moved only by whatever Covey might command. He was able to pull himself away from Covey's control only after an incident that allowed Douglass to regain his strength and perspective,

At the time, Douglass was sick with a fever, yet was ordered to complete a task that was beyond his power in his weakened state. He made every effort to carry out the task but could not. Despite this effort, Covey punished Douglass for his failure. The pitiful slave ran away and pleaded for the protection of his master, Captain Auld. Auld showed little mercy and ordered Douglass to return to Covey. On his return, Douglass recuperated with the help of a superstitious slave named Sandy. She gave Douglass a root for magical protection before Douglass turned himself over to Covey. It was a Sunday, and Douglass found an apparently devout Covey preoccupied with church services.

Douglass, however, was not spared a second beating. The day after his return, Covey grabbed Douglass in order to tie him down. It was at this point that Douglass underwent the fundamental transformation: "I now forgot my *roots*, and remembered my pledge to *stand up in my own defense*" (*MB*, 149). The roots that Douglass severed were not only to the all-too-distant gods of black or white religions but also to the patriarchs who were to protect the slaves as their own children. Douglass jumped back and freed himself from the rope. The power of his initial success encouraged him forward: "Whence came the daring spirit necessary to grapple with a man who, eight-and-forty hours before, could, with his slightest word have made me tremble like a leaf in a storm, I do not know; at any rate, ... the fighting madness had come upon me" (149). The broken-down slave regenerated a sense of self, not through abstract exercises of self-restraint, but through a fighting mania. "I felt as supple as a cat, and was ready for the snakish creature at every turn" (149). Like the predatory cat, Douglass began by playing with his intended prey. Eventually, he drew blood and Covey signaled defeat.

Douglass described the "effect of this combat on my spirit" as the "turning point in my 'life as a slave.' ... I was nothing before; I was a man now. It recalled to life my crushed self-respect ... and inspired me with a renewed determination to be a freeman. A man, without force, is without the essential dignity of humanity. Human nature is so constituted, that it cannot honor a helpless man, although it can pity him; and even this it cannot do long, if the signs of power do not arise" (151).

The slave breaker's technique of breaking the slave is in this variation based solely on a dynamic of power. Douglass had been separated from family and friends and forced to work under extreme conditions of discipline and labor. Like other techniques in race-based oppression, this technique aims to crush the spirit. Its remedy cannot be found in the hands of the master. It is only when Douglass broke from the punitive lawgiver and regenerated the power and the spirit of the huntress—the spirit that he first knew from his grandmother—that he was able to transform himself from property to person.

Significantly, the violence required for the slave's self-assertion before the slave breaker does not simply reverse the roles of predator and prey. When Covey signaled defeat, Douglass stopped the fight. Douglass found himself transformed into a man only because he exerted the requisite force to command a sense of "honor" from the slave breaker. The use of violence was, on this occasion, not criminal but mediating and good. It opened the space for intersubjective exchange that had been closed by the hubris of slavery. Douglass is keen to point out that after the fight Covey showed signs of respect that were previously denied.

For Douglass the transformations did not stop with his victory over the slave breaker in the South. Not long after the encounter, Douglass escaped to the North, where he discovers not freedom but new forms of bondage. "I was soon taught," he writes, "that I was still in an enemy's land. A sense of loneliness and insecurity oppressed me badly" (*MB*, 206). "I was not only free from slavery, but I was free from home, as well" (207). He found a path out of this new form of bondage in his travels to England, where "the warm and generous cooperation" of friends lend him "new life" (225). In fact this warm and generous ethos defined the general atmosphere: "I gaze around in vain for one who will question my equal humanity, claim me as his slave, or offer me an insult. I employ a cab—I am seated beside white people—I reach the hotel—I enter the same door—I am shown the parlor—I dine at the same table—and no one is offended. No delicate nose grows deformed in my presence" (226). If Douglass had earlier decided that the "love of domination" is natural (119), he is also sure that domination is not. All persons, he declares, whether they be black or white, English or American, are down deep "lovers of republicanism" (230). Therefore, Douglass decided to resist the temptation to leave America permanently, or, as he writes, to "allow myself to address Englishmen as against Americans. I took my stand on the high ground of human brotherhood.... Slavery is a crime ... against ... all the members of the human family; and it belongs to the whole human family to seek its suppression" (231).

In many philosophies, the ethical value of the home signifies the comforts of fusion or the politics of identity. As a consequence of these associations, the use of the metaphor of home in modern dialectics of freedom have produced communities or states based on various forms of exclusion. Douglass did not seek a home for those only of his own kind. Douglass sought a home for the extended family of humankind. In this home the spirit will thrive. For Douglass, this is freedom.

9

Narratives of Hubris, Songs of Love

Toni Morrison's Beloved

"For they understood the source of the outrage as well as they knew the source of light."

Beloved

Untouchable Hamlet

" 'The greatest poem of the millennium?' It is no betrayal of the lyric if I name 'Hamlet,' a work as lyric as it is dramatic."[1] So writes literary scholar Helen Vendler as she looks back over the last thousand years of Western history. Quoting from Shakespeare's early seventeenth-century play, she explains: "'Bloody, and unnatural acts, /... accidental judgments,

I am deeply grateful for the rich and insightful conversations (and much exchanging of papers) on Morrison and especially the novel *Beloved* with Barbara Andrew, Amy Coplan, and Pam Hall.

[1] Helen Vendler, "Hamlet Alone: A Celebration of Skepticism," *New York Times Magazine*, April 18, 1999, p. 123. There are many other rich interpretations of the play, some of which might better reflect the historical context than does the modern existentialist reading that Vendler gives. However, Vendler's reading sets up a fascinating contrast between a modernist Hamlet and Morrison's tragic runaway slave in *Beloved*.

[and] casual slaughters' make up the linear plot, but its lyric structure gives us ... Hamlet's high consciousness, tragic and mocking ... over the dramatic action. Though the dramatic Hamlet is provoked by a murder, the lyric Hamlet is moved by all deaths.... Hamlet believes only in death."

Through its "repudiation" of a Christian afterlife, "*Hamlet* marks the philosophical turning point of our Western millennium," Vendler claims. The "reflective loneliness" of Hamlet's "lyric consciousness" replaces the redemptive narrative of Christianity. But this lyric consciousness also replaces drama's classical focus on action and dialogue, she continues. Among Shakespeare's greatest plays, only in *Hamlet* does the single lyric consciousness rule the stage. Other characters in the play do not engage the protagonist in significant verbal or physical exchange. They serve instead as occasions for Hamlet's soliloquies on an abstract and existential question about the self, the question of "'To be or not to be.'"

According to Vendler's existentialist interpretation, the themes and structure of the play set the stage for modern revolutionary times. The death of god and the fall of the feudal system abandon modern man to his own freedom. Images of tragic isolation elicit themes of modern liberation. The "omnivorous worm" that Hamlet contemplates in his soliloquies recalls the bare and liberating truth that "everything human comes to death." Indeed, as Vendler observes, citing lines from the play, "Even the flesh of a king 'may go a progress through the guts of a beggar.' The specter of finality— the omnivorous worm—levels social hierarchies and foments demands for political equality."

The specter of finality also shapes the modern experience of time. "As the deathblow repeats itself in the fortune of each main character," the redemptive and communal meanings that sustain conventional narrative or plot movement are out of joint. This recursive structure characterizes lyricism— more so than drama, Vendler contends. Repetition liberates man from the linear plot of Christianity without returning him to more ancient enactments of sacred law and communal justice. Modern man is free save for death. The end of man is after all just the end of man. There is no more. Death returns man to the abyss from which he has, or imagines that he has, come.

There is, however, more of a story to the "unnatural acts" and "accidental judgments" of modernism than the existential lyric allows. The European prince and his lyrical followers enter into modernity with the privileges and burdens of massive social and economic inheritances. Narratives of colonization and slavery, neocolonization and world monetary policies, recede from the self-reflections of the lyric mind. Untold crimes barely register on the modern consciousness. Still, one wonders if a liminal awareness of modernism's high crimes might not add some element to the ill-defined fear, the angst as the existentialists write, that defines the quintessential mood of the modern subject. Could the subject's failure to register the horror at the periphery of power be total?

"We Flesh"

But then I, too, wonder what is to be called the greatest poem of the millennium.[2] Sometimes the deeper lyricism grows out of the wider vision. In 1993, Toni Morrison became the first African American and the first black woman to receive the Nobel Prize for literature. Her most celebrated novel, *Beloved*, was published in 1987 and was awarded the Pulitzer Prize. Like the earliest of the ancient tragedians, Morrison intends for the tragic tale to be read as part of a trilogy. This trilogy began with *Beloved* and was followed by two more novels: *Jazz* (1992) and *Paradise* (1998). While each of the three novels offers classic elements of reconciliation and catharsis, the haunting lyricism of the trilogy's first novel calls to mind the more bleak reflections of Shakespeare's existential play. In both *Beloved* and *Hamlet*, specters of death elicit tragic songs of loneliness and disjointed tales of murder and revenge. However, if *Hamlet* marks the philosophical turning point of the European subject, perhaps *Beloved* takes us further than ourselves. The bleak and broken narrative of *Beloved* does not collapse into endless images of self-reflection and existential isolation. *Beloved* expresses a more centrifugal force. The novel begins its cathartic song with an epigraph from the ancient text of Romans: "I will call them my people, which were not my people." It proceeds to spin a tale of modernity that weaves across continents and centuries.[3]

The specter of *Hamlet*—the ghost named Hamlet—forges a link between freedom and death in the modern mind. The ghost does not come forth to alert the son to the injustice of his father's death, or at least not on the modern stage. On this modern stage, the ghost serves as an occasion for man to reflect upon the empty ground of his own soul. Death isolates the modern subject. An encounter with death severs the subject from extended sources of meaning, in history, spirituality, and human sociality. It frees the individual to reign supreme over what he names his own.

---

[2] Charles W. Mills develops an analogous contrast between Cartesian and African-American traditions of philosophy in *Blackness Visible: Essays on Philosophy and Race* (Ithaca: Cornell University Press, 1998), Chapter 1.

[3] Toni Morrison, *Beloved* (New York: Alfred A. Knopf, 1987).

The ghost of *Beloved*, also called Beloved, is more difficult to identify. She is the murdered daughter of the fugitive slave, Sethe; but she is also an apparition from those "Sixty Million and more" who were lost in the Middle Passage. The ghost of *Beloved* does not function to engage Sethe in reflections on the ontological loneliness of one's own most soul. The apparition brings back to the stoic Sethe memories of unnatural loss and forgotten dimensions of the self. There are memories of her mother and stories of her people from Africa. But these memories are not only personal; they are also part of unwritten history. Morrison's narrative does not allow the reader to dismiss the ghost as an image from the inner recesses of Sethe's troubled mind. The ghost from the Middle Passage is part projection, but she is also part real. The modern world is haunted by ghosts from earlier times. The world holds memories from events that predate our birth and that exceed our ability to comprehend. These events turn on pivotal encounters of our ancestors, and their blurred meaning reverberates in present time. The historical past—and, sometimes too, the events that were not to be recorded in official archives—brings dimensions of meaning to the cultural and political climate of the present. Through these meanings, the soul extends outward beyond itself and its time. This soul is missing in Shakespeare's modern play. Hamlet's ghost dismantles what *Beloved*'s ghost will not let go: the intimate folds of social space and the woven time of our ancestral past.[4]

The novel warns against the isolation of the self. The novel also warns of the temptation to lose the self in the other. Both the isolated consciousness and the displaced self are examples of lost souls in the modern world. These are souls incapable of respecting the limits that sustain the bonds of social eros. *Beloved* is a story about the bonds of social eros and their limits.

The temptation of the modern mind is to find freedom in isolation, and then to seek release from freedom's loneliness through submersion in another. This is the paradox of modern freedom. *Beloved* tells a different story about freedom.[5] The vision of freedom in the novel carries us past the metaphysics

[4] The ghost functions like the "thought pictures" that Sethe also encounters when she "bumps into a rememory that belongs to somebody else" (36).

[5] In "Love's Ghosts: The Impossible Specter of Love without Freedom" (a work in progress), Barbara S. Andrew presents an especially convincing revision of the modern paradox that freedom leaves one lonely. She argues that "as opposing moral forces, love and freedom set up a paradox: it is not possible to love and to be completely free, and yet, it is only possible to love if one is free, and to be free if one loves." She develops the paradox in her reading of *Beloved*. My interpretation of the novel starts right out by redefining the meaning of freedom so that it is consistent with the needs of the social individual. I argue that autonomy is a means to this higher end of freedom.

of the modern European subject; it expands the soul beyond the domain of its autonomy to the desires of the self-in-relationship-with-the-other.

Baby Suggs, Beloved's grandmother and the "unchurched preacher" of her people, gives us a glimpse into this wider vision of freedom in her sermon at the Clearing. She opens her sermon by calling out to the children: "'Let your mother hear you laugh,' she told them, and the woods rang" (87). Freedom starts that way. Freedom is also the vision that prompts Paul D to stop running from relationships, and to return to Sethe and to her home: "To get to a place where you could love anything you chose ... *that* was freedom" (162). Freedom means something more than the ability to choose for oneself. More fundamental than the ability to choose is the ability to desire. It is the erotic quality and the social relation—social eros—that makes us free, and it is this theme that I explore in Morrison's novel.

In order to explore freedom's deeper meanings, we will need to engage a philosophical anthropology whose elements draw from diverse sources. Among these sources are scientific research into the social life of infants, dialectical conceptions of alienation and recognition, and post-Freudian theories of libidinal drive and unconscious fantasy. (These sources are laid out more fully in an earlier book, *Maternal Ethics.)* [6] The dialectic of subjectivity that emerges provides a template for reading Morrison's lyrical novel.

The drama of the self turns around three central stages, which I will sketch briefly before bringing these stages into a reading of Morrison's novel. These stages are meant to offer a serious corrective to the standard view of moral subjectivity in modern moral philosophy and psychoanalytic theory. The standard view frames issues of existential meaning and moral development around the paradox of freedom. Infancy is understood as an experience of submersion, while maturity is defined in terms of self-control or autonomy. Man is most free when he is most empty. The standard view errs by treating the social drama of the individual as secondary to the project of autonomy. A reversal of perspective avoids posing freedom as a paradox; it also affords a deeper glimpse into the joys and pathos of individual existence.

The first stage interprets the origins of human consciousness (in early infancy) by joining together Irigaray's lyrical discourse on the flesh and a notion of synaesthesia, or "correspondences" among our sensations. The

[6] Cynthia Willett, *Maternal Ethics and Other Slave Moralities* (New York: Routledge, 1995). This alternative frame for development allows me to overcome the assumptions regarding originary narcissism and ontological alienation that Lacan takes from Freud, and that appear implicitly or explicitly in contemporary psychoanalytic readings of Morrison's work. Among the best of the psychoanalytic readings of *Beloved* is Jean Wyatt, "Giving Body to the Word: The Maternal Symbols in Toni Morrison's *Beloved,*" *PMLA* 108, no. 3 (May 1993): 474–488.

latter notion develops out of such diverse sources as the poet Baudelaire, the phenomenologist Merleau-Ponty, and the empirical research of Daniel Stern. This perspective replaces the assumption that the infant experiences no boundaries between itself and the mother (or outside world). The child does not experience as primordial a fusion with the mother. On the contrary, from earliest infancy the child calls out and responds to the mother through lyrical sounds, meaningful touches, and powerful smells. The child's rhythmic touch may evoke a "corresponding" sound from the mother's lyric voice. Or, it may not. In any case, the drama of sociality predates the development of language and intentionality. On this view, an experience of fusion would be read as a distortion of our original sociality and a sign of trouble. Joining together ideas from various writers, one might say that the liminal awareness of consciousness begins (perhaps already in the womb) as an expressive drive for the amorous exchange. Or as Sethe ponders as she recalls the kick of her own child (that "little antelope") within her womb, "Of that place she was born [a geographical area, but perhaps also her mother's body] she remembered only song and dance" (30).

A second significant stage develops as facial expressions and communicative gestures precipitate a sense of self. This stage corrects those theories that anchor the self in the achievement of autonomy (or the boundaries of an ego through self-recognition). The second stage begins several weeks after birth as the child develops the ability to focus on objects, or rather, on faces. Standard theories occlude the importance of the expressive face of the mother (or other social interlocutor) as a first visual object. For example, Lacan interprets the meaning of this encounter through the metaphor of the mirror. He argues that the mother serves to mirror the infant's sense of wholeness. More convincing psychoanalytic theory (Stern) centers the encounter around the face-to-face play between the mother and the child nursing at her breast. This research reestablishes the ethical significance that the face has acquired in the work of Levinas while unburdening his philosophy of the strange and funny metaphysics of the "face from nowhere." Beloved tells Denver she came back for the face of her mother.

A third stage draws from the tradition of social struggle in African-American culture. At this third (and more gradual) stage, the individual develops symbolic modes of understanding, and realizes that its most intimate relations are part of a larger horizon of human sociality. From earliest infancy, the normal child is able to engage and contest proximal sources of meaning. Maturation enables the child to engage and contest distant forces of meaning in the search for wider spheres of human relationship. This stage challenges the view that the child must undergo rites of separation in order to gain moral maturity (or full discursive subjectivity). It is true that Denver cannot mature until she breaks out of the centripetal forces of 124 Bluestone. However, these forces are not normal. Denver matures as she reanchors her self and her home in the wider community.

The wisdom of expressive traditions in an era of globalization is crucial. Classic and modern European philosophies of growth turn on the division of the person into mind and body. This ontological division mirrors and supports class differences between those who work with their heads and those who work with their hands. A more complex understanding of subjectivity is necessary if we are to grasp the many meanings of freedom. From Audre Lorde and Patricia Hill Collins, we have learned how oppressive institutions and their beneficiaries appropriate erotic energy for the sake of wealth and power (Chapter 7). Freedom means reversing this priority. Institutions and communities should release and cultivate erotic energy. But writers like Toni Morrison and Frederick Douglass take us further into the psychology of oppression by exposing what makes it evil. The clearest insight into evil comes from Denver's mature reflections on her mother's murder of her baby sister, Beloved: "Worse than that [than Sethe's infanticide; certainly, worse than the mortal blow that defines the modern subject]— far worse—was what Baby Suggs died of ... and what made Paul D tremble: That anybody white could take your whole self for anything that came to mind. Not just work, kill, or maim you but dirty you. Dirty you so bad you forgot who you were and couldn't think it up" (251).

Antiblack racism (Lewis Gordon's powerful term) takes root in economic processes that alienate labor. But these processes collaborate with social processes that alienate desire. Economic and social processes alienate desire through the appropriation of erotic energy and the abuse of social force. This alienation reaches the point where individuals and communities lose a sense of what they want and who they are. Institutional and community codes need to liberate and redeem the social existence of the individual. This—and not autonomy—is freedom's deeper meaning.

The unnatural acts and casual violations (the existential events) that make up the missing narratives of modernity are not to be measured through the abstract emptiness called death. These missing narratives are to be measured in terms of a more qualified death, what Douglass has described as "moral, political, and social death" (Chapter 7). Douglass tells us that these are the deaths that are visited by those with power on those without (Chapter 8). The ghost of Beloved shows us how these same deaths are revisited by the dead on the living. Stories of violation and trauma repeat from generation after generation, giving us cause to rethink the meaning of justice and the basis for modern subjectivity. The liberal concept of justice is designed to protect the individual from external constraints on his autonomy. Among these constraints are crimes against ownership of all kinds. However, the modern concept lacks the resources to protect the person from violations of his or her meaningful relationships. Perhaps the moribund lyricism of Shakespeare's play clears the space for the reflections of the modern subject. But that lyricism cannot voice the wounds that torment the erotic soul.

As I have argued in previous chapters, the European tradition is not totally without the concept of violation that Morrison and Douglass discern. Crimes against the moral, political, and social existence of the person were represented both in the tragic drama and in the legal theory of ancient Greek culture. The act of hubris (or outrage) exemplifies a lack of moderation and a failure to acknowledge limits. But, as we modernists too often overlook, hubris also constitutes an assault on social bonds. Indeed, according to the ancient plays, the tragic agent, the perpetrator of hubris, might or might not "see" the crimes he or she commits. The boundaries between conscious and unconscious knowing are not always clear. In the ancient world, the failure to recognize crimes against sacred codes of family and friendship does not exempt the perpetrator from the tragic consequences of the act. Indeed, as Freudian reinterpretations of classic drama remind us, blindness itself may be a function of guilt.

The symptoms and effects of hubris do not affect only the immediate individuals involved in the crime. For the ancient Greeks as for the characters in Morrison's novel, acts of hubris take their tow in the sickness of the land. These crimes may be experienced by the victim as degrees of terror. But these crimes are also experienced by the perpetrator through inexplicable fears or mild discomfort, or even in strange acts of avoidance. Centuries-old fears lurk on. I would argue that an ill-defined phobia of the black man is one of the persistent symptoms of white hubris in America since the Middle Passage. It shows few signs of dissipating today.

The Greek concept of hubris tells us much about the crimes of violation that define the tragic plot of *Beloved*. Morrison's novel, however, cannot be read in terms of the popular Greek notion. It is important to remember that the ancient understanding of hubris was limited by a culture where the subordination of women and the practice of slavery were normative. The ancient culture placed a premium on the male virtue of honor. It ranked individuals in accordance with this excellence and promoted degrees of servitude for those who were viewed as lesser types of men. Modern democratic revolutions have led us to question the value of social hierarchies and the virtue of servitude. We seek instead laws and social norms that foster universal egalitarianism and an ethics of compassion. The democratic Athenians failed to see what we understand much better today: a servile character (and its apparent virtues) constitutes a violation of the human spirit. In this respect, *Beloved* is a modern work.

However, unlike Shakespeare's exemplary play, Morrison's novel does not propose that we enter into modernity through an exile from the communal self. Instead, the novel gives us a modern revision of the ancient concept of hubris. Exile or isolation is the punishment for hubris in Morrison's novel as for the ancient Greeks. Separation is not freedom's reward. It is freedom's deprivation. The horror of the American system of slavery was that it routinely separated individuals from friends, families, and communities. This separation of individual from group was not lived as the angst of an existential freedom. Separation means social death.

It is through the perspective of the novel's preacher, Baby Suggs, that we glimpse this moral insight most directly. Baby Suggs is set free from slavery by her son Halle (who is also Sethe's husband). Halle earns her freedom by working overtime on the plantation. Suggs is well aware of the cruel irony of the freedom that her son's labor grants. Halle was the only one of her children that she was able to keep from being sold away from her. When Halle buys his mother out of slavery and sends her across the river to the North, she does not celebrate her freedom. She mourns the loss of her one remaining son. The narrator explains, "All of Baby's life ... men and women were moved around like checkers.... What she called the nastiness of life was the shock she received upon learning that nobody stopped playing checkers because the pieces included her children.... God take what He would.... And He did, and He did, and He Did and then gave her Halle who gave her freedom when it didn't mean a thing" (23).

The ancient Greeks understood that the freedom of the citizen did not lay in his separation from his household and community. It lay in his relation-to-the-other. Morrison's novel shares much in common with these Greeks. For the Greeks, however, the center of the soul is to be found in the honor of the highest caste of the social order. This was the caste that owned and managed wives, servants, and slaves. Control over the self established one's ability to control the lives of others. The ancient codes of justice cultivated the servile demeanor in the lower classes. This demeanor is not a virtue in modern times. Morrison's modern novel makes clear that any variant of the master/servant distinction constitutes a violation of human bonds. However, this modern novel does not displace the ancient bonds with the modern tale of the abstract individual. The lyric narrative shifts the center of these ancient bonds from the masterful skills of the excellent man to the erotic soul of those who have struggled for freedom since the Middle Passage.

As Morrison suggests, it is the magnitude of the erotic soul and not the honor of the feared leader that accounts for Baby Suggs's spiritual role in her community. Baby Suggs deals with having to leave her son behind by turning her attention to her newfound people in Ohio. As the narrator explains, "Accepting no title of honor before her name … but allowing a small caress after it, [Baby Suggs] became an unchurched preacher, one who visited pulpits and opened her great heart to those who could use it" (87). Honor creates social distance and legitimates class distinctions. Baby Suggs seeks instead the spiritual energy and social intimacy of friendship in her community. Through the power of eros that she calls forth at the Clearing, Baby Suggs reworks the ancient notion of hubris and the modern meaning of justice. "Talk was low and to the point—for Baby Suggs, holy, didn't approve of extra. 'Everything depends on knowing how much,' she said, and 'Good is knowing when to stop'" (87).

The tragedy of *Beloved* stems from the failure to heed the limits that allow people to flourish together. The novel takes up narratives of hubris left frayed by *Hamlet*'s vacant subject. The story of Beloved's return stirs old and new memories of excess and violation. The story reminds us that more troubling than the abstract thought of mortality is the actual loss of a beloved. Worse yet—far worse—is to experience that loss through unnatural acts and accidental judgments, the crimes of evil and arrogance that mark our modern time. Acts of hubris pull at the protective fabric of our social lives. Some of these disruptions may be healed through laughter or tears. The greater crimes of hubris—the crimes of the Middle Passage and its aftermath—threaten to damage the fabric beyond repair.

Beloved tells of these most horrifying crimes. Sethe murders her own daughter in order to save the child from the outrage of slavery. The black community abandons Sethe, leaving her alone in the struggle against the white men and the horrors of the past. The compounded hubris of the tragic tale threatens to destroy Sethe and her family altogether. The reader of the novel understands that the grievances of the Middle Passage and its aftermath have not yet been settled. Still, the novel, like its central characters, are able to call forth some saving power. Just as Baby Suggs uplifts her people through what she says and what she does not say in sermons at the Clearing, so Morrison's novel seeks ways to exorcize our modern times through redemptive narrative and cathartic song.

"This is not a story to pass on," Morrison writes in the coda to the novel. The cathartic function of the novel's final song is almost classical. The narrative comes to its end as the ghost and the pathos that she bears disappear. Aristotle had argued that the function of tragedy is the catharsis of tragic emotions. These emotions are fear and pity. The partial closure at the end of Morrison's novel performs something of this classic function. The novel, however, is not Aristotelian. Aristotle's discussion of tragedy misses the human drama of hubris and its mending. Hubris and its repair are at the center of Morrison's novel. The cathartic songs of the novel cannot heal without working through the crimes that the characters have endured. This cathartic work does not exorcize the tragic emotions that Aristotle names without also mending the bonds of family and community. Morrison's novel is also not quite Greek. In the Greek world, the bonds of friendship come and go through contests for glory. Hubris targets the honor that is core to the man. In order to heal the wounds of honor, the offender must return more honor than he has taken.[7] In Morrison's novel, the target of hubris is the libidinal core of the soul—the heart of the subject. The cathartic song must call forth the source of this erotic power in order to repair its wounds.

The power of the erotic begins with the sentient quality of the flesh. Many of the acts of hubris in the novel, from the whipping of slaves and the theft of Sethe's milk on Sweet Home plantation to the rape of the prisoners on the chain gang, aim to humiliate through the element of touch. There are other aberrations of touch. In a discussion of the novel, Morrison notes the white aversion to touching black skin.[8] In the racist ideology, blackness symbolizes what is lowly about the flesh. The general metaphysics of the culture relegates human embodiment to the realm of vegetative or animal life, and below the properly human. The image of blackness is used to intensify the subhuman dimension of existence in an antiblack culture.

Morrison's novel challenges conventional views on the skin and blackness by centering her description of the flesh around the expressive tones of the face. When Paul D encounters the stoic Sethe some eighteen years after their escape from slavery, he sees "a face too still for comfort; irises the same color as her skin" (9). Sethe sees in Paul D's warm face a "peach-stone skin.... For a man with an immobile face it was amazing how ready it was to smile, or blaze or be sorry with you" (7). The flesh is not the locus of subhuman animality. The flesh expresses desire and testifies to wounds through the elements of color, texture, and movement. The face is the center of expression.

[7] Michel Foucault, *The Use of Pleasure*, trans. Robert Hurley (New York: Random House, 1990), 82.

[8] Interview with Toni Morrison on National Public Radio's *Fresh Air*, March 24, 1992.

The representation of the flesh as a dimension of human expression does more than challenge the racist image of "black skin." It also complicates the divide between mind and body. Sociality goes deeper into the natural realm than we have acknowledged. As human beings, we need to be loved and respected through the proper signs of touch and of the gaze. We experience these needs through our bodies. The body is itself a part of our social presence. Respect for our body as part of our self is a need of our spirit. The mind / body divide not only removes us from the impact of the body on the mind; it removes us from social contact. This divide is useful to those who can find no other way to respond to the pathos of the social world than through stoic withdrawal. For Sethe, this world contains the memories of men who stole her milk and then whipped her for telling. The numbing of the scar tissue left on her back strengthens but also betrays Sethe's attempt to block out the horror of the crime. Similarly, the classical or modern philosopher who severs mind from body finds it difficult to grasp the horror and healing of hubris in our social life.

The modern blindness appears in our overemphasis on the importance of autonomy in stories of individual maturation and political freedom. The exercise of autonomy includes among its standard meanings control over one's possessions. Among these possessions is the body. It is not clear to me, however, that such crimes as rape and sexual harassment, or, for that matter, physical assault or even theft can be fully explained as threats to autonomy. The sting of these crimes touches something deeper in the person than the language of ownership can express. The crimes can inflict wounds on the erotic core of the self—sometimes so badly, as Denver learns, that you forget who you are. This is why crimes of violation are better understood as acts of hubris than as affronts to personal autonomy. Certainly, the most heinous crimes, the crimes that make for tragedy, do not mess with our autonomy without also messing with our sense of who we are. Crimes of touch such as rape and physical assault target the self that extends—through the folds of social space—outward to the other. The flesh does not merely belong to the realm of biology. It is also the primordial site for social exchange.

The importance of the body for the soul is clear in Baby Suggs's sermons. To those who have been targets of white hubris, Baby Suggs does not preach that the body is lowly or that the appetites are to be subdued. She does not promise that the last shall be first. And she does not tell her people that they are the "glorybound pure." A regime of discipline, a morality of honor, even a religion of lily-white angels and transcendent gods—these are strategies of detachment and dissociation. Baby Suggs begins her speech by addressing the most elementary desire of the human soul. This is a desire that predates the formation of the subject. It is the desire to be loved and recognized as one of "us" in the flesh. "'Here,' she said, 'in this here place, we flesh; flesh that weeps, laughs; flesh that dances on bare feet in grass. Love it. Love it hard," she calls out. "Oh my people they do not love your hands.... Love your hands! ... Raise them up and kiss them. Touch others with them.... This is flesh I'm talking about here. Flesh that needs to be loved" (88).

But the flesh is not the be-all and end-all of Baby Suggs's erotic spirituality. Her preaching aims to regenerate the soul by mending the bonds that hubris tears apart. These bonds extend across the flesh-and-blood ties of couples and families to wider communities: "More than eyes or feet.... More than your life-giving womb and your life-giving private parts, hear me now, love your heart. For this is the prize" (89).

Sentimental views of human relationships strip love of its emancipatory power. The conventional view of white society represents love as a retreat inward to a private domain, the Victorian refuge from the outside world. Morrison counters the sentimental view by representing love as a way in which one person can lay claim to the self through the recognition bestowed by another. Love moves the self outward. Its force is centrifugal. Morrison gives an image of eros's generative force in a scene of two turtles on a riverbank. In the "pat pat pat of their touching heads," turtle "stretched" out toward turtle, "risking everything outside the bowl just to touch [the other's] ... face. The gravity of their shields, clashing, countered and mocked the floating heads touching" (105). The stoic Sethe knows that if the scars on her back are to begin to heal, she must come out of herself, and seek renewal as she once did with others at the Clearing: "It was time to lay it all down.... Lay all that mess down ... [the] heavy knives of defense" and get "back to the Clearing, back where Baby Suggs had danced in sunlight" (86).

Eros heals as does narrative; it extends the vision of the soul outward toward a better tomorrow. Eros gives time its meaning. It gives life its direction. Baby Suggs closed her sermons by telling her people "that the only grace they could have was the grace they could imagine. That if they could not see it, they would not have it" (88). Baby Suggs did not succeed in finding this grace. Her spirit was finally broken by "the white things"—those who did not know "when to stop." The vision of her soul along with her capacity to care diminished to what Paul D describes as the smallest bits of life, the patches of color that Baby Suggs requests from her deathbed. Still her preaching was not in vain. The memory of Baby Suggs enables Sethe to seek "a Clearing" in the love of Paul D. The memory also enables Denver to find a way out of the tragedy that she inherits from her mother and her mother's past.

In order to better understand the wounds of hubris and the regenerative power of eros, we need to examine further the plot of *Beloved*. In the following two sections, I examine the causes of the tragedy in the novel. As I argue, the central tragedy turns around the violation of bonds between mothers and children. It is from these bonds that we find an origin of human eros and a source of a most basic concept of social justice. Morrison's story of the violation of these bonds has a double structure, divided along the color line.

"The Men without Skin": White Hubris

The most elemental expression of the social eros of the person is the flesh.[9] Morrison's novel is not a story about the shame of human animality (what we find in Plato, Aristotle, Hegel, Kierkegaard, Freud, and Levinas). Hers is a story about the sociality of our human flesh. The cradled baby yet unable to focus on the face of another is driven by the desire to be rocked, caressed, and held against the flesh of those who enjoy its warmth in return. The deprivation of touch, perhaps more so than the other forms of sensory engagement, hinders the libidinal development of the person. The infant who is deprived of touch can become excessively withdrawn or even violent, and incapable of sustaining social bonds in later life. The erotic pleasure the infant takes in the inviting smells and in the warm taste of the mother's milky flesh does not only serve to stimulate and nourish the appetite of a biological organism. What the child finds pleasant in the mother's flesh welcomes the child into the world. Without the warmth of this welcome, the child may retreat from the encounter. Through the rhythmic cycles of those who stay near the child—cycles of restfulness, excitement, fear, and pleasure—the child acquires a sense of meaningful time. Through the social presence of others, the child acquires a sense of its own.

The sociality of the flesh in early infancy comes before the development of a sense of self and other, and before the ability to focus. The diffuse presence of the self-in-the-flesh also preconditions moods of the mature subject. Before our awareness of each other as subjects with specific intentions, we respond to one another as a social presence.

From the story of *Beloved* we learn that just as our most vital social desires are expressed in exchanges of the flesh, so too are some of the most cruel wounds. There are proximal and distal causes of the novel's tragic plot. The character of Sethe is based on the true story of Margaret Garner, a

---

[9] The remarks that follow are a summary of conclusions in Chapter 2 of *Maternal Ethics*, 31–47.

slave who in 1856 escaped with her child from a plantation in Kentucky. The newspapers reported that she murdered the child rather than return together to their white master. A literary scholar, Barbara Christian, has remarked on the irony that Garner was not tried before a white jury for murder, but apparently for theft.[10] Christian argues that infanticide constituted the only way in which Margaret Garner could claim ownership over her child; she sees *Beloved* as challenging the limits of this claim: "Whether children should be owned by parents to the extent of determining whether they live or die is of course partly the question that Beloved comes back to ask" (*CB*, 214).

I mention this interpretation because I think we might push further the complicated remarks about ownership in the novel. While the question of ownership over the child is part of the Garner story, Morrison's retelling shifts the focus from the spectacle of infanticide to more subtle violations of the human soul. This shift in focus expands our perspective beyond issues of ownership and death to less apparent but more vital dimensions of human relationship. The proximal causes of the murder are within the black community of Cincinnati, where Sethe takes refuge from slavery. I will return to these causes later. The distal causes of the tragedy are white.

The white causes of the tragedy do not grow out of the ordinary human vices of character, such as envy, pride, or self-indulgence. These ordinary vices tear at the social fabric but do not unravel it. The more "unnatural acts" of hubris, the heinous crimes of tragedy, work to cripple or destroy their target. The perpetrator may or may not know what he is doing. From a peripheral awareness of the crime comes the strange mix of terror and desire that characterizes the classic agent of tragedy. According to ancient texts, these heinous crimes elicit outrage in their survivors along with fantasies of revenge; they also carry the seeds of social unrest and political revolution.[11] The horror of these crimes is missing from the modern literary and legal mind.

The central crime of the novel is not the mother's murder of her child, but a crime committed by the schoolteacher and his nephews. When Paul D arrives at 124 Bluestone, Sethe's home in Ohio, some eighteen years later, she recalls the day when the slaves made their attempt to escape from Sweet

---

[10] Christian offers these remarks in "A Conversation on Toni Morrison's *Beloved*," with Deborah McDowell and Nellie Y. McKay, in *Toni Morrison's Beloved: A Casebook*, ed. William L. Andrews and Nellie Y. McKay (Oxford: Oxford University Press, 1999); henceforth cited as *CB*.

[11] For a fascinating discussion of tragedy, slavery, and outrage, see Elizabeth V. Spelman, *Fruits of Sorrow: Framing Our Attention to Sorrow* (Boston: Beacon, 1997), esp. 71. On the political meaning of classic tragedy, see Lewis R. Gordon, *Fanon and the Crisis of European Man* (New York: Routledge, 1995), 75.

Home plantation. She tells how the schoolteacher's nephews held her down in a barn and sucked from her breasts. When she reported the crime to Mrs. Garner, the schoolteacher had her whipped. Sethe tries to explain the horror of the violation to Paul D: "Schoolteacher made one open up my back, and when it closed it made a tree. It grows there still." Paul D's response to her story is significant. His focus is on the beating, not on the milk. "'They used cowhide on you?' [he asks]? 'And they took my milk' [she responds]. 'They beat you and you was pregnant.' 'And they took my milk!'" (17). Sethe tries again to draw Paul D's attention to the theft, a violation akin to rape. It is also akin to the humiliation of the whip, but it is not quite the same as either crime. The aim of any crime of hubris is to take pleasure in rendering the victim servile. However, unlike the other crimes, the violation of the breast targets the mother's sense of herself in relation to her children.

Patricia Hill Collins argues that the crime signifies the appropriation of the erotic energy of the slave for the profit of the enslaver (Chapter 7). The fluid from the mother not only nourishes the biological child; it also transmits erotic power to the child. The child needs this warmth and energy in order to grow as a person. The violation, however, is not only about stealing erotic energy from the mother and child. Part of the crime's horror lies in the pleasure that the perpetrator takes in his assault on what he surely knows to be a basic human bond. It is as though he aims to destroy a relationship that does not include him. This secret pleasure testifies to what the nephews and the schoolteacher deny: the black slave is not a beast or piece of property but a human being.

We are all human beings, but there are important differences among us. The fact that Paul D responds to Sethe's story by focusing on the beating while Sethe attempts to get him to see the theft indicates the significance of gender and identity in our experience of violation. Hubris against women may not be the same as hubris against men. Paul D sees the whipping as a hubristic assault against the person. He has some trouble grasping the meaning of the stolen milk.

Crimes of hubris that involve sexuality may also take different forms in women and men. Beloved threatens Paul D's manhood by arousing him sexually in a way that he cannot control and does not desire. This is an assault that Sethe has trouble fully grasping. Sensitivity to differences of sexuality and gender on personal identity would be important in articulating laws or social codes against hubris.

Not all differences are equal. Some modes of sexual and gender difference are inconsonant with social justice. Morrison juxtaposes alternative styles of male excellence and honor at Sweet Home. Mr. Garner is said to define his manhood through his fearless control over other men. His demeanor often leads to fights that go beyond normal friendly competition. "Garner [would come] home bruised and pleased, having demonstrated one more time what a real Kentuckian was: one tough enough and smart enough to make and call his own niggers men" (11). Garner's sense of excellence and manhood sustains a system of honor that does not bring the basic principle of servitude into question. His exercise of virtue is, to borrow from Hegel, the dialectic of the master.

By contrast, the novel identifies the character of Paul D through his expressive and receptive traits. Sethe describes him as "a singing man" (39) and later as a "tender man" (99). The traditional element of mastery also plays a role in Paul D's sense of self. Paul D and his brothers on the plantation are described as training their sense of manhood through exercises of restraint, and in particular through the restraint of sexual desire. The aim of this kind of restraint is not to establish one's worth over other men, although it may have this effect. The aim is to uphold the basis for friendly bonds. It is this kind of restraint that Paul D and his brothers exercise in their response to the arrival of Sethe at Sweet Home plantation. "All in their twenties, minus women, fucking cows, dreaming of rape, thrashing on pallets, rubbing their thighs," they waited for the new girl to choose her man (11). This was the "restraint they had exercised ... because they were Sweet Home men" (10).

The focus of the story's horror is on the white men who replace Garner on the plantation, the schoolteacher and his two nephews. These men assume the classic role of the master-cum-tyrant. They overstep all boundaries of restraint and commit wanton acts of cruelty against the slaves on the plantation. "There was no bad luck in the world but whitepeople. 'They don't know when to stop,'" Baby Suggs remarks as she reflects upon the crimes of her former masters (104). "This ain't a battle; it's a rout," she exclaims as she withdraws to a bed-ridden life in the keeping room (244). Deprived of the ancient means of legal restitution and moral appeal, Baby Suggs wants nothing more to do with people, black or white. Her life diminishes to the desire she musters for patches of color. These patches are unattended by the pathos of the flesh.

Sethe's strong drive to protect what remains of those whom she loves keeps her from withdrawing like her mother-in-law to the keeping room. However, Sethe too works to distance herself from the vulnerability of the flesh. The scar tissue on her hardened back signifies the physical and psychological damage of the past. Like other women in the novel, she knows she can barely afford to care in a world that exposes human relationships to terror. The temptation for these women is to retreat inward in order to protect what little they can. While Baby Suggs searches for her patches without flesh, Sethe "worked hard to remember as close to nothing as was safe. ... [Eventually,] the picture of the men coming to nurse her was as lifeless as the nerves in her back where the skin buckled like a washboard" (6).

The ghost-girl tries to bring her mother back to life through memory and song. For the most part, the memories are not pleasant. She tells of white invaders who tear apart families and communities, and who destroy souls in the Middle Passage. She describes those who inflict pain without experiencing its pathos as "men without skin" (210ff.). The insensitivity to pathos appears throughout the novel as the temptation of those who have power over others. Sethe describes the white abolitionist Edward Bowden as possessing the characteristic "Look" of the man-in-charge. As he rides into the black community, Sethe sees him less as the noble white man that he aims to be and more in terms of the position of power that he acquires as a white in an antiblack society. From this position, he is "above them all, rising from his place with a whip in his hand, the man without skin, looking" (262). The "Look" of the man-in-charge distances even the honorable man from those whom he seeks to aid. This distancing function is not morally or politically neutral. It severs the eye from the face and the face from the flesh. It diminishes social man.

If the crimes of hubris center around the more subtle dimensions of human sociality, so too must the remedies. The novel shows us that the pain that enters through the flesh must also leave through the flesh. When Paul D first encounters the stoic Sethe after years of separation, he reaches her through the touch of his face on her hardened back. He "rubbed his cheek on her back and learned that way her sorrow" (18). His warmth provokes Sethe to ask herself if "maybe this one time she could ... feel the hurt her back ought to. Trust things and remember things because the last of the Sweet Home men was there to catch her if she sank?" (18). Later in the story, Sethe recalls the miracle of her child's birth on the river and the wisdom of the white servant girl (Amy Denver) who saves her and her child. The use of touch in the scene between Sethe and Amy parallels its use in the encounter between Sethe and Paul D. As the narrator explains, this white girl "did the magic: lifted Sethe's feet and legs and massaged them until she cried salt tears. 'It's gonna hurt, now,' said Amy. 'Anything dead coming back to life hurts'" (35).

The healing force of these deeply moral gestures does not work without the transformative power of the imagination. Paul D is able to visualize in "the revolting clump of scars" on Sethe's back "the decorative work of an ironsmith too passionate for display" (17). Amy sees in the same scars "tiny little cherry blossoms" (79). The other who is loved is bathed in the light of a friendly gaze. This is eros's cathartic force. The cathartic gaze has the opposite effect of hubris. While hubris defiles its target, the friendly gaze rekindles the spirit of its object through its ability to see beauty, nobility, or grace where otherwise one might see what is shameful or ugly. The transformative gaze is absent from those "good-willed whitewomen" who take pity on Sethe and her people, "their sympathetic voices called liar by the revulsion in their eyes" (12).

But if a simple ethics of care is not adequate for addressing the horror of the crimes, neither is the undiverted gaze of the witness. As Sethe understands, some crimes are not "to be witnessed without shame" (51). When Paul D is shackled like an animal by the white men on the plantation, Sethe responds with "tenderness about his neck jewelry. . . . She never mentioned or looked at it, so he did not have to feel the shame of being collared like a beast. Only this woman Sethe could have left him his manhood like that" (273). Paul D, on the hand, responds poorly upon hearing of Sethe's crime. He accuses her of animality. It is not until the end of the novel that he is about to shift his focus from the spectacle of the infanticide to the humanity of Sethe's love.

The schoolteacher on the plantation enacts what is core to the white crime of hubris in his representation of a people as part human and part beast. Sethe tells Beloved what she overheard the white man teaching his pupils: "'I told you to put her human characteristics on the left; her animal ones on the right. And don't forget to line them up.' I commenced to walk backward [Sethe says to her daughter Beloved]. . . . Flies settled all over your face, rubbing their hands. My head itched like the devil" (193). The white imagination in and of itself constitutes an assault on the African person.

The effect of this crime on those who are unprotected from its brute force may be madness. When Stamp Paid listens to the "undecipherable language clamoring around the house" with Sethe and her daughter(s), he ponders the source of the madness. "Whitepeople believed that . . . under every dark skin was a jungle . . . swinging screaming baboons . . . red gums ready for their sweet white blood. In a way he thought, they were right. . . . But it wasn't the jungle blacks brought with them to this place from the other (livable) place. It was the jungle whitefolks planted in them. And it grew. It spread. In, through and after life, it spread, until it invaded the whites who had made it. Touched them every one. Changed and altered them . . . so scared were they of the jungle they had made. The screaming baboon lived under their own white skin; the red gums were their own" (198–199).

The crime of hubris undermines the basis for a human relationship between the perpetrator and the victim. The perpetrator both knows and denies the humanity of the person whom he attacks. He represents the other person as part subhuman—but also as part human. In ancient Greece, crimes of hubris were expected to lead to uncontrollable outrage and acts of revenge. These crimes would destroy households and cities. Before laying a hand on the slaves, the schoolteacher commits the crime that releases the ancient terror. He dares to represent Sethe as less than a human being. The crime creates secret pleasure and self-righteous power, but it also brings the fear of social unrest and tragic revenge. This is the jungle that the white man creates. This jungle is America.

"Pride goeth before a Fall": Black Hubris

The more ordinary vices, the excesses of pride, generosity, and envy, are the proximal causes of the tragedy in the novel. The novel's portrayal of the ordinary vices within the black community demonstrates the subtle ways in which social and libidinal forces play a role in individual self-definition. In some respects, Sethe's most enviable characteristic leads to her downfall. Sethe tells of how she managed to get herself and her family out of slavery and across the river to freedom. The community responds to her heroic feat with ambivalence. What Sethe esteems as her strong autonomy was judged by Sethe's community as wrongful pride. "Just about everybody in town was longing for Sethe to come on difficult times. Her outrageous claims, her self-sufficiency, seemed to demand it, and Stamp Paid, who had not felt a trickle of meanness his whole adult life, wondered if some of the 'pride goeth before a fall' expectations of the townsfolk had rubbed off on him" (171). Baby Suggs's meets with similar disapproval from the community. This spirited grandmother who is able to heal herself and her people through her "big heart" was judged by the community as "loving everybody like it was her job and hers alone" (137). "Uncalled-for-pride" and "reckless generosity" were "on display at 124." "The scent of . . . disapproval lay heavy in the air" (137). This time, "it wasn't whitefolks— . . . so it must be colored ones. And then [Baby Suggs] knew. Her friends and neighbors were angry at her because she had overstepped, given too much, offended them by excess" (138).

Sethe's spirited independence provokes her to sacrifice rather than surrender the child to the hubristic whites. The extremity of the circumstances of the sacrifice makes it impossible to decide the ethical character of the act. However, it is clear that the community perceives Sethe's murderous rebellion as part of a larger pattern of excessive pride. This perception holds them back from warning Sethe and her family of the approach of the slave hunters and from extending aid afterward.

Maturation requires understanding subtle ties of sociality and history. Sethe and her family will need to learn how to acknowledge their precious need for friends and community. Denver's mature and spirited act of "stepping out the door" of 124 Bluestone near the end of the novel is not just about gaining independence from her family. Her act of independence is tied to her ability to ask "for the help she needed" from the townsfolks and to have that request respected in return (256). What she finds is exactly what she needs. One of her encounters is with the boy (Nelson Lord) who years ago had "destroyed her with a question." That question was about her mother's crime. The encounter with the boy is different this time. "All he did was smile and say, 'Take care of yourself, Denver,' but she heard it as though it were what language was made for" (252). Separation from family and community is not the milestone for maturation in this novel. Certainly, Denver must possess a sense of self-ownership in order to make her decision to seek help for her family from the outside (267). However, the maturation of the self does not rest abstractly in the capacity to make decisions or control one's passions. Maturation requires the ability to extend the self beyond proximal sources of human contact, and grasp more distal sources of relationship and meaning. Denver becomes her own person as she is able to expand her horizon beyond the centripetal confines of her haunted home into the wider community.

Communities, too, need to develop and mature. The white community in the novel proves unable to deal with the source of its ill-defined fears, or to make restitution for centuries-old crimes of hubris. The black community in the novel matures to the extent that it acknowledges the role of envy in its abandonment of Sethe and her family, and that it reins in its desire to punish the family (cf. p. 258).

The ghost of Sethe's murdered child was too young to understand the causes of the crime against her. She could not have understood what Denver only gradually comprehends, that the mother's aim was not to hurt her child but to protect her against horrors outside the home. As the ghost-girl returns to accuse her mother of abandonment, she articulates what the very young child who cannot yet speak needs most from the mother. It is not a biological organ of nourishment or a quasi-biological act of care: "'What did you come back for?' [Denver asks]. Beloved smiled. 'To see her face'" (75). "In the beginning I could see her. . . . Sethe sees me see her and I see the smile. . . . Her smiling face is the place for me" (211, 213). This welcoming face gives the child not a mirror but a "map of the self." When this face is taken from her, the child loses all sense of boundaries in its mad pursuit: "Her face is my own and I want to be there in the place where her face is to be looking at it too" (210). The fantasy of fusing with the mother does not stem from primordial memories of immersion in the mythic womb but from the destruction of the limits that mark the normal exchange between two social beings. Beloved never recovers from the trauma of irreparable loss. The crime committed against her was too deep to repair. There could not be enough love to heal her. The "girl who waited to be loved and cry shame" will have to disappear. Beloved's "was not a story to pass on" (274).

The novel leaves Sethe's future an open question. When Paul D hears the story of the murder, he confronts Sethe. Sethe attempts to communicate the life-giving joy she found when she escaped with her children to freedom in the North. "It was a kind of selfishness I never knew nothing about before. It felt good.... I was big, Paul D. And deep and wide and when I stretched out my arms all my children could get in between. I was that wide. Look like I loved em more after I got here. Or maybe I couldn't love em proper in Kentucky because they wasn't mine to love. But when I got here, when I jumped down off that wagon—there wasn't nobody in the world I couldn't love if I wanted to. You know what I mean?' Paul D did ... know what she meant. Listening to the doves in Alfred, Georgia, and having neither the right nor the permission to enjoy it because in that place mist, doves, sunlight, copper dirt, moon—everything belonged to the men who had the guns.... So you protected yourself and loved small. Picked the tiniest stars out of the sky to own.... A woman, a child, a brother—a big love like that would split you wide open in Alfred, Georgia. He knew exactly what she meant: to get to a place where you could love anything you chose—not to need permission for desire—well now, that was freedom" (162).

Paul D understands that autonomy is meant for love, and that the destruction of the erotic soul is the core of human tragedy. However, he cannot see how Sethe could carry her need to love her children to the point of killing them. He cannot understand the pathos of motherlove: "Your love is too thick," Paul D says, and he does not stop there (164). He keeps on talking: "'You got two feet, Sethe, not four,' he said, and right then a forest sprang up between them" (165). With these words, Paul D repeats the arrogance of the white man, and then walks away from the family. It is not until some time later that he realizes what he has done: "How fast he had moved from his shame to hers" (165). The story finds its closure in his return to the family. When he finds Sethe in bed, she asks if he has come back to "'count my feet?' He steps closer. 'Rub your feet,'" he responds (272). Sethe tells Paul D that Beloved is "her best thing" and that she is gone. Paul D does not respond immediately. He thinks about how Sixo, a brother on the plantation, had once described the woman that he loved: "She is a friend of my mind. She gather me, man. The pieces I am, she gather them and give them back to me" (272). He recalls how Sethe "never mentioned" that he had been "collared like a beast" so that he would not have to feel the shame. "Only this woman could have left him his manhood like that. He wants to put his story next to hers.... He [then] leans over...and touches her face. 'You your best thing, Sethe,'" he says as "his holding fingers are holding hers" (273).

In the clearing that opens the self to the other, the friend gathers the mind. Eros has the reputation for demanding perfect reconciliations, but this is not true. In our loves and our friendships we seek in the other something that corresponds with our self. We must not expect that the soul of the one is the same as the soul of another. The pathos of shame and the catharsis of love differ for men and women, for mothers and for their children. We grow in spirit as we seek and find those whose stories we can lay next to our own. These relationships do not require fusion. They do not require that we know everything there is to know about ourselves or about one another. On the contrary, sometimes more important is knowing when to look away, and when enough is enough. Eros can bring to our life stories a catharsis that is almost classical.

Almost classical—for Aristotle did not fully grasp the drama of our lives. The pity and fear that fill the house at 124 Bluestone are mixed with the social passions of shame and rage. The violation of the fragile bonds of our humanity elicits tragedy's true horror. Narratives of hubris and songs of love can help us to purge the shame and the terror of tragedy from our lives. These arts convert fear into laughter, and "baptized in [the] wash" (261). The arts of redemption and liberation can also teach us much about the basis for law in the expanding modern world. Freedom's ultimate meaning is not about owning the self and its objects. Freedom is the right to form the bonds that make us human. It is the right of Eros.

Down Here in Paradise

A Coda

"Now they will rest before shouldering the endless work they
were created to do down here in Paradise."

Toni Morrison, Paradise

We live in a deceptively regressive political climate. The managers of
our economies make life and death decisions in the name of globalization.
The numbers of children in Africa, Asia, and Latin America who are aban-
doned on the streets or starve in their homes increase by the millions with
the anti-inflationary measures imposed by the International Monetary
Fund.[1] These children do not count in the same way as do our own. They
do not even receive the resources that we lavish upon our own pets. Lewis

An earlier version of this final chapter was originally written in response to Martin J. Beck
Matustik's *Specters of Liberation: Great Refusals in the New World Order,* and is published under
the title of "The Ethical Heart of Existential Marxism" in *Radical Philosophy Review* 2, no. 2
(1999): 161–169.

[1] The United Nations estimates that six million children die every year as the direct consequence of the IMF's Structural Readjustment Policies. These policies serve to transfer wealth

Gordon describes the racial divide that blinds the white to the pathos of the black man in startlingly accurate terms. Of the black man, Gordon writes: "His death will never rip through the overdetermined anonymity of nature-like existence. He looks around him at the slaughterhouse … and he finds it difficult to distinguish colored life from the array of other animals that sink each day into the belly of consumption, death, and irrelevance. At times of trouble, it is the whites who are scurried off to safety; in the midst of thousands of colored deaths, it is the loss of an occasional white life that rips into the consciousness of the world."[2] The only evident challenge to the invisible narratives of white capital are the all-too-visible spectacles of black rage and revenge. Liberal preoccupations with objective merit, correct procedure, or rational discourse are mocked silly by corporations with the real know-how. These global leviathans know how to cross borders into third-world markets in order to make the cost of labor virtually disappear.

Meanwhile, the devastation of the public school system, along with public subsidies for corporations but not mothers, brings a bleak future of escalating class and racial differences to the centers of power. The entry of the child into the adult world has in most societies required rituals of initiation; as Philippe Ariès observes, in modern societies education plays that vital role.[3] In the past, Ariès explains, "to enter into a society one had to undergo a sort of operation of a religious character, sometimes magical and always ritualistic, which changed the very being of the novice … and joined him to his brothers with an inseparable bond" (*CC*, 244). Since the Enlightenment, a rigorous system of liberal education has replaced the religious rites and apprenticeship system of pre-Enlightenment Europe. While the earlier rites supported an honor-and-class-based society, a modern liberal education claims to promote equal opportunities by teaching disciplined thinking. Today, however, the education system is being used once again to divide us into classes. Those children who do not pass the standardized tests may resist the degradation of a servile life through less conventional rites of

---

from developing countries to the Big Seven. Austerity measures in Nicaragua, Zimbabwe, and the Philippines result in severe cuts to social programs including health care. These policies have brought an end to free public education in Nicaragua. These facts are reported in the documentary film *Deadly Embrace: Nicaragua, the World Bank, and the International Monetary Fund* (Elizabeth Canner, 1996).

[2] Lewis R. Gordon, *Fanon and the Crisis of European Man: An Essay on Philosophy and the Human Sciences* (New York: Routledge, 1995), 75–76.

[3] For a history of the use of discipline in schools and penal systems, see Philippe Ariès, *Centuries of Childhood*, trans. Robert Baldick (New York: Vintage, 1962), esp. 259 (henceforth cited as *CC*). For a discussion of the educational system as a replacement for earlier rites of initiation into adulthood, see 244 and 377.

passage. For one out of four African-American men, these rites take place through an encounter with the white-owned prison system.

It is time to reinvoke the erotic power of an ancient claim, that enough is enough, that good is knowing when to stop. It is time to lay our stories side by side, and to begin to dream of a better tomorrow.

To undertake the work of solidarity, we would have to give up lingering fantasies that some single class, some chosen race, or some nation-state could bear the universal. The fantasy of privileged suffering conceals a desire to be the master. Master narratives of all kinds need to give way to slave narratives, and these narratives must join together for a vision of democracy across political and racial borders. Returning us to the revolutionary vision of Herbert Marcuse, Martin Matustik writes: "The issue is no longer whether or not to seek a revolutionary agency of Refusal. We must ask how multiple refusals may enhance chances for a more just world.... Their joint venture (a multidialectic) conserves subversive hope for justice, indeed, raises specters of liberation."[4]

The collaborative venture that joins old school leftists and new liberals can only work if there is mutual transformation and even, I think, mutual accommodation. It is an old insight of comedy that we cannot come together as friends until we learn to mock the arrogance that keeps us apart. Matustik brings not only Marcuse but also the humor of an Eastern European existentialism to the political debates. At the core of this existential materialism lies the power of the individual to laugh. It is the power to laugh at any attempt to subordinate a person to a Thing, whether this "Fetish-Thing" be the European "Nation-State," the liberal rule-Thing, or the community-Thing. Along with Zizek, "one may discover that when you and I laugh, we already resist stupidity or naked aggression. Laughter is most insubordinate since its outburst cannot be contained, indeed, it can be as contagious as fire. ... There comes a day when [the Fetish-Thing] becomes a tragically comic reality known to all as a denuded emperor" (*SL*, 17–18).

Laughter is existential and liberating, Matustik explains, when it expresses the capacity for dissent that defines the individual. Might an act of dissent be performed in such a way that it does not affirm the core of the individual? Matustik suggests that we can learn more about the dissenting individual from the father of existentialism, Søren Kierkegaard. When I first encountered Matustik's ideas on dissent, I wondered if I would find anything from which to dissent. I thought it would be ironic if I did not find

---

[4] Martin J. Beck Matustik, *Specters of Liberation: Great Refusals in the New World Order* (Albany: State University of New York Press, 1998); henceforth cited as *SL*.

even a single point of disagreement from a project that locates the singularity of the individual in the capacity for dissent. Luckily for me, Matustik makes one mistake. He nods toward Kierkegaard in order to establish the basis for dissent. My question: Will not the existential development of democracy be stalled, unable to give a fully fruitful response to the question of the basis for legitimate dissent, until it learns to laugh hysterically at the Kierkegaardian Fear-and-Trembling-Thing?

Matustik invites us to return to the father of existentialism in order to establish a genealogy for the modern concept of the "dissenting individual." Ironically, while Kierkegaard might be the strongest proponent of the singularity of the individual, as an author there turns out to be at least three of him. Kierkegaard Number 1, as Matustik portrays him, is a neoliberal modernist, who dissents from traditional loyalty to the nation-state Thing "presumably on a private platform of an antisocial, apolitical, solipsistic, if not possessive individualism." Matustik unmasks this Kierkegaard as an imposter. He then proceeds to unmask a second Kierkegaard, the postmodern advocate of anarchic transgressions, as likewise an imposter. The third and most courageous Kierkegaard, as Matustik explains, takes a grand step across the modern / postmodern divide in order to affirm a multicultural dialectic of the existential individual in a democratic society.

Matustik (along with Lewis Gordon and Bill Martin, among other contemporary thinkers) argues convincingly that a strong existential component is a necessary part of any authentic philosophy of freedom. Two years before Marx's *Communist Manifesto*, Kierkegaard wrote words that should be taken as a preface to any social movement: "Not until the single individual has established an ethical stance despite the whole world, not until then can there be any question of genuinely uniting" (quoted in *SL*, 27). Against the "quantitative equality" of revolutionaries, "Kierkegaard restates his claim most emphatically: 'The individual' is the category through which … this age, all history, the human race as a whole, must pass." While earlier revolutionary leaders have too often sacrificed individuals and even whole populations for the sake of larger causes, from Kierkegaard we learn that the individual can only be a part of something larger than him or herself by fully being him or herself.

I question, however, whether the individual emerges intact through that particular rite of passage that Kierkegaard describes in *Fear and Trembling*. There Kierkegaard speaks through the fictive persona of Johannes de Silentio, in order to point his readers toward what is at stake in the transformative rite that marks us as true individuals. As Matustik explains, this rite of passage requires that the individual develop his capacity to dissent from sources of identity embedded in language and community. These conventional sources of identity masquerade all too often as truths for everyone. Johannes de Silentio uses the biblical story of Abraham and Isaac to teach us that the true "individual dissident acts through silences or gaps in propositional speech ... and inhabits the universal through fear and trembling.... Abraham cannot speak about his ordeal with Isaac, [and this incapacity to communicate] teaches ... radical self-choice.... This [radical individual] ventures into an uncertainty of the 'chasmic abyss.' ... The horizon of possible dissent cannot but assume that each individual may embody a sui generis species-being" (*SL*, 28–30).

Let us bring more elements of the existential individual that Kierkegaard portrays into the picture that Matustik begins. As it turns out, the voice of Johannes de Silentio is not created entirely (or "sui generis") out of Kierkegaard's own imagination. One of the external sources for this persona is the Grimms' fairy tale called "The Faithful Servant."[5] The story is about a servant who dares to warn his master of dangers even though the servant knows he will be punished for his loyalty by being turned into stone. Kierkegaard's reference to the faithful servant contrasts with Hegel's account of bondage in the struggle for recognition.[6] In the *Phenomenology of Spirit*, Hegel poses the struggle for recognition as a rite of passage that divides men into masters and servants. The irony of history, Hegel teaches us, is that the servant, whose bondage is initially justified by his lack of spirit, overcomes his fear more completely than the master ever did. The extreme fear experienced by the servant detaches him from his life and his body altogether. As I understand Hegel, this experience of total fear also detaches the servant as well from his wife, family, and community. Sooner or later, the detached servant turns his interest from the mundane world of work toward a sublime world of faith. Hegel terms this stage "unhappy consciousness," and describes this stage in terms of a spiritual belief in an infinite beyond. Through the passage into total darkness and blind faith, consciousness develops the sense of duty, discipline, and disconnection from libidinal bonds that is necessary in the quest for bourgeois freedom and loyalty to the modern nation-state.

Kierkegaard alters the course of the Hegelian narrative of the fearful servant *cum* bourgeois citizen by drawing upon the Old Testament figure of Abraham. Kierkegaard describes how this true servant prepares to sacrifice his son Isaac to God. Without speaking to his wife Sarah, Abraham sets out

---

[5] Alastair Hannay discusses this observation in the introduction to his translation of Søren Kierkegaard, *Fear and Trembling* (London: Penguin, 1985), 10, henceforth cited as *FT*.

[6] G. W. F. Hegel, *Phenomenology of Spirit*, trans. A. V. Miller (Oxford: Oxford University Press, 1977), sections 178–196.

with his son to Mount Moriah. Kierkegaard uses the story of Abraham to provoke his reader to acknowledge the irrevocable mystery of our origins, and to take responsibility for the singularity of the self. He does this by asking that we surrender our bourgeois concepts of duty, reason, and narrative coherence, concepts that we rely upon to make our way in the conventional world. Several times in this discussion Kierkegaard interrupts his narrative, and offers without explanation a variation of the following remark: "When the child is to be weaned the mother blackens her breast" (*FT*, 46). The implication of this recurrent theme is clear. For Kierkegaard, the true individual weans himself from amorous sources of meaningful exchange and practices instead the rigorous discipline of radical self-choice.

One wonders whether in fact the individual can flourish in a rite of passage that normalizes the experience of anguish and privileges the virtue of discipline. In the portrayal of the rite of passage as a ritual of separation, I see the symptoms of a man who is scared silly of women and other, shall I say, libidinal attachments. By returning faithfully to Kierkegaard as the father of existentialism, I wonder if contemporary existential philosophy does not risk transferring the phobic symptoms of Kierkegaard's inability to sustain libidinal relationships into liberation theory.

Moreover, Kierkegaard's basic concept of the individual is not entirely unique. The analogy that Kierkegaard draws between the individuation of the adult and the weaning of the child is not in any radical sense his own. This analogy is both quite conventional and deeply patriarchal. According to the analogy, maturation requires that the individual sever himself from the intimate social bonds associated with the mother, and respond to the unfathomable demands of a divine and distant, if uncommunicative, father. In this encounter with darkness and mystery, the individual discovers who he is. Kierkegaard's *Fear and Trembling* presents a variation of an old story, stock and trade for many a patriarchy, religious or not. Boy leaves home in order to become a man. Boy faces the wilderness alone. If the boy succeeds in his tests, he returns to society having proven himself a man. Kierkegaard's appropriation of the figure of Abraham intensifies the passage through blackness in a way that risks no return, stripping the self of all accoutrements from any given social order. Kierkegaard's true individual, however, does not risk transgressing the demands of the divine and distant father. This is why, for Kierkegaard, Abraham is the father of faith, and, I would add, why faith has to be a father; faith cannot be a mother.[7]

---

[7] Here I echo and return to Kelly Oliver's poignant remarks on Derrida in *Family Values: Subjects between Nature and Culture* (New York: Routledge, 1997).

Matustik's insistence upon a dialectical Kierkegaard Number 3 over a bourgeois Kierkegaard Number 1 and a postmodern Kierkegaard Number 2 offers a bold and salutary intervention in the debates between modernists and postmodernists. As Matustik explains, for the true Kierkegaardian, self-choice "interlocks each individual with the human race, together as singular universals." This Kierkegaard chooses an existential self that is multicultural and democratic; locates the existential individual in a larger project for universal freedom; and democratizes and globalizes, even mobilizes, the dialectical dream of universal recognition.

The existential individual is defined by his capacity to choose himself. The existential choice is, as Matustik explains, the choice of the self. The existentialist's responsibility for his choice of self establishes a prior condition for moral judgment and political commitment. This sense of responsibility is not a retreat to postmodern or neoliberal relativism. The individual's capacity to choose the self is anchored in the multidimensional capacity to say no, dissenting from existing desires, images, and narrative conventions. This rational capacity for dissent need not be discursive; it may take shape in a style of thinking that, as Carol Gilligan suggests, resembles the more amorous activity of making a quilt.[8] This capacity for dissent is already apparent in one-day-old babies, human or not.

Here is where I would like to search for another origin for the existential project. If the capacity for dissent is present at birth, if this spirited capacity to resist is there from day one in the unweaned baby, then why cannot faith be a mother? If the child is not, as Kierkegaard's fairy tale presumes, sealed in immediacy with the mother, if the child is engaged in social exchange from the beginning, and if the condition for this exchange includes the capacity of the child to resist any force that is invasive, then why would the child require a rite of separation from the domain of the mother as a condition for true individuality? Doesn't the child mature by cultivating through the friendships of the classroom and the laughter of play the spirit that is already exercised with the mother? Doesn't this spirit already flourish in the unweaned child, or at least in that child who has not been forced to suffer from the first scarcity, the scarcity of motherlove?

The existential freedom of the spirited child is different from the trajectory that Kierkegaard unfurls. Kierkegaard's individual requires a rite of passage that is potentially traumatizing and always troubling. It is a rite that requires that the individual break all libidinal bonds, and like the self-made

---

[8] Carol Gilligan, "Moral Orientation and Development," in *Justice and Care*, ed. Virginia Held (Boulder, Colo.: Westview, 1995), 42.

man, re-create himself out of nothing. Abraham does not listen to his body, to his wife, or to his community in order to constitute himself as a response. Abraham faces the blackness of the nothing, of human mortality, or of the wholly other in order to constitute himself alone. As I have said, versions of this story are legion, part of patriarchal conventions everywhere. Habermas appropriates Kohlberg's theory of moral development in order to tell a parallel story. In Habermas's rendition, children ascend a vertical scale of moral maturation. This scale begins from a pleasure-oriented stage of early childhood, corresponding with what Kierkegaard terms aesthetic immediacy, progresses toward a conventional moral orientation, and finally advances toward a stage of post-conventional morality. At this final stage, the mature individual is said to be guided no longer by either playful desires or community conventions, but by self-generated (sui generis) thought alone.

There is, in other words, an invisible narrative behind Kierkegaard's existential dialectic; and this invisible narrative may be more conventional than we would have thought. Kierkegaard begins the narrative of self-consciousness in the same way as Hegel. Hegel portrays servitude as good for the slave by demonstrating how servitude teaches through fear and discipline a morality that prepares the way for the modern bourgeois citizen whose ultimate duty is to the nation-state. Like Hegel, Kierkegaard portrays traumatic separation and disciplined detachment as a necessary stage for individuation. It is this origin of individuation that I question. If children are born free spirits, then they do not require a painful ritual of separation in order to discover who they are. Regardless of whether experiences of separation, exile, or isolation induce trauma, these experiences generate anguish and leave scars on the individual soul. Kierkegaard's story, no less than Hegel's, carries the moment of separation to the point of anguish, and then takes the symptoms of anguish as formative of the self. The anguish of separation that these writers recommend does not nourish the person who is already present in the face-to-face encounter at the mother's breast. Rituals of separation can starve the nascent soul of the warmth that it needs.

Why do our myths glorify separation from the sphere of life that the mother represents? Why do these myths portray this separation as a journey into the unknown, an encounter with the nothing, and a penetration into the savage blackness? Do not these myths mask personal narratives of loneliness and alienation, and larger narratives of conquest and submission? Could we not envision a more amorous path for the existential spirit, culminating, perhaps, as Toni Morrison writes, in a dream "of reaching age in the company of the other; of speech shared and divided bread smoking from the fire; the unambivalent bliss of going home to be at home—the ease of coming back to love begun"?[9] This song of solace is lost in the voyages of the anguished self.

Kierkegaard writes: "When the child has grown and is to be weaned the mother virginally covers her breast, so the child no more has a mother." There is then a break in Kierkegaard's text, as though to invite the reader to find his own meaning in the author's spare words. After the pause, Kierkegaard repeats his vignette: "It was early morning, Abraham rose in good time, kissed Sarah the young mother, and Sarah kissed Isaac, her delight her joy for ever. And Abraham rode thoughtfully on. He thought of . . . the son whom he had driven out into the desert. He climbed the mountain in Moriah, he drew the knife" (46–47).[10]

Kierkegaard's elliptical interpretation of Abraham portrays a father ready to sacrifice his son upon the divine Father's command. What if we were to substitute for Kierkegaard's tale of Abraham fragments from narratives not so heavily in debt to a patriarchal past? Bill Martin is right, I think, to insist that the aim of the social theorist should be to assimilate centers into margins, and not margins into centers.[11] How else do we move against the arrogance of power? What if we were to substitute for the biblical tale of god's dutiful servant Morrison's story of the rebellious slave who sacrifices a child that she does not know how to save? Morrison does not tell this story as a test of faith; the loss of the child is real, and this child's sacrifice cannot be redeemed. *Beloved* begins a collection of novels addressing the sacrifice of children before forces that, perhaps like Kierkegaard's, are cruel and beyond our full comprehension. These sacrifices trace back to the Middle Passage—the chasmic abyss of fear and trembling—that initiated millions of Africans to America. For Kierkegaard, the image of the abyss signifies first and foremost the anguish of freedom. For the African who bears the memory of the Middle Passage, separation does not carry the meaning of freedom but of traumatic loss and political oppression. The history of the Middle Passage teaches that freedom cannot rest on the fear and the trembling elicited by the chasmic abyss between man and man. Lest struggles

---

[9] Toni Morrison, *Paradise* (New York: Alfred A. Knopf, 1998), 318; henceforth cited as *P.*

[10] In editing comments on the present essay for *Radical Philosophy Review*, Lewis Gordon remarked that Kierkegaard fictionalized the ages of Sarah and Isaac in his rendition of the story. The effect of this fictionalization, I would think, is to deepen the abyss of irony upon which Kierkegaard builds faith. My suggestion is that Toni Morrison's novels offer a more life-affirming source of spirituality.

[11] See Bill Martin's "Existential Marxism, The Next Chapter: Martin J. Beck Matustík's *Specters of Liberation,*" *Radical Philosophy Review* 2, no. 2 (1999): 145.

against blind arrogance repeat tragic cycles of reversal and revenge, we must tap the more fertile sources of friendly bonds and social justice.

Morrison closes her trilogy's final novel, *Paradise*, with a sermon. The sermon, which speaks to the senseless death of an innocent child named Save-Marie, begins as though it were repeating elements from the story of Abraham and Isaac: "In this single moment of aching sadness—in contemplating the ... incomprehensible death of a child—we confirm, defer or lose our faith.... Here, it is time to halt, to linger this one time and reject platitudes ... about death being the only democracy. This is the time to ask.... Who could do this to a child? Who could permit this for a child? And why?" (*P*, 295).

The reverend who utters these words begins to answer these troubling questions in the conventional manner—as though to remind us of the chasmic abyss that separates us and the discipline of faith. Then he hesitates and alters his course: "May I suggest those are not the important questions. Or rather those are the questions of anguish but not of intelligence.... Do you think this was a short, pitiful life bereft of worth because it did not parallel your own? Let me tell you something. The love [this child] received was wide and deep, and ... that love enveloped her ... completely.... Oh, Save-Marie, you name always sounded like 'Save me.' ... Any other messages hiding in your name? I know one that shines for all to see: there never was a time when you were not saved..." (*P*, 306–307).

Index

5152